P9-APV-376

Healing yourself works
magic on all levels.

SPIRIT AT WORK

Spirit at Work

A Journey Of Healing

By
Lois M. Grant

EMERALD

WAVE

Spirit at Work
A Journey of Healing

By Lois M. Grant

Published by: Emerald Wave
                    P.O. Box 969
                    Fayetteville, AR 70202

All rights reserved. No part of this book may be reproduced or transmitted in any form or by any means, electronic or mechanical, including photocopying, recording or by any information storage and retrieval system without written permission from the author, except for the inclusion of brief quotations in a review.

Copyright © 1997 by Lois M. Grant
10-9-8-7-6-5-4-3-2-1

Cover art: Debbie Rankin
Cover design: NeoGraphics
Cover photo: Keith F. Weiland, AIAE

Library of Congress Catalog Card Number:
96-84870 CIP
Grant, Lois M.
    Spirit at Work: A Journey of Healing
    by Lois M. Grant—1st ed.
    280 pp. 152 x 229 mm
    Includes bibliographical references
    ISBN 0-942531-35-3   15.00
    1. Spirituality
    2. Spiritual healing
    3. Rheumatoid Arthritis
    4. Angels
    5. Channeled Teachings

I dedicate this book to my angel Ariel
and to my
earthly support group—
you know who you are!

You're not that Body,
You're Pure Spirit Soul.
To Taste Love of God is Life's Ultimate Goal.

Dasaratha

A hundred million miracles
are happ'ning every day.

Oscar Hammerstein II
Flower Drum Song

TABLE OF CONTENTS

PREFACE

To the Reader: This book began as a collection of anecdotes of interesting events which I believe are fascinating examples of Spirit at work in our lives. I started writing them down just to help myself remember what had happened to friends and family. I don't remember exactly when—or from whom—I got the idea to make the stories into a book, but as it began taking shape, I decided to begin with this series of vignettes about others and to end with the story of my healing. This may make for a bit of continuity confusion as you are reading, but it all comes together. Trust me!

One other note of clarification: When I speak of God or Goddess or All That Is or The Lord or Creator or Angels or Souls or Spirit or Essences or The Tao or Ascended Masters or Mother Earth or Nature or the entity Michael or Jesus or Buddha or Guides or the Ascendant, I am referring to the Supreme Intelligent Force that Paul Tillich calls The Ground of our Being. I believe that this Power manifests Itself in more ways than our limited human minds can comprehend—and that each of us bears a tiny spark of It deep inside ourSelves. We are taking these opportunities for human experience so we can learn all the lessons we need to become vibrating manifestations of Unconditional Love. That is the only reason for this game we call Life.

PART ONE

Spiritual Awakenings

One

THE BEGINNINGS

After I left my first husband at what turned out to be the nadir of my life, I was living alone—well, with two cats—in unfamiliar surroundings. This was the bitterly cold Michigan winter of 1982 and, besides being unemployed and depressed, I was painfully ill with rheumatoid arthritis. I found a framed drawing of two cats looking at a sunrise through a small forest with this message at the bottom: "Every day, somewhere, something incredible is waiting to be known." I hung the picture where I could see it often, for I desperately needed to believe that the incredible could come into my life. I had left the security of a 24-year marriage to a lawyer whose time was billed at $200 an hour. I had just launched my new career as an architect only to lose my job to an economic downturn. I was not sure I could manage on my own because of my pain and disabilities—I was barely able to walk. On top of all this, I had been forced to give up two of my greatest pleasures, playing the piano and singing, because of the arthritis. (Arthritis affects all connective tissue and vocal cords fall in that category.)

Now, more than a decade later, I have a pretty good idea about what was waiting to be known. My arthritis is under control with minimal medication. I have a successful joint venture/marriage and am a respected professional running an architectural practice out of our treasured home. But more than all of this, I have a rich and beautiful spiritual life and nearly every day it seems that I enjoy another spiritual experience or hear of one from a friend. This life has been such an adventure! I feel I have traveled light years from where I was just a few, short earth years ago and I look forward to the excitement of whatever challenges lie ahead. I have learned to live in the light, to love and heal myself, to make things happen and feel the joy in small things. I am still working toward the complete healing of the arthritic deformities in my hands and feet, having no doubt that this will happen in time. I have learned how to tap into and use spiritual energy and want to share it with you. There's no magic or mystery to it, we may access it whenever we are ready. If you are ready to ride, grab your sled and hang on!

Two

KATHIE'S MOM

One of the first people who ever talked to me about spiritual things was the mother of a woman I knew and liked, but was not particularly close to. Kathie and I belonged to a swim club where our children took swimming lessons during the summer. One day I was sitting by the pool during a lesson and her mother who was visiting sat next to me. We chatted for a while and somehow the conversation came around to angels. "People who believe in angels can ask the angels to watch their house and it won't be broken into," she told me. I was intrigued by this magical idea. Then she told me that she thought I was "an advanced soul." I asked how she could tell and she said by my love of music. These are the only specific fragments of this conversation I can remember after twenty years or so, but it had a profound effect on me and I have considered it many times. I have often invoked the protection of the angels when leaving my car at night to be worked on the next morning, when leaving my home to go on a trip or vacation. It usually works. When it doesn't, I assume that the answer was "no" and there was some lesson to learn or some reason beyond my immediate understanding.

I have always been an avid seeker of knowledge and I began to explore the metaphysical. I noticed that my then-husband, a Scorpio, had several good friends who were also Scorpios and I decided to read about astrology to see if there was anything to it. I found a book that showed how to construct a simplified horoscope. As I began to collect horoscopes of family and friends, I decided that "there is just enough to it that I can't give it up." I have become quite good at guessing whether someone was born in a Fire, Air, Earth or Water sun sign and sometimes can even identify their specific sign.

It is just a short distance from the astrology books in the library to the books on reincarnation and other "new age" ideas which, as it turned out, also intrigued me greatly. I read a book on creative visualization and began to try to manifest simple things, like parking places. I found that it worked best if I thought about and visualized the parking place before I got into my car. When shopping, I learned to visualize exactly what I wanted, which was very helpful since my painful feet made shopping a chore. Visualizing what I want is such a habit now, I am amazed that it is not taught in school. It is easy enough to do: just "see" what you want, believe and accept it, and, providing you feel deserving, it will happen. Oh, and don't forget to say, "Thank you!"

Three

LINDA, CHARLIE AND JOSH

When my sister Linda was in college she met Charlie and fell in love. The only problem was Charlie's Jewish heritage. They dated for a year and became engaged, but neither family was happy about it because of the religious differences and after a while they broke the engagement. Linda and Charlie both proceeded to marry others and Charlie had two children. He lived in California and was a successful corporate attorney for an airline while Linda was a financial writer (she still is!) living in New York. One day in the mid-seventies Charlie was in New York on business. By this time Linda was divorced and he was separated. Charlie knew that Linda was working for Time, Inc., and on a warm spring morning he sat outside the building and watched her go to work. The next time he was in New York, he called her. They got together and realized that they still loved each other after all those years. It was the most romantic thing I had ever heard! I have always felt that they had a spiritual agreement to be together and have often used them as an example why parents should not interfere with their children's relationships. After a time, they were both free to marry and they soon bought a house in suburban New York City.

In 1983 a miracle happened: Linda, at the age of 42, became pregnant. This was a monumental event, since she had always been the career girl in the family and none of us dreamed she would ever have a child. When I told my daughter Diane, "You're going to have a cousin," she was unable to figure out what that really meant! Linda's pregnancy was considered high-risk from the beginning because of her age. She underwent amniocentesis at about five months and was told that the baby was fine, but she began to develop dangerously high blood pressure. The weekend before the 4th of July, with six weeks still to go, she told me that at her last check-up her blood pressure was very high and she was going back to have it checked on Tuesday.

That Sunday I spent some time with my good friend Merry and she invited a friend from her office, a psychic named Sue, to come over for the afternoon. Sue was the first psychic I ever met in person and I was very interested to talk to her. We visited for a couple of hours and just before she left, I asked, "Are you getting anything for me?" "Yes", she said. "Your sister is going to have a hard time with this birth. There will be some problems. But everything will turn out OK. The baby may have a deficit to make up, but by the time he is two years old, he will be fine." I was somewhat troubled by this information and decided not to share it with Linda.

On Tuesday evening, I called Linda to find out how the check-up had gone, but all I got was the answering machine. I left a message and then went out for the evening. When I came home about 10:30 there was no news. I became very concerned, called again and left the message, "I'd like to know what's going on, would somebody please call me no matter how late it is." I went to bed and was awakened by the phone about 1 AM. It was Charlie, sounding very worried. Linda had gone to the doctor with her blood pressure so dangerously high that she had been admitted to the hospital. If things didn't improve quickly, they would take the baby by Caesarean—six weeks early—the next day. I then told him what Sue had said, stressing the part about everything turning out all right. I had no idea what Charlie thought about psychics, but I felt I had to give him, and myself, some hope.

Needless to say, I did not get much sleep the rest of that night. I thought about getting on a plane and I probably would have done so if I had not had six meetings scheduled the next morning. I was designing the renovation of six departments for a Detroit hospital and I was really the only one who could conduct the meetings. One meeting I could have canceled, but not six! So I went to work in the morning and told the receptionist what was going on. I went to the hospital for the meetings and told them I might get a phone call. After the meetings I came back to the office. No, there had been no calls from New York. I worked as best I could until Charlie finally called me at 4 PM. He couldn't bear to tell me the truth. He said that little Josh and Linda were both fine. Well, Linda was fine, but Josh was six weeks premature and his lungs weren't quite ready for air. He had hyaline membrane disease. Linda went home after a few days, but Josh had to stay in the neonatal unit until he gained some weight and his lungs matured. Linda went to the visit him every day. She sat by the incubator and talked to Josh, telling him about all the people who loved him, including his Auntie Loie (that's my family nickname) and how he was going to get big and strong so he could come home. She could tell that he was responding to her voice. Finally his little lungs were healed enough so that Linda could hold him for the first time. Josh was about six weeks old when he attained a weight of five pounds and Charlie and Linda brought him home—their $30,000 miracle baby.

I was thrilled to be an aunt and had a T-shirt made for Josh that said, "Lois's Nephew." Linda quit her job with the Los Angeles *Times* and stayed home to nurture Josh for seven years. He has more than made up any deficit, just as Sue said he would. Recently, at the age of twelve, he scored 1070 on the SAT to qualify for a special summer program at Johns Hopkins University! And he won the *National Geographic* Geography Bee for his entire school which qualified him to go to the state finals. Josh has a wonderful sense of humor and loves the humor writer Dave Barry as much as I do (more about Dave later). He even writes a humor column for the school newspaper. And Josh and I correspond several times a week via e-mail. Thank you, Goddess, for a wonderful addition to our family! The years that Linda spent at home with her son did not derail her career. When she decided to go back to work, she landed the job she wanted writing cover articles for *Fortune* magazine.

Four

ANDY

Andy was an architectural intern (a person with an architectural degree who is working toward registration) at the firm where I worked when I first came to Atlanta in 1985. A slightly manic 26-year-old, Andy was totally uninhibited, creative and great fun to be around. He was quick with the one-liners and wisecracks and I enjoyed matching wits with him after he realized I wasn't a stuffy old lady. (My age, disabling arthritis and scholarly demeanor can mislead young people when they first meet me.) I often drop remarks about astrology as a clue that I am of a metaphysical bent and people who are interested usually pick up on it. Andy was definitely interested. I did a primitive version of his horoscope and explained the basics to him. Then one day when we were working together he confided, "You know, sometimes I have these nightmares. I will be having a dream when I suddenly wake up, not in my room, but in some strange place with people I don't know. It's really scary because I am so disoriented and confused when I first come out of it." I was the first person he had ever told about these weird dreams. I told him that it sounded to me like he was having spontaneous out-of-body experiences. He was relieved to know there was an explanation, since all his life he had thought he might be crazy. After my explanation, he gradually began to be more objective about them, to just "relax and enjoy it." Not too long after he told me about the "nightmares," he related the following story.

The architectural school curriculum where Andy earned his degree included a semester of study in France, so Andy and his classmates all went to live in Paris. One weekend the group took a jaunt to Southern France. Andy and a young woman called "Groovy Julie" because she was usually high on pot—or whatever—decided to leave the vacation spot early and hitchhike back to Paris. Andy was dubious because it was Sunday and there was very little traffic on the highway, but he was a good sport and they began trying to get a ride. It was a deserted area with no houses or towns and, as Andy had feared, no cars passing by. It grew later and later and Andy became increasingly worried that they were going to have to spend the night along the road and they had no water or equipment for camping out. He was on the verge of panic when, finally, a car came along and, to his huge relief, it stopped. The driver suggested that Andy drive the car and he (the driver) would sleep in the back seat. About three hours later, they arrived in Paris. Andy drove to the apartment house and he and Julie, who was stoned, as usual, got out of the car. Andy unloaded their backpacks from the trunk of the car, turned around to thank the driver, and was startled to see that there was no driver and no car anywhere in sight. They had just disappeared! Dumbfounded, Andy tried to get confirmation from Julie that this had really happened, but she was in no condition to remember anything. Again, he had never shared this experience with anyone until he told me. My explanation was that it was his guardian angel or guide who manifested the car to help him and then dematerialized as soon as the job was done.

Andy was "let go" from the firm where we worked together and hired by another office, but we kept in touch and talked on the phone from time to time. One day he told me about the woman who ran the lunchroom in the building where he was working. "She's a psychic. My friend had a reading with her and I'm going to have one, too." That was how I met Lynn. I believe that one reason Andy went to work for that firm was so I could meet Lynn because shortly after Lynn and I connected, Andy moved back to his hometown in Florida. He had always wanted to specialize in residential design rather than the big institutional jobs we had worked on together and when his brother asked him to design a house, Andy decided he was ready to strike out in this new direction.

The house Andy designed for his brother turned out to be a striking modern design built in a noticeable location. Andy's dad owns an automobile dealership nearby and one day a customer made a comment about the house. Andy's dad said, "My son designed that house." "Well, I'd like to talk to him," the man said. This man, as it turned out, owned a firm specializing in residential design/build projects. He quickly hired Andy as his chief designer. Andy was gradually given more and more responsibility, but the best part was that he was so happy to be doing what he loves—designing homes. About two years later, his benefactor had a heart attack and sold the business to Andy, who runs the office in a humane and caring way, always using direct communication. He only takes work for clients he wants to work with. If his intuition tells him that a potential client is going to be a problem, he just says, "I'm sorry, we can't meet your schedule." Among his clients are a pediatric neurosurgeon and a major league baseball pitcher.

Andy's wild dreams and other astral experiences have continued. During one of our occasional phone conversations, he said they were really intense. He told me that when he was staying in a hotel the night before taking the architectural registration exam, he woke up during the night to see a man standing at the desk, looking down at his books. I called Lynn and told her about it. She said, "They are there to help him. Sometimes they wear jogging suits instead of robes when they appear, because it's less frightening." When I told that to Andy, he said, "Oh, so that's what he was wearing." Andy had not told me that his angel was wearing a jogging suit, but Lynn had "seen" it! Andy has since learned to trust the guides and angels, to just let these episodes happen. He no longer worries that he's crazy, nor does he rebuff his helpers.

Five

GOING TO THE LIGHT

DAVID

David is an architect I met when I was loaned out to work on the Underground Atlanta project. A very talented designer, he was also fun and easy to be with and I enjoyed getting to know him. We went to lunch one day and he told me a story he had never told anyone before. David and his wife bought a house in an older area of Atlanta. The previous owner, named Mary, had built the house with her husband in the 1920's. Widowed for many years, she got to be pretty eccentric towards the end, according to the neighbors. She had died in the house.

After living there quietly for a couple of years, David did what architects love to do and redesigned the kitchen. As soon as construction was complete, strange things started happening. David and his wife began to hear unusual noises in the kitchen and find things moved around or fallen to the floor. At first David thought his cats might be making mischief, but when he went to investigate, the cats were usually asleep in the bedroom. And sometimes the cats acted like they were afraid to come into the kitchen. I told David that I thought Mary was mad at him for changing her kitchen. If she was as "weird" as everyone had said, it seemed to me possible that she had not fully completed her transition to the astral plane and was stuck here, haunting her former home. All was well until he changed the kitchen and that made her mad. I told him to talk to her, kindly, but firmly. Explain that this was not her house anymore, it was his and he had a right to improve the kitchen if he wanted to; that he didn't mean to upset her, but that now it is time for her to move on. Tell her not to be afraid, just go to the Light. At the time I wasn't sure David believed me, but a few weeks later he told me that he had talked to Mary as I suggested—and there had not been any more strange incidents in the kitchen.

JOHNNY AND NICOLE

Nicole came into my life during the final stages of working on this book. I first heard of her from mutual friends. I was surprised when she called one day and wanted to recommend us as architects for one of her clients. We began working out a contract and I enjoyed talking to her. She was very straightforward to deal with and didn't mince words when expressing an opinion; in other words, a good businessperson. I wanted to take her to lunch in return for bringing us new work so we met at a restaurant.

As the conversation went on, I sensed a real connection with Nicole. I liked her piercing bright blue eyes and the clear, open way she expressed herself was even more enjoyable in person than on the telephone. About halfway through lunch I decided to mention my book and what it was about even though we had not yet touched on spiritual matters. I knew that my intuition was on target when Nicole grew very excited. She began talking about her husband who had committed suicide, telling me the whole story. As she described these events, I knew I had to add them here because they are such a perfect illustration of Spirit at work.

Johnny and Nicole met in late 1979 when she was assigned to work for him. The working relationship blossomed into a friendship which caught fire and they were married. Towards the end of their twelve-year marriage, Johnny's drinking and depression were more than Nicole could deal with. She told him "I can't do this anymore," filed for divorce and moved out of their townhouse. They remained friends, for she still cared for him, but she couldn't bear to watch him self-destruct. One evening about two months after she had left, Nicole dropped by the townhouse. She noticed the newspaper had not been picked up and Johnny did not answer the doorbell. Because she didn't have a key, Nicole went to the neighbors who called the fire department. The firemen broke the door down and found Johnny unconscious from a drug overdose. They rushed him to the hospital in time and he recovered.

Several weeks later, Johnny was sick with the flu and Nicole stopped in one evening to bring him dinner and see how he was. This time she had a key. When she opened the door and called his name there was no answer. She went up the stairs to the living room and found him dead on the sofa with the covers pulled up to his chin, his left arm hanging down. She thought he had died from the flu and called the police. The first inkling she had of suicide was when she heard one of the policemen say, "Be sure to put the safety on." Johnny had shot himself in the stomach, hitting his aorta, but did it very carefully so as not to make a big mess.

Nicole felt terrible that Johnny had finally succeeded in killing himself. She made it through the wake and funeral but was unable to return to work right away. Even though she knew Johnny was self-destructive, the abruptness of his death was extremely troubling. Her mind continually returned to the deeply imprinted memory of Johnny's lifeless body when she had found him. But each time this happened, she forced herself to replace that horrifying image with a mental picture of Johnny standing whole and healthy with Nicole embracing him. She believes that "What we see, we empower to become reality."

About two weeks after the funeral, Nicole was staying with her mother. She got up on a bright, sunny morning, determined to go to the office, but quickly realized she still couldn't manage it. She let her mother and her office know that she wasn't going to be able to work and then went back into the bedroom where she sat down on the bed, consumed by her grief. Suddenly she found herself in a dark, strange place and she knew that Johnny was there with her. She said aloud, "How is it where you are?" Only silence answered her, but she knew he was still there and she repeated her question. "How is it where you are?" Reaching out with her left hand, Nicole pulled aside what she describes as a "curtain made of something like plastic bread wrappers tied together." Behind the "curtain" she saw Johnny, only from the chest up, standing rather stiffly before her. He was smiling! She sensed that his arms were at his side, although she couldn't see them. "Forgive me," he said. Nicole rose, stepped forward and kissed him on the cheek, saying, "I already have." Then he was gone and Nicole was back in the familiar bedroom at her mother's house.

This moment of contact brought Nicole great solace and relief. It gave her the strength to center herself and to be able to listen to others express their grief, which until then had only increased her own burden.

A few weeks later, one of Johnny's friends told Nicole that he had "dreamed" about Johnny. He said, "We were sitting in the living room of your townhouse, but it couldn't have been your townhouse because Johnny was in a rocking chair and you didn't have a rocking chair." "Oh, yes, we did!" Nicole said. The friend was stunned by this reminder. He then told Nicole that in the dream, he and Johnny had "an absolutely normal conversation" and when it was over, he watched Johnny walk down the hall to the front door and leave the townhouse.

Johnny had a son Tommy and a daughter Ginger by his first marriage. Tommy had died from muscular dystrophy at the age of four. Several weeks after her dad's funeral, Ginger told Nicole that she dreamed that she and her brother were in bed at Johnny and Nicole's townhouse and that Johnny was in the room with them. Johnny told his children, "Don't worry about me, I am fine. I'm going to go to heaven. After I died I stayed around for a while to take care of some things, but I'm going to go to heaven." Ginger was greatly comforted by this contact with her father.

Johnny's mother also had a dream. She was standing in line at the exchange counter in a store when she saw Johnny. She walked over to him and gave him a big hug. Johnny always made a face and rolled his eyes when his mother was affectionate and she was very happy and pleased to see him react this way, "just like the old Johnny."

Donna was one of Johnny's good friends. One night she was driving rather aggressively on a winding country road on the outskirts of Atlanta and was startled to hear Johnny's voice exclaim, "Slow down!" Donna obeyed. When she drove around the next curve, a huge deer was standing in the road. Because she heeded Johnny's warning she was able to stop in time.

One night Donna was asleep, lying flat on her back, something she rarely does. Suddenly she woke up and found herself unable to move. She saw a glowing light at the foot of the bed in the shape of a man and recognized Johnny's profile. Donna wanted to wake her husband up, but she could neither speak nor move. Johnny was happily showing off his newfound ability to be in the light. He was doing flips, dancing and flying around the bedroom. It gave Donna great joy to see this exuberant playfulness, so typical of Johnny at his best. She told Nicole, "It was just like Johnny to say, 'This is so neat, look at this! I gotta show you this!'" Her only regret was that she couldn't wake her husband so he could see Johnny, too.

Nicole says that one of the most important lessons she learned from the experience of losing Johnny was how to pray for him. She knew she was still harboring some anger with him for leaving in this painful way and began to attend healing services at her church. She began by asking for help with healing her anger. The woman conducting the service prayed for Nicole, then started praying for Johnny, asking for his continued spiritual growth, that he be taken into the presence of the Creator and blessed. Nicole could feel the power of this prayer and soon found that by praying for Johnny's healing and growth, she, too, was healed as her anger gradually subsided and was released.

When Nicole and Johnny split up, the only custody issue they had was who would keep their two cats. Since Nicole's job required her to travel frequently, Johnny got custody. The autopsy report showed that Johnny had received scratches on his left hand and his face after he died. Obviously the cats had tried to wake him up. It was several months before they would let Nicole sleep for any length of time.

About a year after Johnny's passing, Nicole was walking on the beach at Hilton Head where she and Johnny spent many happy times. She is in the habit of picking up litter and putting it in her pocket, so she was scanning the sand for foreign objects. This day something shiny caught her eye. She thought it was a pull tab from a pack of cigarettes and bent down to pick it up. It was a gold necklace with the clasp closed. Nicole is convinced that this necklace was a gift for her, although she is not certain from whom. She responded with a heartfelt "thank you" and gains a special warm feeling every time she wears it.

Six

MICHAEL

Shortly after I moved to Atlanta, I went to lunch with Beverly, the marketing director of the firm where I was working. I mentioned to her that I had some strange beliefs, like reincarnation. She didn't blink an eye. Encouraged, I started talking and sharing more of my thoughts and questions. "I have a book for you to read," she said. A day or two later she brought me a copy of *Messages from Michael* by Chelsea Quinn Yarbro and I have never been the same. Michael is an entity of 1050 souls who have all completed their earthly lifetimes. (An entity is a family group of about a thousand souls who all come into existence at the same time and spend many lifetimes with each other in various kinds of relationships.) The last soul of the Michael entity to "cycle off" was called Michael in his final earthly lifetime, so they call themselves by that name. Reunited and now on the mid-causal plane, the Michael Group is continuing their spiritual growth by teaching, which they do by means of channeling through several people on our planet. They have organized their theory of the Universe into what they call "The Michael Teaching." As I read that first book, I became very excited because it all felt so right to me and answered so many of my questions. I started thinking of people and events in my life and analyzing them in light of the teaching. I figured out that my role had to be Scholar—it was the only one that made sense. Michael says, "All is chosen." I struggled with the ideas that my essence chose to be born to my parents to learn the lessons that went with being their daughter and that I chose to stay in my first marriage until it made me sick, but I have come to see that I did.

During the summer of 1988 I was in a metaphysical book store and saw a copy of *The World According to Michael* by Joya Pope. Wow! Another Michael book! I bought and read it immediately. I became very excited because in the back of the book there was information on how I could get my overleaves or soul/personality profile and a personal channeling with Michael. I got pictures together of myself, my husband and ex-husband, my parents, kids and sister and sent them off to Joya. In my letter I wrote, "After I *assimilate* all this, I'm sure I will want a telephone channeling." In a couple of weeks I received all my overleaf charts back. I was right about being a Scholar and the positive pole of Scholar is *Assimilation*! I am a second level Old Scholar with a Goal of Dominance, an Attitude of Pragmatist, Observation Mode, a Chief Negative Feature of Impatience, Intellectually Centered in the Emotional Part and with 65 percent male or focused energy. It wasn't long before I had my first of many channelings with Michael through Joya and was able to get real answers to my never-ending stream of questions. Joya and I have become close friends and I have brought her to Atlanta three times for a week of programs and private channelings.

In that first channeling, Michael told me that I have a teaching agreement with them from pre-Mesopotamian times which means that I want to share the teaching with anyone who will listen. And I do. Some of those closest to me are not very interested in the teaching and resist my Michaelese interpretations of events and people, but I am undeterred and have found many others who enjoy learning about it. I just revel in explaining it, giving the books away and helping people understand one explanation for what is happening in their lives and on the planet. Much of what I am writing about in this book is in the context of, or includes references to, the Michael Teaching, so I am including a summary of the teaching in this chapter and a glossary of Michael terminology along with the names of channels and other Michael resources in the Appendix at the end of the book. There are several wonderful Michael books listed in the Appendix.

The Michael Teaching in brief:

The main goal of the Michael Teaching is to promote or encourage agape or unconditional love.

Michael is a united group composed of 1050 individual Essences or Souls who have completed their cycle of lives on the physical Earth plane and now teach from the mid-causal plane. Many Essences on the physical plane have agreed to learn from Michael, because it is usually on a personality and physical plane level that we gain the most from this teaching. Michael speaks through human channels who have agreed on an Essence level to assist the Michael group with their teaching.

The Michael Teaching views life as a learning game in which Essences choose particular lessons and experiments, many of which continue over several lifetimes. These lessons are experienced by the personality or overleaves which an Essence chooses before coming into the lifetime because certain overleaves will facilitate or inhibit the lessons. Michael describes each of the various components of personality so that we can learn how to use them ourselves and to observe them in others and thus better understand why human beings behave as wisely or as crazily as they do. Michael teaches that life is perfect as it is because each person is learning the necessary and chosen lessons for their lifetime. Even resisting lessons is seen as an interesting growth experience.

The entity Michael teaches as part of their own progression through the circle of existence. This circle is like a great wheel which leads from the Tao (Michael's way of referring to God, Goddess, All That Is, etc.) through five soul ages on the physical plane, six planes of existence beyond the physical, and back to the Tao again. No person, Essence or entity is "ahead of" or "behind" another. Each one simply occupies a different place on the wheel.

Michael's mission is to help the population of the planet Earth to complete the current shift from a "me first" attitude to one of community, in which people will better learn to see others as they see themselves, and realize that all people deserve the same love and respect.

One of the most basic and important principles of the Michael Teaching is that it is not a religion or a belief system. Michael encourages self-validation of all of information received and the use of only that which resonates with or has meaning for the person and seems appropriate for the lifetime.

Seven

HENRY

Henry is a tall, round-faced, very gentle Southerner who worked as a structural engineer on the big Atlanta hospital project with me. We enjoyed getting to know each other and chatted casually about many subjects during the two years we spent on the project. I think I even told him about Michael and loaned him Joya's book. One morning, I entered the break room just as Henry burned his hand on the coffee maker. I went into my motherly role and got some ice and paper towels to help him. He was very grateful.

A few months later Henry hurt his leg playing softball. He was out of the office for several days with his injury and when he came back to work, he was using crutches. One day during the lunch hour, I was working alone in the computer room which was a bit unusual, for it was normally a hub of activity. I looked up to see Henry limping down the aisle in my direction without his crutches, carrying a drink from a fast food restaurant. He looked to me like he was in a lot of pain. I said, "Henry, are you all right?" He told me that he had gone down to the food court for lunch without his crutches and was feeling light-headed. He had apparently overdone. I said, "Why don't you come in here and sit down?" which he did. He repeated that he felt dizzy and I helped him lie down on the floor, afraid he might be about to pass out. I got a cushion from the couch in the reception area and put it under his head. Then I asked someone to get some ice. Others were now realizing that something was going on and came to help. We decided that he needed to go home because he was very weak and one of the other engineers volunteered to drive Henry home, since we couldn't reach his wife on the telephone. I asked the receptionist to call the security guard downstairs bring up a wheelchair. Henry thanked me profusely for helping him and went home to recover.

As I mentally reviewed these events, I reached the conclusion that I must have owed Henry some care to repay karma of some sort and I decided to chat with him about it. When he came back to work after a day or so, I met him in the break room and said, "Henry, have you ever heard of karma?" His eyes widened and he said, "I just got a huge shiver when you said that." We sat down at the table and I explained what karma was. I said that I thought I must owe him some karmic repayment, that the first time I helped him was fine, but it wasn't enough and that's why I had to help him the second time. We talked about what had happened that day in the computer room and he said that when he saw me, "You had the weirdest look in your eye!" I sent for Henry's overleaves from Michael and it came back that he is an Artisan. He confided to me that he really wanted to be an artist, which is quite removed from structural engineering. I asked Michael about our past relationship, but they didn't have much enlightening information to tell me about it. However, my self-validation tells me that something was going on between Henry and me and that I have now repaid whatever it was. It feels complete and I am glad that it was so simple and pleasant

During this time I was learning to recognize other messages from my Higher Self. When I was offered the job to work on the big Atlanta hospital project, Keith and I were talking about it in bed. I wanted this job very much, but he suddenly started in with a lot of negative comments. I thought to myself, "Well, maybe I won't do it." Tears started flowing out of my eyes. I wasn't really crying, but the tears were just running out and I remembered the old song, "I've Got Tears in My Ears from Lying on My Back and Crying in My Sleep over You." I thought to myself, I want to do this. I'm going to do it. I said to Keith, "I'd like to have your support in this, but I'm going to do it anyway." Immediately the tears stopped. I knew this was confirmation that accepting this job offer was the right thing for me to do. And Keith supported me in it.

Another sign was chills or shivers. I began to notice that sometimes when I said something I would have electric chills down my spine. I realized that these chills are validation that I am speaking the truth, just as Henry had felt them when I mentioned karma. These signs had always been there, but I was too unaware and wrapped up in my problems to recognize them for what they are: communication from Spirit. Now my perceptions have expanded to know that the even the wrens singing on the deck outside my office as I write this are confirmation of the joy in my heart.

Eight

CATS

FLUFFERNUT

Fluffernut was born in my daughter Diane's closet in 1970, one of four kittens in our cat Tinkerbelle's second litter. My son Mark picked him to keep and named him for the Fluffernutter sandwich (marshmallow fluff and peanut butter) because his markings were white and tan. I took Fluffernut with me when I moved out in 1982. He was diagnosed positive for feline leukemia two years later, but continued to do pretty well, for an old cat, until the summer of 1988.

July 17, 1988

Last Wednesday evening I was listening to a Mozart piano concerto, which, according to Michael, is supposed to put Scholars in touch with their Higher Centers. Fluffernut came onto my lap and looked me in the eye and I felt a deep emotional surge of something. Was it truth, beauty, love?? It felt positive and wonderful. Whatever it was, it made me cry, just overflowing with love. I picked Fluffernut up and held him close while I wept into his fur. I felt very strong feelings of love and gratitude for Keith and Diane and all my support group.

Two days later I took Fluffernut to the vet on the way to work because he had been throwing up. I thought it was a hairball, but they called me in the afternoon and said he was in kidney failure. I talked to Lynn and told her about Wednesday night. She said, "He was trying to tell you." Then she said her cat Missy was about to have kittens, probably the next week. On the way home from work I stopped at the vet's to visit with Fluffernut. I told him through my tears that if it was time for him to go, I understood, that I loved him, that Mark, Diane, Keith, Duchess (Keith's dog) and Musetta (my other cat) all loved him and that he had been a wonderful cat. Then I told him to find Missy and to come back as one of her kittens so we could be together again. I felt much better after that. The next day about noon Keith and I went over to the animal hospital and decided it was time for Fluffernut to go, for he was not going to recover and was very dehydrated and uncomfortable.

The vet gave him a large dose of tranquilizer and I held him like a baby until it took effect, about 10-15 minutes. He was breathing in occasional short, shallow breaths. Then she took him into another room and finished the job with another injection. It was hard, but it was the right thing to do.

And so he is gone. Seventeen years and nine months—"that's a lot of Meow Mix," as Mark once said. It isn't easy to say good-bye to a being you have shared life with for nearly 18 years. I miss him. But maybe he'll be back—soon!

We adopted one of Missy's kittens, black with three white spots down the front, and named him Misha. He was half Russian Blue and Misha is the nickname for Mikhail, the Russian name for Michael. I let people think it was for Baryshnikov.

In one of my channelings with Michael, I mentioned how I had felt that surge of love from Fluffernut. Michael said, "Cats are out of their bodies about half the time and they often allow essences from the astral plane to come in to channel for short periods. That may have been one of your astral buddies making contact." I immediately said, "Herman!" Michael agreed, "Yes, it was Herman." (Herman was the man I dated after my divorce who had passed away very suddenly—more on him in Chapter Twelve.) Herman had known and liked Fluffernut, but Michael said he wasn't very interested in Misha.

BLACKJACK

I met Merry at the home of a mutual friend a scant month after moving into my own apartment early in 1982. She and I had lived in the same subdivision for years, but never met until after I moved out. I could tell that she was a Gemini (it takes one to know one) before that first evening was over and we decided that we wanted to get to know each other better. We still celebrate that anniversary! She became one of my best friends as I began teaching her about astrology, handwriting analysis, tarot and all that "weird" stuff. She lapped it up, buying the books I recommended, asking questions and learning with me. She let me use her washer and dryer every weekend which gave us lots of time together. She was very emotionally supportive of me during that difficult time and we enjoyed many soul-searching truth-and-confidence-sharing sessions. Sometimes she made me a little nervous, her feelings for me were so intense. (We now know that she is in passion mode.) It was more difficult then for me to accept love and acknowledgment.

Merry (I always say "M-E-R-R-Y") is loads of fun and lives up to her name. She loves to call Keith "Mr. Lois Grant" and it was hard to leave her when we moved to Atlanta. She wrote a touching poem about our friendship which I framed and we have stayed close.

Merry's teen-aged son Todd had a group of friends who spent a great deal of time working on cars and motorcycles in Merry's driveway. One of the friends, James, and his father drove to Florida in a van to deliver a large piece of equipment in the summer of 1988. While James was taking his turn driving, he had to make a sudden stop. The equipment broke loose, slid to the front of the van and killed his father. This was a horrible experience for James and he became quite depressed, feeling guilty and helpless for his part in his father's accidental death. In December, James shot himself in the head and died instantly.

Merry called to tell me about James' suicide. Todd and his friends were, of course, devastated by it. I just happened to have a reading with Lynn scheduled for the following weekend, so I took some pictures of Merry and asked Lynn what she could "see" about it. She said, "I see James with wings, sort of flying around, like he's showing his father how. His father was having trouble adjusting to being on the other side and James killed himself so he could go to help his father." I thought this was such a beautiful aspect to what seemed an out-and-out tragedy. Lynn tapes her readings, so I called Merry as soon as I got home and played that part of the tape over the phone. She, Todd and one of the other boys had just gotten back from the funeral and they all listened to the tape. They felt much better after they heard Lynn's interpretation.

The next summer Merry came to visit me and she asked me to schedule a reading with Lynn, which I was happy to do. During the reading, Lynn's three-legged black cat, Black Jack, who normally is aloof from her readings, became very friendly and jumped up on the table at least twice. The second time, he stretched out before me, purring loudly as I scratched him behind the ears. Then he went over to Merry and laid down in front of her, rolling over onto his back, happily purring and waving his paws in the air.

Lynn was working on Merry's horoscope, and Black Jack went and sat right on the ephemeris. He kept pawing at the book and her hands and she tried to move him out of the way so she could refer to the book. Black Jack then arranged himself with his paws pointing at her, "like an arrow," she later said, and he looked straight into her eyes. Lynn was still trying to read about the astrological phenomena when she suddenly turned the tape recorder off, looked at me, pointed to Merry, and said with a sense of urgency, "Isn't she the one with the son?"

Black Jack then went over to Merry, sat down in front of her and looked her right in the eye. Merry said, "James always dressed in all black." A pause and then, "This cat is James!" Goosebumps covered all three of us and Black Jack slowly arose and left the table. As he was jumping down, Lynn said, "Now that he has been acknowledged, Black Jack/James will leave us alone." Simultaneously, we heard the clock striking twelve noon. James died in the twelfth month, and was buried on 12/12/88, which was also the day that Lynn had done the reading for me regarding his death. Black Jack did not approach any of us again for the remainder of our stay at Lynn's.

When Merry and I returned home, we went to my computer and wrote these events down exactly as they had happened. In a later conversation, Merry remembered that the week before she came to see me, Todd had been in Las Vegas with his sister and he had spent his entire evening at the blackjack table.

Nine

DAVE BARRY

November 17, 1991
Dear Dave Barry,

I am not making this up!

What I am about to share with you is, to my mind, an amazing discovery that I made about six months ago. I have debated with myself whether or not to tell you about it and have decided to tell you about it and let it be your choice how to deal with it—or not deal with it.

About twenty years ago I became interested in handwriting analysis, then astrology, etc. This soon led to reincarnation, psychic phenomena and other "weird stuff." One of the questions that always came to me when thinking about reincarnation, etc., was, "Where is Mozart now?" Music has always been an important part of my life, with works by Mozart among my very favorites. I was thrilled when my son played the Mozart clarinet concerto and I especially love Mozart's operas.

About ten years ago I began reading your writings in the Detroit *Free Press*. I remember so clearly the one you wrote about watching the birth of your son. I saved it and shared it with many friends who were about to give birth. I soon learned your name and looked for your essays which never fail to make me laugh out loud.

About seven years ago I moved to Atlanta and one of my new friends shared with me a book called *Messages from Michael*. Michael is the name of a group of 1050 souls who have completed their cycle of lives on earth. They communicate their wisdom to certain channels. One of the channels is named Joya Pope, who wrote a book called *The World According to Michael* and who is available for channeling by telephone. I decided to talk to Michael through Joya and have now done this several times. Michael has a system or teaching which describes the attributes, which Michael calls overleaves, of people and their souls, such as soul age, role, goal, etc. By sending pictures of people to Joya, Michael will tell what these "overleaves" are. Michael also will advise those who ask about various aspects of their lives and answer questions.

So...one of the first questions I asked Michael was "Where is Mozart now?" The answer was, "He is a writer living in Florida." So I tucked that thought away and mused on it.

Two years ago my husband and I went to Germany and Austria and in Salzburg, we visited Mozart's birthplace. I looked at all the personal mementos of his life, his little violin, his little harpsichord, letters and music in his own hand, etc. I was moved to tears and nearly overcome by very strong feelings. Naturally, I had to talk to Michael about this experience and was told that in a previous life I had been Mozart's aunt. Seeing the actual items brought back these past life memories and triggered my reaction.

Meantime, I was pleased that the Atlanta *Journal-Constitution* started printing your essays on a weekly basis. I look forward to them and my husband can always tell when I am reading them. I began putting things together—about how much I enjoy Mozart's music and how much I enjoy your writing and how you are a writer in Florida....! So last summer I sent Joya a picture of you from the newspaper and asked the big question.

By now you know the answer—that you, Dave Barry, were Wolfgang Amadeus Mozart in a past life.

There you have it. I have no idea what you will think of this information or of me or Michael. If you are interested in pursuing the ideas, I would be delighted to hear from you. Michael says, "All Is Chosen." You may choose to ignore it and that is fine, too.

Keep up the great writing—I always enjoy it.

Very sincerely,

Lois M. Grant

Friday, May 15, 1992

Yesterday I drove to lunch and Mozart was playing on the radio. Nice. On the way home, they were playing the 3rd movement from Piano Concerto No. 22. I thought, that's a lot of Mozart for one day. Well, when I got home, there was a postcard from Dave Barry!

5/11/92
Dear Lois Grant,

    I just got the letter you wrote me last November—the Atlanta paper was apparently in no hurry to forward it. Anyway, I'd like to know more about the person who says I'm Mozart. Please write directly to me at the address on the other side.

    Sincerely, Dave Barry

    I tried to meditate, but had trouble concentrating. I just sat there, grinning and laughing. I felt like I had made a real connection and I was <u>thrilled</u>. I called Joya to ask her to send him a copy of her book and answered Dave's postcard.

May 15, 1992
Dear Dave,

    It was a great surprise for me to receive your postcard today! I had pretty much accepted that I was not going to hear from you and I am so pleased that you are interested in knowing more. I have called Joya Pope and she will be sending you a copy of *The World According to Michael*, which is my gift to you.

    It was interesting to realize that when I went out in my car at lunch time today, Mozart's music was playing on the radio. I didn't think too much about it. But then when I drove home after work, one of my favorite Mozart piano concertos was on the radio almost all the way home and I thought it was a little strange to be hearing so much Mozart in one day. When I read your postcard, it all came clear to me. There are no coincidences!! As I am writing this, I now remember that on Tuesday night I played a recording of another favorite Mozart piano concerto—was that the day you read my letter? ("Doo-doo-doo-doo..." Theme from "The Twilight Zone".)

    If, after reading the book, you want more information, please let me know. There are several other Michael books on the market and there is a newsletter. There may even be a Michael channel in Miami. Or you can write or call me any time, as I love talking and teaching about Michael. I am right now trying to arrange for Joya to come to Atlanta to do lectures, channeling, workshops, etc. She is a wonderful person and we have become very good friends. And, of course, if you ever get to Atlanta, I would be delighted to get together with you in person.

(If you are interested in knowing more about me, I am the subject of the third chapter of a book called *Take Two* by Jo Brans. It was published by Doubleday in 1989 and might be at your library or the "self-help" section of your bookstore.)

Thanks for writing...everything!

Very sincerely,

Lois Grant

September 13, 1992

Dear Dave,

I heard the Overture to "The Magic Flute" on the radio yesterday and it made me think of you. How did you fare in the wake of Hurricane Andrew? I have been wondering how you are and hoping you and your family live north of Miami and were not too badly affected. It has been heartbreaking to read about the devastation.

I enjoyed your columns from the two political conventions and realized that you couldn't come to Atlanta to see Joya because you had to go to Houston! (That's a joke!) She had a great visit to Atlanta and we filled all the slots for channeling. She is tentatively planning to come back here in April for another week, FYI. I realized that I did not include in my previous letters what little information about your overleaves that I do have: Mozart was a 3rd level mature Artisan and you are 5th level mature Artisan. (The Artisan part never changes. Fifth level people tend to be quite eccentric.) I don't know if you care about this or not, but as long as I am writing, just thought I would mention it.

Your column about your son going to the dance recalled memories of my son's first dance in jr. high, about 20 years ago. When I picked him up afterwards, his comment about dancing was, "You know, Mom, it's just random body movement."

Take care,

Sincerely,

Lois M. Grant

September 28, 1993
Dear Dave,

 Last evening I saw in my Oxford Bookstore newsletter that you will be signing your book *Dave Barry Does Japan* next Thursday. I became mildly excited because, being a Scholar, the Oxford is one of my most favorite places on the planet and you are one of my favorite writers. Also, you may remember, I am the one who wrote to you about Michael and Mozart.

 I plan to attend the event at the Oxford, but I would like to visit with you, if that would be possible. There is a neat Caribbean restaurant just down from the Oxford, if you would care to meet my husband and me for dinner. I know these travel schedules can be extremely tight, but thought it was worth asking. I will see you at the signing, regardless.
Sincerely,
Lois M. Grant

 When I got home from work the evening of the big event, Keith said that Dave's secretary, Judy, had called and said he would not be able to meet with us because his son's birthday was the next day and he needed to fly home immediately after the book-signing. I was thrilled to have any kind of response.

 I was excited about this book signing, needless to say! Keith and I left home early and ate fast food. We got to the bookstore about an hour before the appointed time and all the seats were already taken—we had to sit on the stairs! Finally we saw him come in with the escort. He was casually dressed in jeans, a navy shirt and tweed jacket. He did about twenty minutes of commentary—stand-up comedy, actually—and had everyone in stitches. I laughed until my sides hurt. Judging by the warmth of the audience, I was certainly not his only fan in Atlanta. When we came in, we were issued ticket number 123 and when it was time for the book-signing we lined up in numerical order. I placed one of my business cards in the front of *Dave Barry Does Japan*, which I had just purchased, and also brought my copy of *Dave Barry's Only Travel Guide You Will Ever Need*, which my sister had given me for Christmas. When I got to the table, he saw my card and I could tell he recognized it right away. He looked up and said, "Did my secretary call you?" I said yes. We chatted briefly. A photographer was taking pictures and I asked if he would take one of us. Dave jumped up, put his arm around me and posed for the picture. It was so gratifying to meet Dave and for him to be so open and friendly and fun. He truly seemed like an old friend. I just glowed all the way home. When I got home, I opened the books and was taken even higher. He signed one, "To Lois, with great passion, Dave Barry." The other was inscribed, "For Lois, with best wishes—Dave 'Wolfgang' Barry."

Ten

PROTECTION

I have learned that it is very important to follow your feelings, hunches, urges, or whatever you want to call them because these are basic ways Spirit communicates with us. I have three anecdotes to demonstrate this advice.

This first time this became so obvious to me was a Wednesday evening when Keith had gone to North Carolina and was supposed to get home around 6 PM. I came home from work and there was a message on the answering machine saying that his flight had been delayed about two hours. I fed his dog Duchess and ate my dinner while reading the mail and newspaper. There was a newsletter in the mail from the Oxford Bookstore and I decided to take a run over there. I browsed around and I think I bought something. As I was getting into my car, I looked longingly at the yogurt store wanting a cone of chocolate frozen yogurt. No, I told myself, I don't need it. "Doggone it, I want one," I said. I walked over, bought a cone and wandered leisurely around the shopping center, enjoying the yogurt and the beautiful Atlanta evening. Then I got into the car and drove home.

By now it was well after 8 PM and time to take Duchess for her evening walk, which Keith normally did. I put the leash on her and we went outside. As we started up the condo drive, I saw a car from the Atlanta *Journal-Constitution* passing by. Hmm. That's interesting. Then a minute later, here came a broadcasting truck from one of the local television stations. One of the neighbors was outside and I asked him, "Is something going on?" "Yes," he replied, "There's just been a murder-suicide at the end unit." It turned out that a jealous lover had driven through the complex around eight o'clock and rung the bell at his former lover's condo. The new roommate answered the door and was shot at close-range. Then the spurned man shot himself. Spirit kept me from harm with chocolate yogurt. Keith, meanwhile was kept circling overhead in an already delayed flight that experienced further delays before being able to land. If he had been walking Duchess at eight o'clock and a car had sped by him, he probably would have yelled at the driver to slow down and who knows what might have happened.

Not long after that, my daughter Diane, who was then a medical student at Emory University, was doing a rotation in the training hospital Emergency Room. She and one of her colleagues were looking at an X-ray for one of the emergency patients and they were having trouble discerning something. They decided to go up to the Radiology department on the fourth floor to discuss this particular X-ray with a more experienced physician. It was a little unusual for them to leave the E.R. floor, but they felt they needed another opinion and it took them about twenty minutes to run this errand. During this time an angry man walked into the Emergency Room with a pistol. He shot and killed both his wife, who was a patient, and the man on the stretcher next to her.

My third example is not quite so dramatic, but was still very meaningful after we realized what had happened. One of my co-workers, Keith and I decided to go to an American Institute of Architects meeting where well-known architects whom Keith has worked with were showing slides of their work. The meeting was held at a country club where parking was rather limited. Even though we thought we arrived in plenty of time, Keith was forced to park in an illegal spot. We went to the meeting, ate lunch and enjoyed the presentation, but time began to wear on. Suddenly, we all three looked at each other and in unspoken agreement got up to leave. We walked out to the parking lot to find a wrecker just about to tow Keith's car. This proved to us that Spirit is always there to help us and not just in matters of life and death, if we just choose to pay attention.

When "bad" things do happen, it is useful to play them back in your mind and see what intuition or messages you ignored. Spirit may have tried to warn you, but you chose not to notice. It's like the man whose house was flooded. He went up on the roof and proclaimed, "The Lord will save me." A neighbor came by in a rowboat to take him to safety. "No, thank you, the Lord will save me," he said, so the neighbor left. Later a policeman in a motorboat approached, but again the man declined, saying, "No, thank you, the Lord is going to save me." After a while a helicopter appeared overhead and lowered a rope, but they were waved off and told, "The Lord will save me." Darkness fell, the water continued to rise and the man drowned. When he met the Lord in Heaven, he said, "Why didn't you save me?" "What do you mean?" answered the Lord. "I sent a rowboat, a motorboat and a helicopter!"

Eleven

KENNY

SEEDING

Kenny is an engineer from Texas who was working in the architectural/engineering (A/E) firm which moved me to Atlanta. He is a soft-spoken, very gentle man with a wife and four kids, a faithful Southern Baptist family. He wasn't very sure of himself when we first met and whenever anyone asked him a question, his first response was a long "ahhhhhhhhhhhh" while he thought about what he was going to say. Even after he started to talk, there were frequent long pauses which reminded me of the old Bob and Ray routine of the world's slowest talking man. I, having a chief negative feature of impatience, often felt the urge to jump in and help him with his apparent struggle to finish his sentence or thought. Kenny and I worked as part of a team of architects and engineers and we, along with several others, were a bit of a clique who went to lunch and socialized fairly often. I met Kenny's wife Elena at office parties and picnics. A heavy-set Hispanic woman, Elena didn't seem to like me very much. I always aimed to make friends with the wives of the men I worked with and was usually able at the very least to talk to them about their kids, but Elena always remained distant and somehow disapproving. I surmised that she was somewhat jealous or resentful of me, that perhaps she felt I was a threat of some kind.

After a couple of years, the workload in the office began to drop off and one day, seemingly without warning, Kenny was "let go." (This is an A/E firm's jargon for firing without cause. It happens all the time because when an office gets a lot of work, they hire and when work slows down, they fire. Fortunately, there is no penalty career-wise for an engineer or architect who moves around a lot. I call it "Musical Drafting Boards.") Kenny was shocked and hurt and all of us in the clique were outraged that this had happened to him. A week or two later, the unemployed Kenny called me and when I realized it was him on the phone, I said in a very earnest and concerned way, "Kenny, how are you?" There was silence. I could tell he was choking back, or trying to, the tears. He soon got a job at another A/E firm in the same building, so our group was still able to get together for lunch every so often.

One day after we'd had lunch, Kenny, Andy and I were standing outside on the sidewalk when the president of the firm came by. He said, "Kenny! You never came to say good-bye." Kenny answered immediately and rather forcefully, "Good-bye!" When Mr. S. walked into the building, we all erupted with laughter. It was so spontaneous and so unlike Kenny to speak up like that. What a great moment!

As work continued to decline, I was loaned out twice to other offices, one of which was where Kenny was working. They soon offered me a permanent position and I accepted. Once again, he and I were working together. He started asking me questions, for by now my arthritis was in remission due to the methotrexate and the spiritual work, such as meditation, which I had begun to do. (More about this in my chapter which follows.) One day he said, "I thought if you had arthritis, you would have it for the rest of your life." I responded: "That's if you don't change any of your thinking patterns," for by then I was heavily into applying the philosophy which says we create our physical problems by the thoughts we think. I was using positively stated affirmations to counteract the habitually negative thoughts which had been drummed into me.

I like to say, "God only knows and she's not telling," delighting in the shock value. One time after I said that, Kenny seriously replied, "Oh, no, God is male." He would bring up controversial issues, such as abortion, and I would rebut in a friendly way, simply stating my opinion. I knew that Kenny had high blood pressure and it was about this time that I learned he also had hepatitis B. I wanted to share the spiritual causes of liver problems with him, but felt he wouldn't "get it." Daniel Condron says that liver problems are caused by feelings of worthlessness and uselessness. The remedy is to build self-respect. Michael says, "The liver has to do with how much you stand up to what needs to be faced. If you are a person who tries to hide from yourself, who won't tell yourself the truth, you'll have liver problems." Say, "I find tranquility, happiness and love everywhere."

One of the project managers in this office was interested in Kenny's professional development and sponsored his attendance at a workshop called "The Path of Least Resistance." I could tell a difference in Kenny after this confidence-building experience, for he didn't seem to hesitate as much before speaking. But there was still a wall there. Elena, however, experienced these changes as very negative, for Kenny began asserting himself in forceful and unpleasant ways. "He yelled, ranted and raved over the least little thing," which put a lot of stress on their relationship. During this period Kenny developed and expanded his hobby of making decorative objects of stained glass. One Christmas he brought in some stained glass angels he had made and I bought one from him.

After a couple of years, I left this office to work on the big hospital project. During this time Kenny and I would occasionally get together for lunch. I remember one of these lunches in particular because he seemed to be very painfully tongue-tied. I had the feeling he was holding back for some reason. I was holding back, too, because I didn't feel I could discuss any of my spiritual adventures or try to help him express what was in his heart, for he seemed to be still in the grip of a negative fundamentalism. I decided after that lunch that there probably wouldn't be any more because we obviously had so little to discuss. It's not much fun for me to sit one-on-one with someone and not feel like I can openly express myself.

A year and a half or so later, I was asked to work with yet another office on a new medical office building. Imagine Kenny's surprise when we both reported to work on the same day. I was waiting in the lobby that morning when he came in and said, "What are you doing here?" I answered, "Workin'." We both were somewhat amazed that here we were, working together in yet another, our third, office, isn't it a small world, blah, blah, blah! Little did we know that profound changes were in store for both of us, that amazing adventures lay just ahead, that we had a spiritual agreement which we had not yet begun to fulfill.

This time we sat in adjacent workstations in a team arrangement for the project. We were like old shoes for a while, remembering stories from when we had first worked together, catching up on the news about former co-workers and mutual friends, like Andy. We enjoyed discussing television programs. For example, we both liked "Northern Exposure," but every time we discussed it, Kenny would mention how Elena hated it. I had concluded by this time that people who liked that program were usually late mature or old souls and it was proving to be a pretty good indicator or "litmus test." Kenny and Elena were perfect examples. Then the deeper questions started coming up. He started asking me about metaphysical issues, such as astrology, reincarnation and past lives. And what about evil? Kenny knew I was pretty far out in my beliefs and willing to talk about them. Because of his conservative leanings, I tried to be delicate, to protect him from what I really believed (when am I going to learn!), but he seemed so genuinely interested that I held back less and less. I began to think that we must have a teacher-student monad going and had better get on with it.

Finally one day I said, "Kenny, I am going to have to tell you about Michael." So I gave him the introductory lecture and brought in a copy of *The World According to Michael*. He asked more questions and really seemed to be interested. When he asked me what I thought his soul age was, I said "late mature." I was guessing that Elena was a baby soul because of her many fears. After reading the book, Kenny said how relieved he was about the concept of evil. His church had made him feel so responsible and guilty about the existence of evil in the world and he was stressed out because he felt so helpless—he just didn't know what to do about it. "I grew up with the God versus Satan mindset and the book helped me to look at these issues in a new and different way. I never heard anybody say that it was just experience or how reincarnation and karma worked." Now that he understood the place of infant, baby and young souls in the scheme of things and their sometimes ruthless experiments with life and death and creation of karma, he realized that he could cease feeling guilty about the actions of others who are at a different level of development. I felt this was a real step forward for him. He stopped drinking so much coffee and noticed that the veins on his hands didn't stand out as much, a obvious indication of reduced stress.

Elena continued to be a concern, because she just didn't care for any of these new ideas and he was trying to be very open about sharing them with her. I sent for their overleaves: Kenny's profile came back as a sixth level mature Artisan and Elena is a second level young Priest, still under the influence of her family imprinting and not yet manifesting her true soul age.

I urged Kenny to start meditating, the first step to spiritual growth because it lets the Higher Self come through. I also told him to look at himself in the mirror and say "I love you," two hundred times a day. While he didn't talk a lot about his health, I knew that the hepatitis B and high blood pressure were still lurking. He also had suffered from a series of illnesses such as strep throat, the flu and an ear infection. His doctor gave him antibiotics for everything, which made me cringe. I started introducing him to the spiritual causes for physical dis-ease. When he started having nosebleeds, I hesitated to tell him the real reason—feeling ignored—but when I did, he said it was right on.

Howard is a Kahuna healer who I invited to come to Atlanta (more about him in Chapter Twelve). Kenny kept asking about him, showing unusual interest and curiosity and then he totally surprised me by saying he wanted to see Howard, even though he felt "skittish" about it. He made an appointment, but it was such a stretch for him I wasn't sure he would actually show up. Well, he not only showed up, he loved it and even went back for a second session the next day. The following week I could tell that Howard had done more than work on Kenny's body. He had opened him up spiritually as well.

Kenny later told me, "As we talked about Howard I knew that I had to see him. I was skittish, but fully convinced of the need to go. When Howard worked on me I had visions and we communicated spiritually. I saw the face of death—my own death. Howard told me it was the power of death being overcome."

Kenny told me that during the previous fall when he had been unemployed, he had felt a sensation like a wrecking ball thudding against corner of the house. He felt the house stand firm and solid and thought that this was a good thing. He also received a message that he would get a job that he would not have to do anything to get, which turned out to be this medical office building job. We had been brought together again for a reason: there was more than just a building to work on! A couple of days after Howard had worked on him, Kenny was lying in bed digesting what had happened with Howard and once again felt that the wrecking ball was swinging toward the house. Suddenly he sensed in his mind/soul a loud crash, something like heavy glass shattering and falling down. The defenses of many years were breached and truth and light came streaming in. Kenny immediately knew on a very deep level that this was better than the old house standing firm. Soon after he reported this event to me, I noticed that his eyes were brighter than before, that he was not as hesitant to speak his thoughts and generally seemed happier and more at peace with himself. We could only conclude that a great step had been taken in breaking down the old walls he had so carefully spent a lifetime building around himself.

Kenny's 17-year old son George had been the source of some problems. It sounded to me like normal teenage rebellion—wearing weird clothes, not wanting to go to church, hanging out with some not-so-neat guys, etc. George also had problems with his feet, bad enough to keep him from running track.

About a month after seeing Howard, Kenny went by himself to visit his parents in Texas. While he was sleeping, he was awakened by a "voice" speaking to him. "The voice was clearly outside of my body and it had a sense of urgency. The message was repeated several times and there was no doubt whatsoever that this was the most important thing I would ever do," he told me. "I even pinched myself to make sure I wasn't dreaming." The message had two parts: First, that he should trust his son during the next week and, second, that he was a teacher for Elena. When he asked who the voice was, the answer was, "Archangel Michael."

I was very excited when Kenny told me about this fantastic event. I suggested to him that he might be able to do automatic writing in order to record the messages he was receiving and I told him how to protect himself with light and prayers. (Visualize a shaft of bright white light from high above, like a spotlight, surrounding you. Say, "Let no evil enter here, let only good and truth come through," and repeat the Lord's Prayer.) He started to receive the automatic writing with great success after only a couple of halting attempts. One of the first sentences he channeled this way was, *"I have much to teach you about the ways of the Universe."* When he showed this to me, I felt indescribable joy. I gave him a big hug. I was thrilled—and a little jealous. If I can teach others how to channel, why can't I do it for myself? (Probably because I would spend all my time asking questions!)

One afternoon Kenny came by my desk and just sort of hung around. "What are you doing?" he asked. I replied, "Workin'." An awkward pause. "I'm supposed to take your hand." "OK." I gave him my right hand and he held it with both of his. I felt warmth and vibrations. "Here, do the other one." More warmth and vibrations. One of our co-workers came by. "What are you guys doing?" "Holding hands," I said. Nothing more was said. Kenny and I just grinned at each other.

A week later Kenny called me in the evening, which was very unusual. He told me that one of George's friends, the trouble-maker, had committed a heinous torture-murder of a homeless person. He had tried to get George to go along, but George later said that he had had a "gut feeling" that he shouldn't go. He recognized at the time that a very real and powerful spiritual force prevented him from going. It was unusual that during the weekend when the murder was committed, Kenny and Elena knew where George was for the entire time. He had worked, stayed home, watched a movie with the family on Saturday night and gone to church. That, combined with the message of the angel's voice to trust George, helped Kenny and Elena to deal with this awful turn of events and to trust that George had not been involved in any way. I told Kenny, "The reason George is having trouble with his feet is that he has been going in the wrong direction." Talk about a wake-up call! When Kenny told George the story about how he had received the angelic message, it helped George to deal with the situation. Realizing how close he had come to being a part of something truly awful, he knew he needed to refocus his goals. George has since shared the angel story with others, including writing about it for several of his college classes.

Kenny began to keep a journal of the transmissions he was receiving from Archangel Michael, which included some beautiful prayers and affirmations, such as this one:

> *As I rise this morning, I thank you for this day.*
> *Send my roots deep into the Creation.*
> *Raise my crown high unto the Creator.*
> *Cover me with healing and balancing energies.*
> *Wash me with the renewing River of Life.*
> *Set my feet in good directions.*
> *Tune my ears to hear your voice.*
> *Set my heart to speak your love.*

Soon after this, Kenny was told that he is a healer for me.

Archangel Michael: Lois has many hurdles to overcome. She has to stop running away from conflict, which prevents her from dealing with the root causes of her arthritis. You need to show her this if you are to help. By touching her hands you helped to initiate the next stage of her healing. Both of you must be ready to deal with what happens when you are on the other side of the healing process. Wholeness/Wellness is a great gift. To whom much is given, much is required. Be sure you are ready to walk in the light after your healing is complete.

One day we went out for lunch and Kenny suggested that I should open doors and push revolving doors with my hands instead of using my forearms, as I was in the habit of doing because my wrists tend to hurt less that way. The next day Kenny gave me this message:

Archangel Michael: Your role in Lois' healing will continue. Your message Friday about using her hands to open doors was from me. As she uses her hands more and more, doors will be opened to her. The doors she opens are the key to her dealing with the hurts her mother has caused her. As she opens the doors, the pain will be gone and her healing will be complete.

The following Sunday I hurt my foot. I stubbed my right little toe very badly and I stayed home on Monday because I couldn't wear a shoe. Kenny called to see how I was, so I suggested he ask the angels why I did that to myself. I was very excited and intrigued to have this new resource for guidance.

Archangel Michael: Your feet are the means to travel on your path to wholeness and healing. Your spirit is very attuned to your healing and is already there. You have accepted your healing spiritually. Your emotions have not accepted your healing. There is much fear and anxiety about opening the doors to your heart. Your fears are well-founded because the unknown can be frightening, but you must trust me to guide you through the journey to your healing.

During your meditations, ask for information on the doors which <u>must</u> be opened. I will show you, love you, and guide you through this journey. Remember that your condition was many years in the making and it won't be resolved overnight. Your desire is great, but the journey is hard. My love is sufficient to carry you *through. Keep asking for messages, and continue to act on my instructions. All for now.*

Kenny told me he had a vision of Elena leaning against an old split-rail wooden fence. I said, "Maybe you are the fence." The next day there was another, more comprehensive message for me:

Archangel Michael: Lois, these words are hard. You have spent many years building these rooms and closing these doors. (I thought that the architectural terminology was interesting.) *You are now surrounded by love. Dwell in it and start opening the doors. Your angels are with you and will guide your every step. The Love of the Universe is with you.*

Kenny: What is your name?

Archangel Michael: My name is Michael. I am your angel.

Kenny: Is it time to ask about directions for Lois?

Archangel Michael: Yes. Ask in humble obedience. Be prepared to follow through. As I said last night, time is of the essence. We have much to do.

Kenny: Where do we start?

Archangel Michael: With doors. Lois has shut many hurts in her life away in many rooms in her heart. Our job is to help her open these doors.

Kenny: Will you tell me the doors?

Archangel Michael: Yes. The first door is to open herself to feel the hurt and disappointment of all these years.

The second door, the first inside, is the hurt she feels over her sixth birthday party. She blames her mother for the bad time she had.

The third door: The pain she felt about her mother's ridicule of her when she would make a mistake. This happened many times. Lois tried to be perfect, but she couldn't, wouldn't, let herself be who and what she is. Her sister is involved in this hurt. Lois feels some anger because her mother relates better to Linda and doesn't judge Linda as harshly.

The fourth door: The pain she felt about her mother's recognition of her friends' achievements while seeming to ignore her accomplishments.

The fifth door: The pain...

Kenny: (Here he wrote, "I stopped.") Thank you for your answers. I am feeling a lot of anxiety right now. I don't want to hurt Lois' feelings. Please give me something that doesn't hurt right here.

Archangel Michael: Lois is a very important component in the rebirth of your planet. Her book is a key to this rebirth. The focus of her book is friends whom she has helped, but the real focus is Lois. That is why she must be healed.

Kenny: Thank you.

Archangel Michael: The fifth door: The pain Lois feels over leaving behind so many friends and acquaintances from her former life in Michigan. She had to move on, but she did not release her guilt. She avoided the pain of good-byes.

The sixth door: When Lois gets to this door a trip will be involved. If she follows the list and opens her heart to this pain, she will recognize this door, this hurt when she sees it. Red is involved. Lois has the key to this door, but she has hidden it. When she opens this door and experiences the pain and releases herself of the guilt (remember, these are emotions, not intellect) she will be free to move on.

When we reach the end of this journey, her healing will be complete. If she chooses, her hands and feet will be restored to their former beauty. Her love of music is a key to this healing. Praise can flow from her hands, which can be a great comfort to her.

Kenny, do not be afraid. You are in my hands. Lois was correct about your vision last night. As Howard said, you are to be supportive and loving toward Elena. In your vision, she was a young girl. You were the old fence, beautifully weathered gray (look in the mirror).

There are no accidents in this life. All things are for a purpose. Keep looking toward me, the Light, for your immediate guidance. You both, Lois and Kenny, are in a delicate place right now. Attune your ears to hear us. We have much for you to do. Love is the essence of all that we are. Give this to Lois.

Well, that was a lot to absorb all at once. I could not even remember my sixth birthday. Maybe it will return to me, or maybe it doesn't need to. I was thrilled by the depth and clarity of this message and that there was yet another source of spiritual knowledge I could tap.

I couldn't help asking for more and soon gave Kenny a list of questions I had made. I suggested that he could channel answers for me and I would pay him for his time. This was a most agreeable arrangement for both of us. I had easy access to Universal Wisdom through him and I could afford it. Kenny needed the money and it encouraged him. It also made the whole business more acceptable to Elena. Before the morning was half over, he came back with this:

Lois: Do I need to confront my mother, even though I don't think it will do either one of us any good? (Howard had been telling me it was necessary.)

Archangel Michael: This is a question that only you can answer. When you come to this point, you will know the answer. The key here is that you will not be confronting. You will be forgiving. Believe it or not, this is not one of the first doors you must open. Regardless of what forces or influences led us to shut ourselves away, we did the shutting and closing. We must open the doors. The bulk of your work is completely internal. When you get to the last door, it won't be what you are now anticipating. You will not choose the last door. You will find and recognize it. The act of opening will symbolize all that you have achieved. Please try to put this on the back burner, while you work on the other doors. You are being healed. This is about you, not your mother. You can be healed whether your mother ever responds positively or not. The key is Lois Grant's feelings and emotions.

Lois: Can't I just forgive and forget?

Archangel Michael: Lois, you have been trying that all your life. Look at your hands and feet. What does that tell you? To feel the greatest joy, you must feel the greatest pain. To be the most effective writer of your book, I want you to feel joy beyond measure. When you feel emotions rising in you, let them come, rising up from the deepest recesses of your heart. The tears and the feelings you release will cleanse you and soften your heart to feel and experience love. You have looked in many places for your healing. Your healing must come from within. Wait for a while.

I gave Keith the messages to read that evening and he became very serious. He said there was a lot of wisdom in them. He also knew intuitively that there was no way Kenny could have made this up. The next morning Kenny was waiting for me with this:

Archangel Michael: Lois, your fears and concerns right now are grounded in a belief that you will find something dark and horrible tucked away inside your heart. That is not the case at all. The problem is that your heart has these closed areas—closed up hurts, not horrible things, just hurts. They are events that hurt you deeply at the time. They are real. They just got closed away. Many times you did forgive and forget, but you tucked the hurt away. You didn't release it. Try this release:

> *Good morning, All that is Beautiful and Holy,*
> *Flood over me. Fill every space, every pore of my being.*
> *Search out the closed rooms of my heart.*
> *Each day open three doors.*
> *Wash away these hurts. Replace them with your love.*
> *As these doors are opened, multiply them by seven.*
> *I envision all my Heart, all my Soul, all my Spirit, as one,*
> *Balanced, Loving and Flowing in the Love of the Universe.*

This prayer is one that I have used in my meditations nearly every day since I received it.

Kenny and I both felt the need for him to take my hands that morning, so we went to lunch together. We found a quiet corner and after eating, I gave him my right hand. I envisioned us in bright light with all our angels above and around us. We could hear talking and laughing in the restaurant, but our little corner was very quiet and we knew that no one paid us any attention. Then I gave him my left hand. When it was finished, I started to cry. I was deeply moved and could have cried a lot louder and longer if we hadn't been in a public place. When we left, Kenny said he was sure that the tears meant that it was a good beginning, a good release. I felt very light afterwards.

About this time I reduced my hours in the office with Kenny because my own firm with Keith was getting busy. Now that my spiritual work with Kenny was underway, we didn't need to be in the same office every day. We talked frequently by telephone and he started faxing my angel messages to my home office. I went downtown for lunch with him whenever we could schedule it. Every time we had lunch, however, Kenny mentioned how Elena didn't like it when we got together. One time I replied, "Tell her I'm not interested in your body!"

On August 28, Kenny had this conversation with our unseen guides:

Kenny: Dear Michael, Please be with me on my journey, as my guide and inspiration. Thank you for all the help you have been so far. May my heart be open, my eyes be open, may I learn the truth, speak the truth, and grow in peace with all of life. Please accept my love and gratitude for your teachings.

Archangel Michael: You are most welcome. My response to you is clear and loud enough to penetrate the cacophony in which you have chosen to live.

Kenny: Michael, I want to help Lois in her search and want your wisdom in ways in which I can ease her healing. What is her angel's name?

Archangel Michael: Ariel.

Kenny: Michael, May I ask questions directly of Ariel?

Archangel Michael: Yes.

Kenny: Dear Ariel, It is an honor to address you. I want very much to help Lois in making direct contact with you. I care deeply for Lois and want her healing to be complete. I sense the reluctance she feels in trying to communicate directly. Are there some more words that I may share with her to help her open her heart?

Ariel: Yes.

Kenny: May I open a door in her heart?

Ariel: No, only Lois can do that.

Kenny: May I tell her your name?

Ariel: Yes.

Kenny: Why is it so hard for Lois to break through?

Ariel: She thinks too much! Why do you think she has a sprightly angel? She needs all the help she can get to lighten up!

Kenny: What else can I do to help her?

Ariel: Just love her. Pray for her. Lois has set a mighty goal for herself. She is going to be triumphant over the limitations of her human body and disease. Her witness is powerful and will be magnified many times over. I am a sprightly angel, but I speak with

*a small voice. I have to be heard in the stillness. Your Michael can
penetrate the noise of this world. I am in the depths of Lois' heart.*

Kenny: Thank you so very, very much.

After receiving this transmission, Kenny faxed it to me with this
accompanying note:

Lois, There aren't enough words to express my joy in finding
out what is inside of me. Your teaching me has unlocked so many
doors in my heart and soul. I will forever be in awe of the power of
the Universe. Thank you for having the wisdom and courage to
teach me and to be patient with me as I learned.

Watching Kenny's enlightenment has been one the most exciting
things I have ever witnessed. He is like a rose, opening to the glorious
light that shines from the Creator and I am thrilled to have played a
small part in this miracle.

Kenny gave me pictures of his family and I sent them to Joya
with newspaper clippings about the murder to get all the soul ages and
personality overleaves. I was betting that the killer was an infant soul.
We were somewhat astounded when the overleaves arrived and he turned
out to be a sixth level mature soul, pretty far along in his development to
be committing murder. However, the sixth level of any soul age tends to
be fairly karmic. Joya's note said, "This young man was absolutely
clearing an old and violent karma with this homeless person, whom he
has known and liked in many of his past lives."

George is a first level young priest like his mother. If he had
gone with his friends, he would have formed a murderous karma,
something his essence and guides and instincts prevented. Torture and
murder are the most horrifying human behaviors to contemplate. But
Michael reminds us that this planet's human species is very aggressive
and we all, especially in our early lifetimes, have taken lives, paid the
price and learned that this kind of behavior is not rewarding. We learn
these lessons by experiencing them and feeling the emotional intensity
that is characteristic of karmic acts. Many spiritual teachers state with
emotional detachment that there is no "good" or "bad" experience; there
is only experience. George's former friend pleaded guilty to the murder
charge and is now serving a prison sentence.

About this time Kenny began to see Patsy, who is a practitioner
of Inner Nature's Integration (see the Appendix for a description) which

has the stated goal of "restoring human potential." It was a pretty far out thing for him to do, as this work deals with spiritual burdens and very subtle layers of reality. He also did it despite Elena's disapproval. She didn't like Kenny to be seeing a woman and she certainly didn't approve of this "weird stuff." One thing that came up for him right away was Liver Chemistry, which was interesting in light of his history of hepatitis.

Growth is difficult and painful, as Kenny was learning. He continued to have upper respiratory and ear infections. According to Michael, all these problems in his head suggested that he was fighting the messages that were trying to come through from above or there was too much going on and he was suffering from mental confusion. He wrote this on October 11, 1993:

In the name of Jesus of Nazareth,
I release all the blocks in my ear passages.
I release the inflammation that has clogged the canals, the channels.
I release the fear that has kept me from acting, from moving forward.
I release the anger that interferes with my acceptance of life, my
　　　acceptance of who and what I am.
I release my reluctance to move forward.
I lovingly and graciously accept my healing.
Thank you.

The angels answered by giving him the following meditation:

By drinking this water I cleanse my being.
Attract all that is impure, toxic and dead to the water
molecules and
Carry these impurities from my body.

As I walk in the light of His glorious presence,
So shall I be free.
As I hear in the light of His glorious presence,
So shall I be free.
As I speak in the light of His glorious presence,
So shall I be healed.

By these words My life, My heart, My will, My ways,
My fears, My dreams, All of me, then, now and forever,
I entrust to your guidance.
I entrust my heart to your love, My hand to your hand,
My feet to your ways.

Late in November of '93 he asked:

Kenny: Michael, I feel really disoriented. What is going on?

Archangel Michael: There is very strong energy flowing through the Universe right now. Major shifts and changes are taking place which is causing anxiety and discomfort. You are feeling strange right now because of the processing going on in your body and soul and spirit. Much is being worked out in you even as we speak. Here is an exercise:

Picture yourself at the edge of a cliff. Look down. Describe what you see.

Kenny: I see rocks and a stream in the valley. I see grass and flowers, beauty all around. The beauty far exceeds the rocks below.

Archangel Michael: Now picture yourself jumping.

Kenny: I am flying, being carried by you. We are touching down in the grassy meadow. Flowers are everywhere. The beauty is intoxicating. I did not see you, but I knew that you were there. I did not fall, I floated down. There was no fear.

Your provision for me is abundant.

My willingness to follow your leading is complete.

All the choices are mine.

There are many ways to follow. Many choices. All are OK.

Some lead more quickly to growth. I choose to grow.

To be in you.

Nov. 28, 1993 Archangel Michael gave this prayer to Kenny:

My life and all that is I give completely to your leading.
My goals are your goals for me.
I open my hearing, my ears to hear
    what you have for me to hear.
I release my reluctance to hear and speak the truth,

Truth as only comes from the Father.
I choose now to act on this belief.
I sever my ties with all that holds me back.
I am free. I am at one with the Universe.
I choose to see what life has to show.
I love you,
    Archangel Michael

Nov. 29, 1993

My life, my heart, my total being.
I place in the Hands of the Creator.
I accept my role chosen for me.
I accept my place chosen by me.
I accept the Love and Care of the Creator.
My life, My heart, My total being.
All is in harmony. All is at rest.

By our Oneness, By our Beings, By our Love
I free myself to be Yours.
I honor You, I commit to You, I love You as my own Soul.

Kenny and I met for lunch before Christmas to catch up with each other's progress and to exchange gifts. I gave him a copy of *You Can Have It All* by Arnold Patent which is a wonderful resource for prosperity, an area where Kenny and Elena, as do so many of us, need help. This book taught me to say, "I can afford it," instead of, "I can't afford it," because whichever idea we pronounce, we create that situation for ourselves. Kenny gave me an angel of leaded glass which he designed and made. I have the one that he made about five years earlier and the contrast is a perfect illustration of the change in him. The old one is stiff and angular and a little bent over. The new one is graceful and flowing, alive and dynamic. It is a stunning addition to Keith's and my collection of Christmas ornaments.

After the New Year, Kenny began to notice a change in the angel's voice, so he asked what was happening.

Kenny: Is it your intention, Michael, to move on, so to speak?

Archangel Michael: No, but your more immediate communication should now be with Azriel.   He is your personal guardian angel.   I was selected to bring you to the state where you can truly begin to serve.   That is my mission.   As you look at your life, you certainly see changes.   Continued growth is what is in your plan.

Kenny: Azriel, How can I tell the difference in your voice?

Azriel: My voice is a little more gentle. I will not be as able to cut through the clutter. You will be required to maintain your end of the relationship. I have always been with you, but you have not known of my presence. As Archangel Michael told you earlier, you have often heard our voices, but you almost always discounted them. I would like for you to ask me more specific questions.

As Kenny continued to expand his awareness of the loving presence of Spirit in his life, Elena continued to resist it. She managed to find fault with nearly everything he brought up, even the angels, but especially other New Age ideas, such as the entity Michael. I thought he was being too open with her, that it wasn't necessary to share everything when she was obviously so resistant and could turn it on him, but he continued. One night they were having a discussion and for a change Kenny did not retreat from Elena's negativity, but stood his ground. He sensed a sudden release and felt his spirit shoot upwards, "as high as it could go." He felt he had been set free. And there before his eyes was a glowing vision of Jesus! This was an incredible confirmation of the rightness and sacredness of his new growth, a transformation supported by the words he continued to channel from the angels.

Feb. 7, 1994

Good morning, Universe!
I am happy to be alive. I am grateful for another day.
As I open my heart to the Universe,
Fill my total being with Light,
The Light of all Creation.
Shine the Light into my darkest corners.
As feelings and fears come to my mind,
I release them to the Creation.

As I open my heart, Fill my heart with love,
The love of All Creation.

April 19, 1994

Use this affirmation to lower your blood pressure:
See yourself in a pool of light.
See the world around you a cool blue, almost glowing.
Place a gauge in front of yourself.
See the gauge drop a few points to the left.
Say: Open my heart to the peace of the Father.
Calm my soul. Clear my vision.
I am one with the Father. I am one with Life.

August 6, 1994

A message from Archangel Michael and Azriel for Kenny:

Today you are called to greatness. Your acceptance of your gift, your role, is opening in your heart. There are many ways that your gifts can be used. There is much that you need to learn in this regard. There are many teachers who could help you. The teacher who is our choice to help you is Howard Wills. Howard knows that this is in his life plan.

Spend the next two weeks in prayer and meditation about this. You will know when it is time to call Howard. Use this meditation upon arising and upon retiring. There is much power in the thoughts of your heart and the words that you speak.

My Life I surrender to spirit.
My Heart I surrender to spirit.
My All I surrender to spirit.
May all that I am, all that I want
Be in total harmony with spirit.
This day I take to be the day of my new beginning.
My Heart, my All, my Life, I open to the universe.
I am. I am wonderful.
I am on my journey to surrender, to surrender to greatness.
To the One who is All in All, who knows all,
Be the source of Light Everlasting.

This last message was the most astounding yet. Kenny and I were truly in awe of what was happening: my healing and his rebirth! The events of the previous summer when the angels first became manifest in our lives, which we thought were so miraculous, now paled in comparison. To say we were excited and thrilled does not begin to express our feelings. We could hardly wait to see what would happen next.

Next turned out to be a reading by my psychic, Lynn. She came by the house to do a reading for me and I took about two pages of notes of rather general and positive information. Then she started talking about Kenny and I very quickly took four pages of notes! The next morning I "just happened" to have a meeting downtown. Kenny was able to meet me for lunch and I gave him the following:

From Lynn for Kenny: You are one of the Forerunners. Your crown chakra is opening up. In a previous life you mastered wizardry and black temple ordainment. In this life you had to be closed down so that you would not practice until you were ready. You shut yourself down out of fear, a fear of not using your gifts properly. Now it is time to set it right. You know all there is to know, but chose not to remember until now. You hold much power and must use it well and with right action and discipline. There will be temptations that you must not give in to. They will be severe and great. You must remain in alignment and on the right path and not allow the negative ego to come in as it did in that past lifetime.

At this time you are enjoying the sweetness of Spirit. Enjoy it and be grateful. As the teachings become more intense, you will need to remember where you came from. We, your guides and angels, will be there with you. All you need to do is ask and it will be given to you. You will be allowed to make choices. In the next one and a half to two years you will have many tests. You will quit your present job and move to a different kind of work to have more time and a better environment for learning the teachings. Your family will not go with you.

The Southern Appalachians are in a major spiritual vortex—Tennessee, Southern Kentucky, North Carolina. You need to go there for spiritual rejuvenation. You will be healing with or through the stars, doing night work and dream work. Prepare for night duty.

Kenny, you have <u>a lot of power</u>. There is much light surrounding your head, like a big, bright cloud. You have yet to realize how powerful you are. Thank God you started with the angels. I see your left eye like a laser coming out in a triangle, then becoming a circle. You will guide through your sight. Howard will train you to be a shaman. You will do release work.

Kenny was excited and impressed by this profound message. The next day he actually called Lynn to thank her and discuss the message, the first time he had ever talked to a psychic. Then he called me and asked if there were any books he could read that would help him understand it. For once, I couldn't think of a single one! Then on Saturday this came in on the fax machine:

> *In my surrender, give me Peace.*
> *In my surrender, give me Grace.*
> *In my surrender, give me Understanding*
> *Of the boundless love of the Universe;*
> *Of the unlimited power that comes in total surrender.*
> *Surrender to the forces of spirit, to the assumption of roles.*
> *Roles laid down since the beginnings of time.*
> *Since the beginnings of my adventure in Spirit.*
>
> *Praise be to the one who is—I AM.*
> *The total encompassing Oneness of Love.*
> *Praise be to the One who is All, is in All,*
> *Who transforms All into Light Everlasting.*

This day, like many others, is a time for reflection. Reflection on who you are, who you are becoming. You have agreed to a role in this life, a role which will transcend all the glories that you can imagine. It also will be the most difficult thing you have ever done in any lifetime—ever. Remember who you are and why you were chosen. Only those who can fulfill their roles are chosen. You can and will do this great and wonderful work, which is being laid before you, even as we are speaking.

This is from your guides, who surround you with both the mighty Power of the Universe and the gentle strength of the unfolding flowers which herald the arrival of Spring. Praise be to SPIRIT.

I requested Kenny to ask the angels, What is a forerunner?

Archangel Michael: A Foreruuner is one sent to prepare the way for the return of the Master, the Ultimate Essence. Many are called to this work through the ages. You, Lois, have been instrumental in bringing many people to an understanding of their role in this task. The imminent return of this Essence requires much preparation and you are a facilitator in this work. You bring the Forerunners to their life fulfillment. Your scholarly understanding of the ages is the tool that you use to do this work. The name for the souls who awaken the Forerunners is Lightbearer. You carry the light to the Forerunner whose mission it is to take the light and run with it.

It was about this time that Kenny reported to me that he could now look in the mirror and tell himself, "I love you," without hesitating. Now that's progress!

Aug. 22, 1994

This day be granted unto me peace.
Peace in the midst of chaos.
Peace in the midst of pressure.
Peace in the midst of uncertainty.

This day be given understanding;
Understanding of who I am.
Understanding of what I am about.
Understanding of the love of the I AM.

Uncover within me all that is good and pure.
Disclose all that is right and positive.
Praise be to the One who is ALL.

I confess my fear, my really great fear.
I release my fear to the powers of the Universe,

Into the Creation, To be transformed,
Transformed into something beautiful and glorious.

During the fall Kenny was working hard to get the engineering work on a major project completed on time. This meant making many visits to the site, identifying problems, working with the contractors to correct mistakes and convincing the Owner to pay for it. He noticed he was feeling tired, but there was too much to do for him to take time out, or so he thought. After Thanksgiving he noticed his ankles were swollen and went to his regular doctor who referred him to a gastroenterologist, Dr. F., but he put off making the appointment for fear of what might be discovered. Right before Christmas Kenny talked to his Inner Nature's Integration practitioner Patsy who referred him to a chiropractor she regards as a superb diagnostician, Dr. L. Dr. L. sent Kenny a homeopathic remedy for his liver. After the first of the year Kenny started seeing Dr. L. on a regular basis. He added herbs and nutritional supplements to the regimen and Kenny began to experience considerable improvement. He finally got his courage together for an appointment with Dr. F. in February. Based on Kenny's history, Dr. F. immediately scheduled two days of medical tests, including a CAT scan, ultrasound and bloodwork. He mentioned the possibililty of a transplant.

The night before the tests, Kenny was lying in bed, trying to relax and prepare himself mentally and emotionally for the testing, praying for help. Suddenly he saw two glowing oval bright purple lights at his feet. They traveled up his body and settled on each side of his abdomen, one over his spleen and one over his liver. Kenny felt a deep sense of peace and was able to sleep soundly.

Several times during the tests, particularly the ultrasound, the technician told the person in training that what they were seeing was not nearly as bad as what was expected in a liver transplant candidate, but when the test results were complete, Dr. F. told Kenny that his liver was in serious trouble and that a transplant might be required. I was horrified by this and I said, "That's the last thing you want to do, because if you do, it will be about the last thing you will do." He went to see Dr. F. every week for several weeks and the test results began to fall somewhat. The visits became monthly, then every two months and three months, for almost a year; Kenny was still seeing Dr. L. and Patsy during this time.

Before long his hepatitis B virus count was very low and soon went to zero "on its own," to everyone's amazement.

April 14, 1995

> I release my burdens.
> By the power of Spirit and the simple act of my will,
> I lay them down. I turn away.
> I do not look again on them or reclaim them.
> I lay them down.
> I release this energy back to Creation.
> I accept the fullness of Spirit today.
> I accept the sight that I am given.
> I open my eyes to the wonder of the Light.
> The knots in my neck and shoulders I release.
> My burdens are lifted. My stubborn will is yielded.
> I continue in my chosen way.

BLOSSOMING

Kenny called me in May of 1995 and asked to set a lunch date. The night before we were to meet, he called me again and said there was something he wanted to tell me and that it would be "heavy." I said rather flippantly, "I can handle it." I was curious, but didn't think all that much about it. We had hardly sat down at the table when he asked me if I knew how he got the hepatitis. I started to reply something scholarly, like, "from contaminated food," but he interrupted me with, "Unprotected sex with men." I nearly fell off my chair. I was completely surprised, since I tend to accept people as they appear to be. When I asked him if he were gay, he said he wasn't sure, maybe bi-sexual. I gave him the Michael angle on sexual preference, which says that it is a choice made on a very deep essence level prior to birth. All of us occasionally choose lifetimes with attraction toward the same sex. Some essences choose it a lot and tend to "specialize" in it. Homosexual lifetimes generally throw us to the edges of "acceptable" society and teach us to love ourselves regardless of society's criticism. Being part of a minority of any kind usually makes for intensified learning.

Kenny was pleased that I was so surprised. "Sometimes I feel like a walking billboard." He told me, "I had my first contact years ago, one weekend when Elena was out of town, and it developed from that. I was consumed with desire for this type of sex—it let me be me in an anonymous way." He began to use misunderstandings and arguments with her as a rationalization to go to the gay part of town and find someone to have sex with, although it had now been years since he had done that. Well, he was right, it was pretty heavy.

All of the work he had been doing with the angels led Kenny to realize that he needed to tell somebody the truth if he was going to move forward and if he was going to be healed, both physically and emotionally. I was the first person he told because he knew it was safe, that there would be no change in our closeness. But it still took a lot of courage for him to reveal his secret.

Fortunately there was a gay man named Gabriel at the office. Kenny realized that he needed to find a way to deal with his sexuality. "I recognized that not doing so was a major block to my spiritual growth." He reached out to Gabe, knowing he was gay, and the two began to go to lunch and take walks together. During their second walk, Gabe let Kenny know that he was gay, confirming what Kenny already knew. One day the two men were standing in the break area with one of the secretaries. She mentioned to Gabe that she knew that Kenny meditated. This gave Gabe and Kenny a spiritual connection and deepened their fledgling friendship.

The week after Kenny had confided in me, Gabe made a remark to Kenny about clearing the air and Kenny "came out" to him, admitting that he, too, was gay. Gabe has what he calls "gay-dar" which enables him to recognize another gay man, so he already knew. But he was glad for Kenny's sake that it was out in the open, out of that soul-stifling closet. The next day, Kenny received a message from the angels which said that one of his closest and longest-term friends, Hank, was his chosen partner for this lifetime. The first time Kenny saw Hank at a distance when they were in college, he said to himself, "We're going to be friends," and proceeded to initiate the relationship. (I believe this was an example of soul recognition, which occurs when two people with an agreement to have some kind of relationship during the lifetime first meet.) Hank is married with children and lives in Chattanooga. The two families have gotten together fairly often over the years. Kenny says that his friendship with Gabe is a lot like this older friendship in that he chose them both to be his friends and he needs them both in his life.

As one project in the office was completed and another one began, Kenny and Gabe were moved to adjacent workstations which further facilitated their friendship. Gabe began to bring in books and magazines about the gay lifestyle which were fun and helpful to Kenny. It was a true blessing to have someone he could talk openly with and Kenny was grateful to Gabe for being so patient with him at this crucial juncture in his life. I could be helpful and supportive, but sharing with Gabe gave Kenny a closer connection to reality. At one point during their discussions, Gabe put his arm around Kenny to comfort him and show his support. This gave Kenny a very warm feeling and he began to feel attracted to Gabe, even though Gabe was already in a long-term relationship. Kenny introduced Gabe to his family and the subject of homosexuality began to come up in the family conversations. Kenny's teen-aged son was quite negative about the subject, as he had been taught to be, but Kenny pushed him to be more tolerant of Gabe's situation.

When Kenny had his channeling with the entity Michael and Joya in April, Michael said that he had unglued himself from a very stuck place and that he was now manifesting his full soul age—second level Old! Michael also said that Kenny and I are doing a Leader/Follower monad (spiritual agreement). In this type of relationship, the people involved take turns leading and following each other and I can see that we are doing just that. According to Michael, Kenny and Elena had 18 or so years of karma to accomplish in this lifetime and that it was now fairly complete. They are now free to figure out what they <u>want</u> to do with the relationship: mellow it, stretch it, quit it or keep suffering.

The next time we had lunch, Kenny was really struggling with his situation. He told me, "It would be easier for me to kill myself than to do what I have to do," meaning to be honest with Elena and his children. I nearly choked on my sandwich and the sudden tears that came up. I told Kenny, "I love you a lot and I'll help you any way I can." It took me seven years to end my first marriage, so I could relate to his ordeal. During this time of reading and learning to begin to accept himself, Kenny was continually reassured by his angels that the time for telling Elena would work out and all would be well. Needless to say, he was not convinced and the specter of it worried him greatly.

The first time he had gone to Dr. L., Kenny denied that he'd gotten the hepatitis B from homosexual activity because Elena was with him. But after declaring himself to me, when he next went back he told Dr. L. the truth, another big step. On another visit, Dr. L. asked Kenny if he had any fears and of course the answer was yes. Dr. L. gave Kenny a homeopathic preparation to counteract fear and soon he could feel a genuine difference as the old fears began to retreat.

A few weeks later, Elena went to visit her parents for a weekend, which happened to be Gay Pride weekend, celebrated with parades and events in cities all over the country. Kenny took a major step, literally and figuratively, by marching with Gabe and his partner and thousands of other gay and lesbian citizens of Atlanta. He was exhilarated and empowered by the sense of strength and rightness he felt by publicly affirming himself.

One evening Elena and Kenny invited Gabe for dinner and then Kenny and Gabe went to see a local theater group perform the gay play "Torch Song Trilogy". When Kenny returned home after the play and they were getting ready for bed, Elena said, "Can you imagine having sex with a man?" Kenny hesitated just long enough for Elena to sense the real answer. She became very upset, of course, and they spent most of the night talking and crying, trying to find a way out of this seemingly hopeless situation. I was sure that when Elena found out, she would kick Kenny out without a second thought and I had offered him our guest room if he needed it. But she didn't. Elena deserves an enormous amount of credit for sticking with Kenny and searching for a solution they can both live with. She told me later that the words she spoke that night and in subsequent discussions were not from her. The angels were guiding both of them every step of the way and giving her the words to speak at these critical times. Elena has steadily grown in this ability to follow the leading she is receiving from Spirit.

Kenny wanted me to meet Gabe, so we scheduled a lunch. I liked him immediately and it was fun to share incidents from our two very different friendships with Kenny. During lunch Kenny was still in awe of the fact that he and Elena were talking about how to salvage their relationship and trying to work it out so they could stay together. He was so grateful that they were able to discuss it at all. Later that afternoon, when I was back in my office, Kenny called me. "I want to know what you think about my situation," he said. "Are you sure?" "Yes." "Well," I responded, "I think you are trying to do the noble thing by letting everyone down easy and making these compromises. But I don't think you can really be true to yourself if you do that." "I knew that's what you thought." "Thank you for letting me say it." I really enjoy having a friendship where I can express myself so freely. It's very satisfying.

At one of our occasional lunches Kenny told me that Elena no longer gets upset when he and I get together and that my long-time feeling that she was jealous was true. She told him, "I knew you were hiding something," and assumed it was another woman. She has commented several times that since Kenny and I began fulfilling our Leader-Follower Monad, he has changed into a new person. Actually, what he has done is to throw off the old masquerade and reveal the individual he truly is, the extraordinary person that he kept hidden for almost half a century!

In Kenny's own words:

I had thought I was closing off a very small part of myself, but discovered that I had stifled <u>all</u> of my personality. Only in opening myself up did I find out who I truly am. Elena has been very helpful in this search and flowering. She has pointed out my changes as they occurred and the more I changed, the more she reflected them back to me. Initially my changes were disturbing to her, but as the process continued, she began to see me for who I really am and we both began to understand that the real me was much better than the old, closed-up me. The new me is free to grow and I'm now a lot nicer to be around. She is often the catalyst for deepening our relationship because she doesn't hesitate to bring up issues and we have spurred each other in a synergism of spiritual growth. She has learned to follow her leading and the more she does, the more she grows and recognizes what she needs to do.

The angels gave Kenny this perspective on what was happening:

Your wife was given all the words that she has shared with you. As she reads the scriptures, she will see things in a more open way. Your friend Gabriel's role in your journey across the chasm which you had dug for yourself will ultimately be too difficult for her to reconcile. Remind her quietly that you needed a physical manifestation of Spirit as you crossed over that chasm. When Gabriel put his arm around you, he was following his leading. The gentleness, the safety, the total peace that you felt were all from me, for I was there with you every step of the way. You were never alone. Think of all the books that you read as he shared them with you. Those were my choices. The thread through all of them was the search for understanding of who each person truly is. Love was the dominant theme.

As the Scriptures say, "To whom much is given, much is required." You are going to discover the real joy of living. We told you to hang on and enjoy the ride. The ride is about to get really exciting. You have everything that you need to do whatever you choose. All your affirmations and the homeopathic remedy for fear have succeeded in dissolving much of your fear. Ride the crest of the wave, for the view is ever so spectacular!

Kenny: What is Elena's angel's name?

Archangel Michael: Azriel. You have the same angel right now as you are dealing with the changes in your relationship. This will change as your relationship matures.

Aug. 2, 1995

Kenny, your life has taken a giant step in a wonderful direction. While you are coming to terms with yourself, you will notice many things that you always took for granted being shifted ever so slightly. At first it will hardly be noticeable, but as you grow, it will become more pronounced.

Your analogy of the razor-blade-edged tightrope came from me. You are being chosen to do some wondrous things. We are going to give you some meditations to use as you begin your new growth. Because you listened well, you are ready now to begin learning the tools for your healing work. You already know them subconsciously, but we will bring them to your conscious awareness.

These are your new meditations:

MORNING

As I rise this morning of a new day,
Thank you for the light.
Place in my heart the joy of now.
Place in my spirit the joy of being.
Place me in quiet rest.
As I open my heart, as I open my eyes,
As I hear the voice of spirit,
Open in me the wellspring of life.
Thank you for this day.
Bless this day, these hands, this heart.
Open my hands to serve and to receive.

WORDS TO LIVE BY:

My life, My joy, My spirit be One.
I love and approve of all that I am.

EVENING

This day has ended. All is well
May the sweet peace of rest enfold me now.
May I rise in service to the higher planes.
Send the gentle strength of the quiet Spirit.
Hold me in Your hand.
Bless me now, for All Is Well.

August 25 , 1995

Archangel Michael: Kenny, There is much to be accomplished in your lifetime. It is of paramount importance that you return to using and sharing your gifts. Continue to share with Gabe. There is much healing and awakening that is to take place in his life and you have much to learn from him. This weekend, as in tonight, start your exercises and your meditations. As you return to this way of dealing with life, you will be completely healed and, indeed, will advance to the next level.

As you enter the light, let it shine from within.
Turn your eyes inward as you look down life's pathway.
In your heart, know that All is one.
In your spirit, know that All is now.
In your life, know that All is beauty.
Rest in the Oneness of All That Is.

My life, my all, My calling, my call.
I accept this life, which was laid down before the ages:
To awaken the light, the ancient wisdom,
The knowledge of All That Is;
To be in the light, To walk before the light;
To walk before the light and be guided by All That Is.
Peace.

As I was working on this book Kenny and I talked often about whether to include the part about his being a gay man. We finally agreed that this part of his story needs to be told, even though there are risks and Elena was not pleased with the idea. He said that when he first heard Archangel Michael's voice, he thought to himself, "Wow! I must not be gay," for he actually believed at that time that the angels would not bother with, much less love, support and approve of, a gay man. He now realizes that the angels are not so limited, that their love and the love of the Creator is boundless and unconditional, that a person's sexual orientation is not a strike for or against them.

I began to write my questions for the angels on my computer and copy them to a diskette for Kenny. He channels the answers at his office computer during his lunch hour. At the end of one of my transmissions, he added:

Lois, I really enjoyed doing the questions on the computer. The answers flowed more freely. It seems to be the way to go. Your love and compassion and concern for me is satisfying beyond measure. I feel I have unlocked a key or door, so what I visualize or create comes to be. Join me in this planning. Thank you.

Kenny came over to my house one weekend to read his chapter in progress. When he finished, he said, "Wow!" He had a couple of minor comments and then I showed him the photos from a party we had given in October. His picture was especially wonderful because he was wearing a big smile and his eyes were so bright and clear. He later asked me for a reprint because of the following message.

Nov. 13, 1995

As you looked at the photos at Lois' house yesterday, you saw joy in your face. There was real happiness. This outward reflection of the inner presence of light is what is available as you walk in the light. Get a copy of the photo from Lois. That is the real Kenny.

Words change, ideas change, but the Eternal presence of Spirit, of Light, in the lives of people hasn't changed for thousands of years. As ideas become codified by philosophy and religion, sometimes they get stagnant. As time passes, fresh infusions of life are necessary to get things going again.

People tend to accept a pittance of the presence of Spirit. They are afraid to ask for more. Behold! Ask and it shall be given. The truth will set you free!

At one of his regular checkups with Dr. F., the hepatitis virus factor was elevated again. Chronic illnesses advance and recede, waiting for any weakness to let them rise again. They challenge us to grow and grow and then grow some more.

Dec. 2, 1995

Kenny: Michael, bring me words of direction and comfort to carry me forward in my journey.

Archangel Michael: Dr. F. informed you that the hepatitis B was active again. In its active state it can easily be conquered. The secret is in your believing what we have told you, that you are called to a place of wonder, of healing, of Oneness.

You are a man with a homosexual nature. This is who you are. You must accept yourself for who you are. As Elena said, you don't have to change, just be yourself.

Yesterday wearing the AIDS awareness ribbon was an important step. Do not fear being yourself. Truth is an intoxicating freedom. Don't censor your feelings or thoughts. Let them out. As you have seen, your honesty with Elena has transformed her love for you. If that doesn't defy all human logic, what on earth does?

As you deal with the active hepatitis B, recognize what part of yourself is represented by it. During your meditations, make lists of all the times, events and feelings which come to mind. You have invested so many years in disliking yourself that you need to go back and release all those hurts and fears. You have put the real Kenny off in a corner and not allowed him to be seen because you are afraid of who you truly are.

In times past, you did abuse your power greatly. You knew when you came into this lifetime that you had chosen a great goal for yourself. As you open yourself to this very real part of you, you need only to keep your focus on the Creator and all will flow smoothly and richly. Total transformation is your goal.

Wear your feelings proudly. You don't have to tell the whole world everything you think and do, but you must open your heart and let the Oneness of Spirit shine forth from your face.

Total healing is yours. The healing is not just of hepatitis, it is also the setting in place of all that you are. Remove from yourself what is not the real Kenny. As you discard the fears and hurts that you carry as a shield, you will discover a lightness of being that is totally transforming. This growth can be a very enlightening experience. Expect to be surprised at things you discard. What you are doing is reordering the priorities in your life.

While there are sacred places where you can perceive the presence of God more clearly and more focused than in your present environment, you can also know God very clearly in the midst of your everyday life.

Liking yourself makes the process of living a powerful and fantastic experience. Disliking yourself produces the tortured existence to which you condemned yourself for so long. Let yourself be free. Let yourself be whole. Let yourself be healed! You have a very important assignment on the planet. We want you to enjoy fulfilling your role. There are two alternatives. You know in your heart that living free and whole is the way that you would prefer to let the light shine forth. Grasp the ring! Go for the gold! Be the person that you are!

Over the next several days, Kenny responded to this message by writing the following affirmations to himself:

Dec. 4-7, 1995

I forgive you for the hepatitis B.
I forgive you for all the sexual activity.
I forgive you for following your desires.
I accept wholeness. I accept wellness.
I accept a liver free of damage.
I accept antibodies to hepatitis B, the disease over and done.
I accept my homosexuality.
I release the guilt that I have carried all these years.
I accept whatever lies ahead in terms of relationships.
I accept my gift of creativity with stained glass.
I release my procrastination about getting started.
I release my fear of communion with the forces of Spirit.

I release my previous conclusions about the way God works.
I accept my sexuality, the totality of my being.
I accept Elena's love for me.
I accept wholeness. I accept my good health.
I accept my role as healer and conveyor of angel messages.
I release my fears and doubts.
I no longer want to hide behind my illness.
I am free. I am whole. We are One!

I choose life.
I accept the promised abundance.
I accept my Self.
I love myself.
I choose to be free.
I choose to be true to myself.
I am Wonderful!

Thank you, Creator of us all.

December 7, 1995

Archangel Michael: Kenny, this is a day that you will always remember as the beginning of seeing the path that you have chosen. Life paths are reached, not by feeling, but by the simple act of choice. By choosing to see, you see. By choosing to be, you are. By choosing life, you have it and abundantly, many times over what your physically-bound eyes are currently seeing. By choosing healing, you have it. When you choose a goal, the paths open before you. Remember that for your protection and safety, some of your vision is limited. Use this meditation for yourself and anyone with whom you choose to share:

> *Today I choose the light.*
> *I choose the light of seeing.*
> *I choose to be, I choose to be free.*
> *I choose to be the creator of my reality,*
> *My reality in alignment with my chosen path.*
> *I choose healing.*
> *I choose to live in the center of the golden light,*
> *The golden light of transformation and healing.*

During the holidays, Kenny and Elena spent an evening with two couples they have known for many years. They took a major step forward by confiding in their friends about the problems they were having and Kenny openly stated that he was gay. While it wasn't easy to share this, both were gratified and encouraged by the love, concern and support that were expressed to them.

At his last office visit in 1995, Kenny's virus count was up to 124 and by January it had increased even further to 196. Dr. F. wanted to give him a new drug known as 3TC when it was under development and Kenny agreed to try it. After only two weeks, the count was down to 10! When Kenny went to the office to get the results, both Dr. F. and his nurse were so excited that Dr. F. forgot to give Kenny his new prescription! They fully expect the virus to be defeated. There was true joy and enthusiasm in Kenny's voice when he called to tell me these results and I was thrilled for him. While 3TC is being given the official credit, I believe that Kenny's spiritual work is the engine driving his recovery.

Feb. 27, 1996

Today is a new beginning. You have discovered much and responded well in the last few weeks and events are unfolding before you. Your health is greatly improved. You are at a crossroads in your life. You can choose to stay on your path and grow at a rate that is determined by how well you are functioning as Elena's teacher. As she has shared with you repeatedly, she is hearing the voice of her angelic guides much more readily than ever before. The other pathway for you is to branch off more on your own. You do not have to give up your family if you choose this path. They are with you and will be with you. The relationships may be altered somewhat, but their essence will stay the same.

You are feeling a very strong pull to this other pathway. It is a glorious way and much can be shown to you in this pathway. To aid you in your decision, use the following meditation:

My life and All That Is, My life and all that I have chosen,
My life and all that I have accepted, I now receive.
I open to receive the blessings, the light,
The golden light of understanding.
I place mySelf in the center of the golden light.
I receive in my heart the power of knowing who I am,
Who I have always been,
To know the All In All, the center of Being,
The light of understanding,
The awakening of my hidden Self;
To blossom;
To rise in Oneness with the All That Is, the great I AM.
Thank you, Spirit. Wash over me.
Cleanse me and purify me to walk in the Light,
In the wonderful Spirit of Peace.

As I worked on this manuscript, I gave Elena and Kenny a copy and asked for their comments. I knew it would be painful for Elena, but she wanted to read it. I wrote her that if she felt that her part of the story was not properly told, it was because I didn't feel I had access to it. She answered with a long letter which can only be described as honest and courageous, the result of much growth and soul-searching. She wrote:

> The Lord has worked miraculous changes in our marriage. It defies all logic that Kenny's being honest with me could bring about the wonderful changes within our relationship and within ourselves. Praise God that we were open enough to Him and each other to allow this healing to take place. Kenny had closed not a small part of himself from me, but his entire wonderful self. I am thankful to the Lord for giving me the opportunity to get to know my wonderful husband. <u>The Lord must receive credit</u> for the amazing healing in our marriage and our lives.

Kenny and Elena's story is still in progress. In fact, I suspect that it has only just begun. As they continue to take the steps toward the fulfillment of their goals for this lifetime, doubtless another equally exciting chapter is waiting to be written. We can hardly wait to see.

PETALS

This section contains more of the prayers and meditations that Kenny has channeled from the angels.

August 28, 1993 Words from Archangel Michael, given to Kenny to share with his father when he was ill:

Daddy, I love you. I care deeply about you and all that happens to you. Thank God for His hand in bringing you through a most difficult healing experience. Thank God each day for His little miracles: for each breath you breathe, for each bite you eat, for each step you take, for all the love that surrounds you. Your body is His temple and He has chosen that you dwell in it for several years yet to come. You are in His hands. Love your wife and let her know how much her love means to you.

Oct. 8, 1993 When Busy and Stressed

As time rushes by, grant me peace.
Enfold me with your wings.
Clear my vision, Bless my heart.
Grant me peace.

Jan. 8, 1994 Expression of Gratitude

As a child of the Light, I fully open my heart.
I praise the Creator
For all the glorious fullness,
For all the glorious oneness,
For all the glorious Joy, Peace, Love
Which flow in unceasing streams.

Jan. 24, 1994 Before Sleep

In the evening As the day is ending
So my day's journey takes a rest.
My spirit rejoices As the rest of sleep comes.
Sleep frees the spirit to stretch and grow unfettered.

Each evening as I rest upon my bed I trust my soul, my
    spirit to the powers of the Universe.
I give my body to rest, to sleep.
I free my spirit to soar In the heavens. To dust among the
    stars.
To soar with the angels. To be with the Creator.

Feb. 14, 1994 Prayer for Guidance

As I open my heart to the Universe, Cleanse me.
Lead me in my chosen path. Guide me in my chosen ways.
Clarify unto me my vision.
For Life, For my Service, For my Mission.
Thank you for opening the doors of opportunity.
Thank you for the transformation which comes from total
    surrender.

Feb. 18, 1994 In the Morning

As I rise each morning I greet my day.
By all I am, By all that I have, I release.
I release mySelf to the Creator, to become the Creation
To become ME!
We have been here before, We will be again.
Our lives are interwoven with the Universe.
We can become one, One with All.
I release me.

April 6, 1994 Prayer of Surrender

My life, My all, My being, My oneness, My relationships
I release To the Creation and the Creator.
I accept the Perfect, the Harmony of the Universe.
Spirit, flow through my life,.
Wash over me in abundant waves of love, joy and peace.
Bring me life and joyous abundance.

Sept. 19, 1994 Praise and Blessing

Today I see the glory. Today I see the light.
Today I see the splendor.

Open your eyes. Lift up your head. See. Believe.
The Lord is coming!
Majesty and Glory belong to the One Who is ALL,
Who IS IN ALL,
Who transforms All into Light Everlasting.

Jan. 13, 1995 Letting Go into Love
In all things, give thanks to God, The Father of us all.
In all things, give praise.
Praise to Spirit, who empowers. In all things express joy,
Joy overflowing Down like unending streams of light.

Look deep within your heart.
Release everything that comes to mind.
Release facts, thoughts, ideas, feelings, hurts, joys.
Return everything back to the Creation from which all
*   things come.*
You are Creation.   You are created.   You are one with
*   Spirit.*

March 3, 1995 Before Eating
Bless the food which I now intake.
Transform this food to the energies that I need.
Bless my body with healing.
As the temple for my spirit and soul and mind,
*   I consecrate my body to your service.*

PART TWO

Healing

Twelve

LOIS

HERSTORY

I started having arthritic pain in the spring of 1975, when I was considering going back to school to get a degree in architecture at the "advanced" age of 37, an idea less than enthusiastically received by my husband Jack. I now believe that the arthritis was the physical manifestation of my inner turmoil, a conflict between my true Self, which knew that I needed to move forward and strike out on this path, versus my lifelong programming, brainwashing, if you will, to be content to be nothing more than a housewife and mother and keep my thoughts and true feelings buried as deeply as possible. So-called negative emotions, particularly anger, were forbidden in the home where I grew up as well as in my marriage. Michael later told me that Jack and I had twelve years of karma to complete, so the relationship was due to end around 1970. We were actually having problems at that time, largely because I didn't like his workaholism, but Jack decided to change jobs and so we patched it up and stayed married for another twelve years. No wonder I got sick! The arthritis was symbolic of my not moving on in my life. We both were the products of hypercritical, perfection-expecting parents who either withheld their love or parceled it out only under stringent conditions, thus teaching us to deny our feelings and rendering us incapable of true intimacy. I was never able to please my mother, though I tried mightily. I have to this day never had anything but a superficial conversation with my emotionally unavailable father. While he is a kind man who provided well for his family, he has never been able to express in a meaningful way how he felt about anything.

One of my main motivations in opening up a new life for myself was the example of my mother who had an excellent mind but who never did anything substantive with it beyond creating a home and playing bridge. The lack of a meaningful outlet for her creativity caused unacknowledged and repressed frustration which was turned into an intense, microscopically over-managed style of parenting. I vowed I was not going to do that to my own children and when aptitude testing showed that "medicine, architecture or composing" would be suitable careers for me, I opted to look into becoming an architect. I learned that there was an architecture school just a fifteen minute drive from my house and decided to try it. I entered the school as a sophomore and whenever they gave me an assignment, I said to myself, "I can do this."

Although school was intellectually challenging and exciting, it was also stressful and created a lot of problems at home. I am convinced that it was these new stresses, added to my habitually repressed emotions, which precipitated my rheumatoid arthritis. The arthritis quickly progressed into a clinically severe case: pain in nearly every joint in my body, especially my hands, knees and feet; extremely difficult walking; continuous low-grade fever and fatigue. Jack was not sympathetic and I later learned he didn't believe that it really hurt; he thought I was doing it on purpose to inconvenience him and to get out of doing physical things like housework, yard work and his favorite activity, backpacking. Well, maybe I was, but not consciously. He was also mystified that one day the pain would be in one knee or the other, then the next day in my shoulder or ankle or elbow.

I fought back in every way I could think of at that time. I started going to a rheumatologist who gave me gold shots, Motrin, cortisone injections in my knees, and tons of aspirin. With this seemingly untreatable agony, I finally felt I had a good reason to consult a psychologist, which I had considered doing for years. Russ was a member of our church and it was acceptable to Jack that I see him. His advice and gentle acceptance of my idiosyncrasies helped me recognize some of my destructive thought patterns and behavior, such as always taking the blame for anything that "went wrong" at home or literally punishing myself with pain and illness when I made a mistake. I had for years denied to myself that I was ever unhappy. If I was unhappy, I rationalized that there was something wrong with me and denied my right to feel anger and dissatisfaction. Russ also pointed out to me that expecting my mother to love my children was a fantasy. Through the counseling I began to learn how to express my anger constructively instead of holding back and stuffing it into my body. I learned how continual depersonalization (treating someone as if they are less than a full person) had made me feel a helpless rage. An example of this was Jack's attitude when I was writing documentary radio programs for a well-known Detroit radio personality. When one of my programs was presented on the air, I got pretty excited, but Jack never seemed very interested. However, he was truly thrilled when he came home one night and I had painted the basement stairs. He praised me repeatedly with unusual enthusiasm. It was obvious that using my brain did not impress him, which is a real problem for a Scholar. No wonder my pain and disability continued to get worse! My hands and feet became deformed. Finding shoes to fit my knobby feet became a major concern because shoe stores don't carry the wider sizes and it was embarrassing to show my feet to a shoe salesman. I soon found that ordering by mail was the best solution.

In spite of my illness, I enjoyed the architecture courses and in five years I had earned a Bachelor of Architecture degree. I quickly landed a job in my new field working on hospitals, which I loved. I really felt launched into this carefully planned new phase of my life: My son and daughter were both in college and I had a brand new career! A year and a half later, however, the Detroit area was hard hit by recession and my new-found career came to an abrupt halt when I was "let go." Unemployed and struggling to find a new job, I began exploring alternative therapies. Russ recommended a chiropractor/kinesiologist who put me on a low-stress diet which eliminated foods which are stressful for the body to digest, such as red meat, caffeine, refined flour and sugar, citrus fruit and dairy products except for yogurt. I still observe these guidelines for most of my diet. I tried yoga, but it was a sad joke because I couldn't get up off the floor by myself. Then I attended a "stress seminar" at a hospital. Their main recommendation to combat stress was to relax twice a day, which was nothing more than sitting in a chair with my eyes closed for ten minutes, morning and evening. I started doing this, realizing that it is akin to Transcendental Meditation, yoga, prayer, exercise and other traditional stress-easing activities which allow the brain to go into neutral. I believe that taking those few minutes twice a day to just *be* allowed my Higher Self to come through. Within six weeks I was convinced that if I were going to have any hope of stopping the progression of my arthritis, I must begin to remove agents of stress from my life. The most prominent of these was Jack. Before I moved out I told him, "I need to find out if living without you is as stressful as living with you." I was so incapacitated that I wasn't sure I would be able to manage living alone, but I had to try it. Two weeks after I left him, I knew I had done the right thing. I remember waking up and feeling more relaxed, as if I were on vacation. And no wonder. If I didn't want to clean up a mess, I didn't have to. Nobody got hurt, nobody got sick, nobody got mad. I was able to do, or not do, anything simply because I wanted to. This new-found freedom was wonderful and led me to recognize how much I had been doing all my life to please everyone else and how little to please myself. It was as if my own needs and feelings had had no validity in my world. But now they did. I liked it. I now believe that my Higher Self engineered my job loss so that I would at long last confront these issues and take the necessary action to rebuild my life. While I was working, I could keep going in the same old way, but without that structure I had to face the reality of my life, how unhappy I was.

As I struggled to create a new life for myself, I continued reading everything I could about my illness. Scholar that I am, I have always been a great reader and library hound. Now that I was unemployed and single I had time to pursue this favorite pastime as much as I wished. I became more and more intrigued with the idea of psychic healing and many of my "relaxations" were spent visualizing myself getting well, my joints becoming healthy again. I also began to absorb the idea that we create our own reality and experimented with visualizing things like parking spaces opening up for me. It worked pretty well.

A friend who had an architectural practice in his home asked me to do some free-lance work for him and that helped me a lot Then in the summer of '82 I actually returned to work at the firm that had let me go and also enjoyed a comfortable relationship with Herman, an architect who was twenty years older than I was. I now know that we were doing what Michael (see Chapter Six) calls a Pivotal Facilitator Monad, an agreement made before the lifetime that one person will come into the other's life, make a big impact and turn/pivot the other around. Herman was so good for me. He made me feel loved, accepted and able to relax. After my divorce became final, I bought a condo and was actually beginning to enjoy some happiness. But I still was very sick. I had a hard time walking because my feet were terribly painful and deformed. Many times I counted every step because of the pain. Someone recently asked my what it felt like and I replied it was like having buttons taped to the ball of your foot. If that doesn't sound very painful, try it! I had what I called "attacks" regularly. Technically known as flare-ups, they usually occurred late in the day. I would start to feel achy and as the day wore on, the pain would get progressively worse, like having very sore muscles everywhere. I would spend the evening just lying down. Getting up to take a shower and get ready for bed was an agony, although the hot water was the only thing that really felt good. I took Darvon for the pain, which didn't really help much—it usually kept me awake with a dry mouth and made my head spin. Usually the pain was less by morning, but it often took 48 hours for an attack to really end.

My rheumatologist recommended that I start taking methotrexate in pill form. This is an immuno-suppressive drug used in chemotherapy which seemed to be having good results at low dosages for patients with rheumatoid arthritis. It had a few drawbacks, though. First of all, by definition it suppresses the immune system. No one had ever taken it for twenty years. If I quit taking it, I was told, I would be likely to have a relapse in three or four months and then be worse off than before. Methotrexate is very hard on the liver, so you can't use any alcohol: "I don't even want you taking Nyquil!" After continuing to endure more pain and thinking about it for several months, I decided to try it. The routine meant that I had to go to the hospital lab to have blood drawn every other week, wait several days to get the liver enzyme readings and then call my doctor to find out how many pills I could take. After a time (nothing for arthritis works immediately) I started having somewhat less pain. I still had the "attacks," but they didn't seem to last as long.

Herman passed away suddenly in December of 1983. He had always told me, "I am not the man for you. You are going to meet someone else, someone who doesn't care about your hands and feet." This bewildered me and made me cry because I loved him. He had stabilized me and prepared me for the next phase of my life by opening me up to love. I didn't realize that his lifetime was complete and he was about to check out. On the Sunday before he left, he said, "You don't understand, now's the time to go." I said, "But what about me?" And he answered, "You'll feel bad, but you'll get over it." I was depressed by this, but didn't know what to do about it. I found him in his apartment the following Friday morning when he didn't come to work, apparently the victim of a heart attack. Herman was right: I felt very bad. I grieved for him every day. But Herman was also right about something else: In March of 1984 I met Keith. Keith's first wife Jean had passed away a year earlier (the same month my divorce was final) due to complications of multiple sclerosis. She had been in a wheelchair for twelve years, so he was very considerate of my disabilities and my deformities didn't bother him at all, just as Herman had predicted. I was amazed that he could be interested in someone with another chronic illness, but he said, "As a matter of fact, it attracted me."

There was another major source of stress that I needed to remove from my life: the cold, damp, gray Michigan climate. Winter seemed to be endless and I came to feel like it was being done to me. Putting on heavy coats, boots, gloves, etc., was all very painful and time-consuming. Walking on snow and ice was very difficult—I couldn't walk easily on a carpet! And I was afraid to go out when it was icy because if I fell down, I couldn't get up by myself. At this time Seasonal Affective Disorder (SAD) was just beginning to be recognized as a syndrome, but had not yet been named. This is a condition in which depression is brought on by light deprivation. I remember reading about the studies in the newspaper and laughing because they used people from Michigan for the studies! It is nothing in the Detroit area to go for a week without seeing the sun and in the winter it gets dark at 4:30 in the afternoon. Every year I had to talk myself through December. After December 21, I would tell myself, "The solstice is over now, so the days will start getting longer." One year I was so far down that in the spring when things started turning green and I could hear the melting ice running in the gutters, I was truly surprised, for I felt like it was going to be gray and cold forever. I am now convinced that this lack of light aggravated my illness. So on our third evening together, I asked Keith how he felt about Arizona. I wasn't going to get involved with anyone who had to stay in Michigan!

Keith's son Scott and daughter-in-law Sue were living in Atlanta, Georgia. In the spring of 1985 Keith and I decided we were ready to make a commitment to each other and he asked me to marry him. Jack's name is a difficult one to spell and pronounce and after the divorce I had gone to court to reclaim to my exquisitely comprehensible birth name. I told Keith I didn't want to change my name again for anybody. He said, "I don't want to wear a ring," and I said, "Deal!" Then one day he asked me, "What would you think about moving to Atlanta?" I said, "Great, let's do it!" Four months later I had a job and an apartment in Atlanta. Keith soon found a job, too, and we were married in August. We never intended to have a traditional married relationship. Rather, our announcements said, "We have created a joint venture." Two other miracles happened that summer. Sue got pregnant with little Mark who I believe decided to come in once he knew his grandfather Keith would be in Atlanta to mentor him. And my daughter Diane decided to move to Atlanta so she could attend Emory Medical School. The only blemish was Keith's nephew Jody who resented me, feeling that Keith was being disloyal to Jean by ever loving or marrying again. Jody had been very attached to his Aunt Jean and Keith was like a father to him.

I found a new, self-described "aggressive rheumatologist," Dr. M., who started giving me methotrexate by injection, which is easier on the liver than taking it by mouth, and Trilisate, which is related to aspirin but doesn't cause stomach problems. This meant a weekly visit to his office for bloodwork and the shot, which was a bit of a chore and expense. But within a year and a half I was in remission. I remember realizing that I didn't seem to need as much sleep as I had before. And then one morning I came down the stairs and my knees didn't hurt! This was unheard of. I also think part of it was due to the Atlanta climate. I didn't realize it until I experienced my first Southern winter how much better I felt, simply because the days were so much longer. At 6 PM on December 21, the sky in Atlanta is still pink! What a wonderful difference! No more SAD! Another factor in the remission was that Keith and I were very happy together. He gave me emotional support I had never known before. We lived for a year in an investment condo and then bought a condominium townhouse. We stated at the time that this would be our last move. It was my fourth move in four years and I was ready to stay put.

The remission of my arthritis was real and I enjoyed regaining the ability to do many things that had previously been painful or impossible, such as clap my hands, open a can of Coke, put on pantyhose or take off a jacket without pain, use a stapler, iron standing up, and hold a baby. It was wonderful.

In addition to the weekly office visits and weekly and monthly lab work, I was instructed to have a liver biopsy each year. I did this twice. A liver biopsy is performed by driving a foot-long tube into your side to extract a sample of your liver tissue. Yes, it hurts and it requires a day in the hospital because they need to be sure you don't hemorrhage. The second time I submitted to this, the assault had to be repeated and I went into shock. I remember lying in the hospital bed thinking, "There has got to be another way."

A co-worker introduced me to the channeled Michael teaching (see Chapter Six) and I became truly fascinated by it. I had my first channeling with Joya Pope in the summer of 1988 and Michael told me that I would cure my arthritis and that I could become a "medical curiosity." Michael gave me many tips on diet, vitamins, and exercises. One of the most helpful recommendations was to read *You Can Heal Your Life* by Louise Hay. I typed up and carried the applicable affirmations with me, repeating them to myself often. I especially liked the one for Nervousness, "I am on an endless journey through eternity and there is plenty of time," and the one for Bruises, "I am kind and gentle with me." I found myself becoming more relaxed, especially when driving to an appointment and I stopped bumping my shins on the dishwasher or ramming my hands into things. I bought Louise Hay's tape called, "Love Your Body," and played it in the car while driving to and from work until I nearly memorized it. I began to love myself and also to love my body. And I kept getting better. The only place that really still hurt was my feet.

Other interesting tidbits from Michael were that my daughter Diane and I are from the same entity, which helps explain why we are so close. We never did go through the typical teen-age-daughter-mother problems. And when I asked what my healing animals were, they answered, "Cats, bears and your husband."

I still had problems relating to my mother. I went to visit her (and my dad) for Thanksgiving in 1988. We had a disagreement because I was looking at one of her books. The conversation went something like this:

"Don't touch that book, that's one of my book club books."

"I'm just looking at it, I'm the last person who would hurt a book!"

"I don't like the way you talk back to me. After all, I'm the adult!"

"Well, I'm 50 years old. When do I get to be one?" No answer. Later I tried to hug her and told her, "I love you." She did not respond. When I came home, I wrote the following:

November 26, 1988

Pain is what you feel when someone doesn't want you to be who you are. It is very painful when that someone is a person you would like to have a good relationship with;

...it is especially painful when the person is someone you want very much to have a loving relationship with;

...it is excruciating when that someone is your mother.

Yes, she is sick. I know she is incapable of showing me love. And I shouldn't let it hurt me. But it does.

I felt the strongest I have ever been while we were there. I want to believe that I have made progress. But when I say, "I love you," and there is no reply, yes, it hurts. When she doesn't want me to do anything but agree with her, it is difficult. And when she treats me like a six-year-old child getting jelly on her book, it seems pretty hopeless.

Well, I have tried recently to be honest with her and I have gotten nowhere. Will I try again? Not for a while. Because it hurts.

Some time after this I had a dream. My son Mark was swimming in the pool where Linda and I learned to swim. He was wearing a green bathing suit. Mark always liked to swim underwater and I was watching him. He stayed down for such a long time, I started to be concerned. Finally he came up, making a very painful moaning cry when he broke the surface. I woke up and was very worried. Was something wrong with Mark? I went to work and tried to call him— there was no answer at either his home or work. I asked a friend who channeled his guide to ask for me if Mark was OK. The answer came back that Mark was fine, the dream was about me. I should sit quietly and recall the dream and its meaning would come clear to me. It was not until the end of the day when I got into my car and began driving home that I started thinking about the dream. I had a true flash of understanding. Mark is my firstborn, I am my mother's firstborn. They are both Scorpios. Scorpio is a water sign. Water represents emotion. Green is the color of healing. The sound he made represented the release of all the emotional pain I have kept submerged for so many years. The tears of confirmation came and I knew this was the correct interpretation.

One of the greatest days of my life (so far) was Mother's Day of 1989, the day my daughter Diane graduated from Emory Medical

School. She had worked extremely hard and attained a perfect 4.0 average! She was the third person in the history of the school to accomplish this and, of course, the first woman. My sister Linda and my son Mark came from New York, Jack and his parents came and we had a dinner celebration for Diane at the Ritz. It was very special. I will never forget feeling that sense of pride and exultation when Diane walked across that stage, Summa Cum Laude, to prolonged applause from her classmates and the rest of the audience.

In December of 1989 I attended a business seminar on stress management. I was truly amazed when they recommended the Relaxation Response, which consists of sitting in a chair for ten to twenty minutes with your eyes closed. This is almost word-for-word what I had learned at the hospital stress seminar in 1982. There must be something to it! I had let my relaxations slide somewhat, but decided this was something I must make time for and I resumed this simple act of doing nothing for fifteen minutes twice a day.

It was a great day in April of 1990 when my doctor allowed Keith to give me my weekly methotrexate shot at home and reduced the lab work to only once a month. Now I was in control of the dosage. I had decided that I just did not want to take a chemotherapeutic agent for the rest of this lifetime and wanted to see how well I had done with my emotional healing work. I began very gradually to reduce the weekly amount and in October I stopped taking the methotrexate completely. I continued taking the Trilisate, two 500 mg. tablets twice a day.

Two weeks later I went to see my doctor and told him what I had done. He was not pleased and predicted a relapse in three or four months. Little did I know the adventure that lay ahead!

I worked on a very large hospital job for three years managing the specifications and code compliance. It was quite challenging—and stressful—as big projects with multiple deadlines are. I basically enjoyed it, since I like an intellectual challenge and was working with some outstanding people who are very good friends. I was well-known in the office for my ability to control the elevator. Our office was on the sixth floor and I developed the habit of asking for the elevator to go all the way down without stopping at any other floor. Most people were mildly amused by this and tried to ride the elevator with me. One evening another architect was in the elevator lobby when I came out. I knew Ted was a very negative thinker. He had been recovering from pneumonia when I joined the office, but continued to smoke. He was always hurting himself, and I had often heard him set himself up for disappointment by saying things like, "I just know this isn't going to work," when he sat down at the computer. When I pressed the button this particular day, I said to Ted, "Are we going straight down?" He answered, "Oh, that never happens." "It happens for me all the time." Well, sure enough, we stopped at the fifth floor and a woman got on and pressed the third floor button. We stopped at the fourth floor and another woman got on and pressed the second floor button. The elevator stopped at every floor! Jokingly, I told Ted I was never getting on the elevator with him again! The trick to something like this is that it only works if you believe it! I believed it, but Ted didn't. Negativity is heavier than positivity and I still have difficulty overcoming the negative attitudes of companions.

Another useful visualization is from *The Bridge of Light* by LaUna Huffines, which Michael recommended to me. It involves seeing red and green lights, asking a question and seeing if the red light or the green light blinks. I tried this one night and asked if I was doing the right thing by going off the methotrexate. I wanted very much to see the green light blinking and thought I did, but I was afraid to trust what I was seeing because I wanted it so much. So I said to myself, "If it's true, I'll see green lights tomorrow," not really sure where I would see green lights. The next morning when I drove to work, all but two of the eighteen traffic lights between my house and the parking deck were green, some of which I had never made before! I was truly amazed and grateful for this sign of confirmation.

During medical school and her residency Diane was spending a lot of time working at the same hospital that I was working on architecturally which enabled us to meet for lunch on occasion. She was between relationships and living alone, a little discouraged about ever finding the right man. On New Year's Day she decided to declare what she wanted:

HERE'S TO '92! MY GOALS FOR 1992
What I want to happen in my life this year,
What I want to create and manifest...
PERSONAL:
I want to create space for a man in my life.
I want to love and be loved.

I want to open up to intimacy.

I want to trust myself enough to be vulnerable.

I want a significant love relationship.

A man with vitality, a love for life, for himself and for others. Someone capable of loving, honoring, respecting; who expresses himself and is open to other's expression. A man whose eyes sparkle and dance with life and love, whose smile captivates my heart.

Someone who is intelligent, but can act stupid. Someone who is capable and confident but not afraid to be like a kid. A man who loves his career, but knows that balance is important. A man who is not afraid of a strong yet feminine woman.

Honest. Open. Supportive. Capable of sharing and caring. Who knows his values but is willing to hear others out. Considerate. Someone with a big heart.

Attractive. Sexy in his own way. A man who appreciates his body and who enjoys physical pleasure. Masculine, muscular. Sensual but not overbearing. Healthy.

Interesting. Interested in trying new things, enjoys music, movies, wining and dining. Likes to seize the moment.

A soulmate who knows that a relationship takes work and working things out. Someone who is willing to talk and to listen. A monogamous man.

Someone who wants a family. Who might even want a house and a big white dog—and a swing in the back yard. Who understands the importance of my career and is willing to help out.

I want to open myself up to love. To not be so afraid when opportunities arise. To enjoy the attraction and the fun of courting. To think about what is happening at the moment, without getting so caught up in the past or worrying about the future.

After writing this on her computer, Diane printed it out and put it in a desk drawer. Early in February, on the way to an aerobics class at her health club, she noticed a television crew. The newswoman stopped Diane and explained that she was interviewing women about the female condom which had just been approved by the FDA and asked if she had an opinion about it. Diane agreed to go on camera. She had just spent three months working in Fulton County's Sexually Transmitted Disease

Clinic and said she was in favor of anything that would help stem this epidemic. The weekend this news segment was broadcast Keith and I were out of town, but little Mark spotted Diane on TV and called Scott into the room to see it. Shortly after this Diane and I met for lunch and she told me that someone else had seen her on the news, a man named Hobie, whom she had met at a party a year and a half earlier. They had actually gone out once, but nothing clicked. When Hobie saw Diane on TV, he remembered her and called, saying he very much wanted to see her again. They had gone out a couple of times since then and she really liked him. As she told me about Hobie during that lunch, my eyes filled with tears of joy. We both felt right then and there that he was the one she had been waiting for. The Universe had heard her request and answered it swiftly and completely.

PUSH AND PULL

When the big hospital project was winding down, I realized that I needed to move on and started meditating to create my new perfect job. I felt I had been reacting too stressfully to all the deadlines and complexities of the big project and needed a change. There was an ad in the paper for a Specification Writer and when I looked into it, found that it involved the computer programming of specifications for automated question-and-answer-format spec writing. It is an ingenious system invented by a man named Rick, a friend of one of my good buddies on the hospital job. I was excited to know such a spec writing system existed and decided I wanted to be part of it. I had to go to Washington DC for a confirmation interview and the job was mine. While this was going on, Keith retired—or tried to. Problem is, he loved being an architect so much that he had never pursued any hobbies, except stamp collecting. He brought his collection up to date for the first time in forty years and put it away. It was done. Then he had to put his 14-year-old dog Duchess to sleep. He was depressed and miserable. When I came home from work he would be watching cartoons. He had sinus infections and then, finally, back surgery. I knew we had a big problem. That summer we also had water coming up through the condo slab after heavy rains.

Deepak Chopra came to Atlanta for a weekend seminar at a church. I didn't go to hear him, but called the church and ordered the set of tapes from his sessions. They were pretty interesting and I decided to look into the Ayurvedic medicine approach he promotes. I bought his book *Perfect Health* and went to see an Ayurvedic physician. I started the diet, the herbs, Amrit Kalash (a jam type of preparation which is full of anti-oxidants and other good stuff), the sesame oil rubdown before my morning shower and I learned Transcendental Meditation which takes twenty minutes twice a day.

About the time I got "the perfect job," I went to see Dr. M. for the first time in a long time. He immediately spotted some newly inflamed joints in my left hand. (What's a joint like you doing in a nice girl like this?) I told him about the stress of the big hospital job in general, my new job, Keith's illnesses and difficulties adjusting to retirement. My body is a walking stress indicator and I knew that all these events could be enough to send me over the edge, back into the rut.

Dr. M. immediately wanted me to restart taking methotrexate. I recoiled, a huge "NO!" rising up from my guts. I said I didn't want to because I felt it was a defeat. "Methotrexate is your friend," he argued. "Think of it as a vitamin." I could not agree and said I believed methotrexate was poison and I didn't want it in my body. There had to be another way. So as a compromise he suggested doing the internal medicine thing, meaning all kinds of diagnostic tests, and I went along with that. I actually had X-rays and an EKG that afternoon.

When I got home I cried in deep, painful sobs for about half an hour. Keith was very sympathetic. What bothered me most was that Dr. M. said not one word about stress management, only how to treat my symptoms. I haven't been back to see him since that day.

I called Lynn, my psychic. She asked right away, "Have you been doing your affirmations?" The answer was really no, I'd been concentrating on creating the perfect job. I asked if I should go back to my chiropractor. The answer was, "Your chiropractor and more." When I asked her why I was having so much pain, she answered, "Because you're on a spiritual path," meaning that I still have more clearing work to do and I'm trying to get along without Western medicine.

The next day I called Joya to make an appointment for half an hour with Michael. Basically Michael said I am doing the right thing, that those deep sobs were from my essence which was saying loud and clear that I could find other ways to heal myself and that not going back on methotrexate was the right thing for me to do. Aggressive, young soul, yang Western medicine does not agree with my essence. Ayurveda looked good for me and they said Hellerwork would be a "9" (out of 10). This is a form of deep tissue bodywork, an evolution of Rolfing. Its goal is to loosen the fascia, which is a network-like membrane that lies between the layers of muscles. The theory is that emotions which are not released or expressed get stored in the fascia, as well as other parts of the body (such as joints!) which causes the fascia to lose flexibility and the body to become stiff, asymmetrical and painful. The bodywork/massage helps to soften the fascia and release the emotions. Joya's partner Duane Hall is a Hellerworker. So, as the new job developed, I worked the starting date so that I could go to Arkansas for a week of Hellerwork before starting the new job.

I decided to keep a journal of my experience. (From now on journal entries are dated and indented; narration will not be indented.)

April 11, 1992 Fayetteville, Arkansas

Here I am in Arkansas for Hellerwork! I can't wait to experience it. This morning after meditating, I did my Ayurvedic sesame oil shower massage, got dressed very leisurely and went out for a walk. I'm staying at the Hilton, which is very close to the city square. I walked over to the square and there was the Saturday Farmer's Market! So I just walked around and bought a few little things. Everyone was so sweet and small-town friendly. Joya and Duane met me at the hotel—I knew them right away! We walked to breakfast which was yummy. Then we went to their house to begin the Hellerwork. It consists of eleven sessions, each with a different area of emphasis and a catchy title. We did the first session in the morning and the second in the afternoon.

Later: All I can say is, "WOW!" Hellerwork is work, but good, but good. I really ran the gamut and stuff really happened. I talked, I laughed, I cried, I shrieked, I moaned. It is a very personal procedure, well, it's bodywork. Duane is wonderful with a very gentle demeanor. He likes the planet enough to keep coming back and this is an extra life for him as a 7th level old Server. He said I did very well with breathing into the pain to release it. I had some wild reactions: lightheadedness, dizziness, saw blue stars on a black background, felt streams of energy vibrating in my hands and flowing out, especially the fourth and fifth fingers. Also had some pains in my jaw, which indicates a wish for retaliation. He said I was releasing a lot of energy and old stuff.

Duane told me that the left big toe represents mother and the right one father. My left big toe and its bunion is my biggest arthritis problem. This fits with the basic premise that the right side of the body is masculine and the left is feminine.

What an adventure! "The only way out is through."

Joya and Duane are so much fun. I love to be with people who talk "Michaelese" all the time. They have figured out the Role and Soul Age of nearly everyone in the area and, jokingly, even some of the neighborhood dogs!

April 12, 1992

Day Two: Two more very powerful sessions. The fourth session ("Control and Surrender") was incredible and I really expressed a lot. My emotions were first triggered by a Strauss polka on the tape player which got me thinking and feeling about Vienna. Then a little later, "The Moldau." Well, the river really flowed. Herman and I used to listen to this musical description of that great Eastern European river and I sobbed and cried very hard for a long time, so much that Duane was moved, too! It had been a long time since I grieved for Herman like that—it went so deep. I saw myself riding a raft down the river and into the ocean where I was floating adrift on a sea of emotion. Then the sun came out and I was heroically rescued. That session lasted an hour longer than normal! Duane just patiently works the painful areas until it is all taken care of. I have a lot of stuff in my body and it takes a lot of work to release it. I saw colors, mostly green, some bright purple/magenta. But the tingling, vibrating, pulsing energy in my hands flowed up to my wrists and then I felt it go to my elbows. It was wild. I felt like I was flying. I exclaimed, "Let my fancy flow free, let my fancy flow free," (a quotation from the healing affirmations of Paramahansa Yogananda) and while he worked, we played with a lot of clichés, such as "shooting from the hip," "sitting on those feelings," etc., etc.

I called my mother tonight. She said I sounded "so invigorated." If she only knew!

April 13, 1992

Day Three: Morning session today was pretty easy. Not so much stuff in my guts. Well, I'm glad there is some part of this body that is not loaded with emotional garbage! The afternoon with my back was another story. Not as intense as yesterday, but I really have some stuff near my right shoulder blade where it felt like an arrow was piercing my back. Later I wondered if I have been crucified, because the area across both shoulders is so stiff and much of the trauma of crucifixion is felt there. I really sobbed over that.

April 14, 1992

Just one session today, called "Losing Your Head." It was fairly intense. Stirred up a lot in the back of my tongue and some in my sinuses, too. I really felt a tingling aliveness in my arms and legs as I released the old energy. My neck is improving and Duane says I am making good progress. There's just so much junk in my body. No wonder it's deformed! When I asked if everyone has this much trauma to release, he answered, "You're definitely in the top five percent." Duane says it is usually Scholars like me who hold the most in their bodies because we don't want to forget anything, not even arrows and crucifixions. My feet are the most deformed he's ever seen and he's never seen an Achilles tendon lump like mine. Well, I've always been at the top of the class! The tongue part is all the things I've held back from saying. When I stood up I felt pressure on my shoulders as my weight shifted down through my body, everything feeling very heavy. I've certainly had many sensations this week that I've never experienced before, at least not in this lifetime.

Since the afternoon was free, I drove up to Eureka Springs, a small Victorian tourist town in the Ozarks and the site of an architectural gem, the Thorncrown Chapel, designed by E. Fay Jones who lives in Fayetteville. It was a beautiful day with a sunny, blue sky full of puffy clouds. I drove through the hilly countryside taking in the blossoming dogwoods and spring wildflowers, just thick in some areas. I sang "The Sound of Music," my "I Am Healing" Song, and made up a new one to the tune of "Muss I Denn:" "Let it go, let it go, I don't need it anymore. Oh, let it go, I don't need it anymore. All that energy so negative, goes back to the Universe. I release it all now, I don't need it anymore. Oh, let it go, I don't need it anymore."

The chapel is fabulous. Hardly anyone was there when I arrived (I had asked for it not to be full of tourists). It's framed in wood with lots of glass so you are in a place of worship, but feel like you are sitting in the woods because they didn't clear the land around it, not even one bulldozer width. All the materials were hand-carried in to preserve the natural woods right up to the building. Truly exquisite. I sat there quite a while and nearly broke down, but I wasn't alone, so held back. It was still a pretty good release to feel the emotions. I took pictures and walked around, then went into town, did a little souvenir shopping and drove back. This week is going very quickly. I am so glad I have taken this time for myself. It has to have a healing effect.

April 15, 1992

Day Five: Two more sessions today: first the feminine, then the masculine. Surprisingly the feminine was comparatively easy. Duane noted that this was the first session during which I did not have an emotional outpouring! But masculine was a different story. My shoulders were full of old stuff, and I felt that arrow point in my right shoulder blade again, plus a lot of sadness which sure feels like Indian lifetimes. It's hard to know if I'm reliving a past life or remembering "Dances with Wolves" which touched me deeply. It doesn't really matter, I guess, as long as I let it go.

After the second session today, I sat in the hot tub and did my meditation there. I felt so refreshed in body, mind and spirit. Joya made dinner for her sister and some neighbors and it was great—she's a creative, intuitive cook. Chicken breasts, salad, lots of vegetables, like baked carrots in herb sauce. It was delightful.

I'm looking forward to getting home. This will be a real new beginning: springtime, new job, new healing experience behind me— onward and upward! New levels await. And I want Joya and Duane to come to Atlanta. Hopefully I'll have more time for things like that now with my new job.

April 16, 1992

A change of pace day! We drove up to their neighbor's cabin near the Buffalo River in the Ozark mountains. A pretty drive with no billboards, very rural, picturesque. The cottage is true minimalist, but has some nice features. We tramped through the forest until about 3 PM. It was great to be out in the woods and I saw many wildflowers. As we were leaving, I saw an eagle flying around, then he sat in a tree right where we would be sure to see him

One last day coming up, then back to reality. I wonder what Dr. M. would say. I am walking easily and feeling great. Happy and very alive.

April 17, 1992

Last Day: Two sessions today—supposed to be one last session—No. 10, Integration—followed by the final interview and pictures. However, Duane gave me two real sessions—three hours in the morning and almost as long in the afternoon, followed by a brief interview/evaluation session. I sure got my money's worth!

He worked really hard on my feet in the morning. Asked me if I had any past lives in China when my feet might have been bound. Answer: not that I know of, and it didn't make me cry to think of it. (I did write six radio programs on China in 1973 and really enjoyed doing the research.) I saw colors like the mandala unfolding, red-to-orange-to-yellow and lots of green (the healing color!), chartreuse, orange fireworks, then the ultimate outer space/Star Wars/Star Trek black sky full of glittery silver, blue and purple specks. Was this a view outward or inward? Are they the same? It was beautiful, a great release. My right foot, especially, felt very light afterwards. I was pretty high when we stopped for lunch and then I took a hot tub break. Nothing like sunshine and warm bubbly water to soothe my body.

In the afternoon Duane worked on my back and shoulders. He was working on my shoulders, pulling my arm up over my head and said something about "going all the way." I quipped, "I wasn't allowed to go all the way." That really opened up some anger. Also recalled how my mother always said, "Beauty must suffer," with the implication that if you didn't suffer, you sure wouldn't be beautiful. I released quite a bit of that old trash.

At the end of the session, when he took all the negative energy away, I cried with an appreciation of the power at work, with joy at the release of so much old stuff and with some sadness that it was over. I have released a cartload of stuff. All the work I've been doing has been prologue to this.

Back home to Atlanta tomorrow! It is going to be very interesting. Keith said my employment papers came in the mail yesterday, so it's all coming together for my new, perfect job. Well, of course! I created it!

Duane is really the first person to say yes, I definitely can heal myself. All the way. Hey, Mother, I'm going all the way! Watch me! Yeah!!

11:40 CDT Saturday, April 18, 1992 On board Delta's vibrating commuter flight 7401 from Fayetteville to St. Louis:

As the plane was taking off, I saw six hawks—or maybe eagles—huge birds circling near the airport. They said to me, "Soar with the eagles, Lois!"

April 19, 1992

We weren't out of the airport yesterday before Keith said, "You're walking as flat-footed as I am!" No more buttons on the balls of my feet! I was glad to see him and I always feel good when I come back to Atlanta. It really is home.

April 24, 1992

I talked to Lynn. She said, "In '94 you'll be going into something else—you're becoming too enlightened." Too enlightened! Is that possible? I'm not sure exactly what that means. Guess I'll have to wait until '94 to see. In the meantime, I have started working at my new position in what I have asked to be "the perfect job" for me. Rick's right-hand person Karen introduced me to Paula and Elise who welcomed me and invited me to join the Birthday Club. Right now they have no one else in the club whose birthday is in June.

April·28, 1992

I hate to admit it, but for the last week, I've been pretty discouraged. Little pains here and there, a stiff neck yesterday, it's all keeping me awake, which is also somewhat depressing. And makes me tired! I keep remembering that Dr. M. told me I would relapse after stopping the methotrexate.

I had another chat with Michael and Joya on Saturday. When I asked if I had had an arrow in my back, they said, "Many arrows!" One of the most painful was from a lifetime out West when I was a white settler who was working with the Indians. I had to inform them that they would be giving up more land. As I left them, one of the angry young braves shot an arrow into my back and killed me. I was very sad to leave that lifetime because I had a family living on the prairie. Keith was my wife and we had a son, so there was a lot of grief over that.

Michael recommended alternating baths in bentonite clay with baths in sea salt and soda. Both help soak out residues that had been released. They said to take two or three baths a week of bentonite (one pound in a tub of hot water for half an hour) for a month and then repeat with sea salt and soda (one pound of sea salt and two pounds of baking soda). They also recommended a book, *Medical Assistance Plan (MAP)* by Maechelle Small-Wright. I've been doing quite a bit of the Ayurvedic routine for a month now. Hopefully some of that will start kicking in. It's hard because I invested all that time, money, emotional and physical effort in the Hellerwork and am still having pain. I want it to work! I want something to work. I don't want the methotrexate. More than anything, I don't want that. Am I being impatient? Unrealistic? Stubborn? Am I missing something?

Oh, God, oh, my guides, please help me, heal me. Lead me to the TRUE CURE. I want to be well, whole, perfect; pain-free, drug-free, energetic.

April 29, 1992

Thank you, my chiropractor! She says yes, I can do it! Best of all, she said it is normal for me to be going through a "cleansing flare-up" after the deep bodywork. She thinks that Dr. M. essentially programmed me to flare by telling me I would have a relapse after going off the methotrexate. Even though I still have some pain tonight, I feel better emotionally. Also, stiff neck is lots better than yesterday.

Sooo, onward and upward. Merry called. She has been getting my distress signals! We talked for nearly an hour.

April 30, 1992

And the answer is: Better! When I woke up this morning I felt much clearer. My Ayurvedic Aroma F and two herbal concoctions arrived yesterday, plus the shark collagen and tachyon bead from my chiropractor. Could those things have made the difference? Who cares! Maybe it was just her saying, "cleansing flare-up." And telling me, "Yes, you can do this." <u>YES, I CAN DO THIS!</u>

May 2, 1992

Wednesday night I was achy again by the time I got home from work. Keith was out for the evening, so after I meditated I went to the health food store and bookstore to buy the MAP book that Michael recommended. Then came home and took a bentonite bath. I felt a lot of tingling in my hands during the bath, but afterwards was still very achy. When Keith came home he comforted me.

Thursday and Friday were very good days, just a little pain in my right shoulder Thursday evening. My feet felt especially good yesterday. The MAP book tells how to meditate and call in a healing group of guides to help heal you and then you lie quietly for 40 minutes to receive their healing. Only problem is, you are supposed to lie still and no one else can be within three feet, including the cat. I hope to try one this weekend. I feel wonderful this morning. Keith and I have been very happy together.

Later: Just did my first MAP session. I felt quite a bit of warmth and tingling in my hands and feet. Are these signs of my heavenly healers at work? I hope so. The book also tells how to do muscle testing to get a yes or no answer, basically applied kinesiology, which is useful to know. So, I have added two more weapons to the arsenal.

May 9, 1992

MAP healing number four. Lots of shivers and tingling, some over my whole body. The book suggests giving the healing group a name and "Red Lily" was confirmed. I recently moved a big, beautiful volunteer red lily that came up by the dumpster to the garden outside our bedroom window where I see it first thing in the morning. "Red Lily" is a comforting name to me. I've also found that doing TM helps the time pass. Forty minutes is a long time to lie still, especially for someone who is impatient and who has arthritic joints which tend to "jell" and stiffen when not moved.

May 11, 1992

Bath four last night. This morning I feel really good—both swollen tendon sheaths seem smaller and better. Maybe something is working.

May 12, 1992

Bath five tonight. My Achilles' tendon sheaths both feel significantly smaller tonight, especially the "goober" (as dear Dr. M. called it) on the right. I can't feel it now when I point my toes and I had been feeling a slight pain there when walking.

I felt pretty achy when I first got up this morning, but improved greatly by the time I got to work. Work is really great. Two friends both said they could see a real difference in me. Just took a break to listen to my favorite Mozart—what a lift.

May 14, 1992

My chiropractor said I looked more relaxed, like when we got back from Europe last fall.

May 16, 1992

Bath six last night. Talked to Lynn and she said I sounded more relaxed.

May 21, 1992

Bath eight tonight. Seven was Monday or Tuesday but the weather was so hot and muggy that I just couldn't stay in it more than about 15 minutes. But tonight's was the full 30 minutes. Also did a MAP yesterday morning. I am losing count. This week hasn't been quite as good as last week. I've had several aches and pains.

Talked to Joya Sunday night and we set the dates for her visit to Atlanta in August. I am so excited that it's really going to happen. She will give a talk at the bookstore, have a book signing and do private channelings.

May 25, 1992

Yesterday we went to Chattanooga to the new aquarium. I was tired at the end of the day, but basically pain-free. Friday night I had stomach pain and did not sleep well. Did a MAP process Saturday and today.

Tonight I went for a walk. I'm optimistic again after being a bit depressed and in pain last week because of the difficulty of learning how to do my job. It seems to be fairly understandable, but I keep hitting snags because it's so far outside of my past experience and it reminds me of when I was taking calculus. It's really not spec writing, but computer programming, which means getting a whole bunch of numbers in the right place. I hope I'm over the hump with that. Rick and Karen invented it and it is a brilliant program, but I don't think they realize how tricky it is to learn. They've assigned me to rework the carpet specification section. I have completely restructured it, which it needed, but I didn't realize how hard it would be to get all the nuances worked out.

June 1, 1992

Took the first of three sea salt and soda baths Thursday and really had less pain afterwards. Had a bit too much pain for comfort last night, but my Higher Self through kinesiology says I can cure it.

Work went really well this week. I did not have the doubts about learning the programming that I did last week.

June 3, 1992

MAP with the Red Lily group last night. Yesterday and today my feet were terrific—I hardly felt them! This morning I put on my new navy pumps and five minutes after getting to the office forgot I had them on. Truly remarkable! So I called up and ordered the same shoes in white. It's so easy to be optimistic when you're not hurting. Also I think the swellings on my left hand that Dr. M. noticed are somewhat smaller. This is the seventh week since completing the Hellerwork.

June 6, 1992 Saturday

Keith left early this morning to attend a niece's graduation in Michigan. He'll be gone for a week.

I had three great days in a row this week. Took _no_ Tylenol all week—first time in several months, I think.

June 8, 1992 My 55th birthday.

Birthday Club at the office is nice because all the members wish you happy birthday all day long. Keith's flowers were delivered to the office and I was touched because he signed the card himself when he ordered them last week. I had a fun lunch with five of the guys from the big hospital project and Birthday Club was at 3 PM. Paula made chocolate cheesecake for my celebration.

Just got back from dinner with Diane. We had a wonderful time talking and relating and loving each other. What a joy she is. She made an interesting comment tonight that she senses I still hold a lot of resentment towards my mother and that this may be holding me back physically. Hmmm. Maybe I need to work on that. She's a 5th level old Priest and when she has something like that to say, I think I should pay attention. (According to Michael, the Scholar's job in the Universe is to remember everything, while Priests see where people are blocked and inspire them to change.)

I'm tired now and my knees are hurting. I just took the first Tylenol I have taken in ten days! This has been one of the most celebrated and fun of all my birthdays. I was just remembering the worst one, exactly ten years ago, when I so sick, unhappy, unemployed and living alone. I've come a long way, BABY!

June 13, 1992

I hate to say how discouraged I am. Yesterday and today have been very difficult—knees, hands, etc., have been achy and inflamed. Yuk. I've cried several times this week, have tried to get in touch with feelings, guides, etc., but something seems to be blocking me. I keep asking for help, guidance, etc., but don't really feel like I'm getting it. I just don't know where to turn.

On second thought, the only person I can turn to is myself. I can do this. After last week, I was so pleased and excited, thought I was really getting there. Took a bentonite bath last night. Tried MAP this morning, but my cat Misha came in halfway through and I had to quit. Keith is due back from Michigan soon. Maybe he can help get my spirits back up.

June 15, 1992 Monday

What a difference two days make. Saturday night was hell, the worst night I've had in so long. Keith came home and I cried when I told him what Diane said about my resentment towards my mother. I and did a MAP process that weirdly felt more like a Hellerwork session, but with no release or resolution. My hands were on fire, especially across the knuckles—like a hot vise, very steady pain and heat. It was awful. I slept half an hour, came downstairs for drugs and tried to sleep with Keith. Went back upstairs, finally slept from 3 to 7:30 AM. We took Diane and Hobie to brunch for her birthday. In the afternoon I took an hour nap, then slept very well last night. I hope it was the last "cleansing flare-up." I have added some affirmations from a book I read on Silva mind control: "I will always have a perfectly healthy body and mind." "I will always have a perfectly healthy immune system." "I will always have perfectly healthy bones and joints." And, "I release, I let go, I forgive." Maybe the pain in my hands is symbolic of holding on to the resentment.

Today was very good—about 90% better than any day last week. I appreciate any progress.

June 29, 1992

Had an incredible Red Lily MAP session one night last week. I was breathing through the pain in my hands and they began tingling. It developed into a very powerful surging of energy or something, all across my chest, centered, I think, in my heart chakra and out through both arms to my hands. I was breathing very heavily and my whole body felt very alive. I was able to experience and release a lot of energy. I wonder now if that was kundalini energy.

Last week was very strenuous. Tuesday night we toured the new Georgia Dome, then the Construction Specifications Institute's National Convention was in Atlanta and Thursday night our office gave a party for former employees who are here for the convention. I worked our convention booth on both Friday and Saturday, attended hospitality parties Friday night and Saturday went to a shower. Yesterday we just took it easy. I did very well with all this activity and felt great today.

I turned in the carpet section again today. I have 3-1/2 weeks to de-bug it, think it should work pretty well. They also asked me to write a new wall and corner guard section.

I have been sleeping much better lately. I lost a lot of sleep recently worrying about the arthritis and the specter of going back on methotrexate. I'm not sure how to know what's working, but will be keeping it all up for a while.

A former associate has asked Keith to design a house on Lake Keowee in South Carolina. This is a godsend, as he has been so bored with retirement. It's the perfect answer. Thank you!

Keith's nephew Jody and his bride Jan came down from Louisville for a week and brought their two big dogs. It really made the condo seem small, especially with our two cats. Even brave Misha was afraid to come inside and poor Musetta spent most of her time under our bed. Jan is expecting. It was a fairly congenial visit, although I still feel that Jody has never really accepted me and he keeps his distance. Jan is more friendly and she's interested in some new age ideas, which gives us a connection.

July 12, 1992

Let's see: Bentonite bath last Sunday, sea salt and soda tonight. Last week I was pretty stiff 'cause I was very concerned about the carpet section. Got my printout back and learned how to edit it myself, then felt great the rest of the week. Last night when Keith and I went swimming, I swam twelve lengths, two of them in the crawl! This means my shoulders are feeling good.

Did MAP healings several times last week. I think I'll do one tonight. They make me feel relaxed and cared for.

July 19, 1992 Sunday

It was a very good week; I took Tylenol only once. Friday we drove up to North Carolina to see one of Keith's college buddies. On Saturday he took us on a tour of buildings he's designed over the years—fascinating! His wife prepared a delightful lunch and we enjoyed visiting in their unique home. Then we departed for Lake Keowee to see the site for the house Keith is designing and later met friends for dinner. It was a pretty long day and by the time we got home, I was exhausted and my left knee was hurting. But between having this house to design and buying a beautiful travel van, Keith is back on track. He had owned a converted van when Jean was in the wheelchair and every time we saw one on the road, he'd wistfully say, "There's a nice van." He decided to shop for and found the perfect one, only a year old and in great condition. It was a little more money than he wanted to spend, but I encouraged him to go for it and he has thanked me for that. It is great to travel in.

So now I have five days to finish the carpet section. Worked all afternoon on it today—did two hours of input at the office. So we'll see how the "day of completion" (that's my new euphemism for "deadline") stress goes and if I can get it all done. Yes, I can. I can do it, I can do it, all I have to do is <u>do</u> it—<u>Believe</u> that I can do it, I believe that I <u>can</u> do it!

July 22, 1992 12:19 AM

I've been trying to fall asleep for two hours. I have counted backwards, done neck rolls, relaxation visualizations, taken Valerian, Tylenol, etc., etc. There's a huge bug in the carpet section. I've <u>got</u> to fix it tomorrow. I <u>will</u> fix it. Wall and corner guards section needs so many changes! Well, I need to sleep so I can get it done. But it's not happening. Bentonite bath tonight. My wrists and knees were hurting. I <u>can</u> do it. I can heal myself and I can meet this deadline. And get some sleep.

July 29, 1992

Well, euphemisms aside, I guess the lesson is: "A deadline is a deadline." I have experienced my first quarterly deadline at my perfect job and it was not fun. I would have been sunk if Karen hadn't gone over the section twice in great detail. I'm still on the learning curve and there are certain refinements that I simply could not intuit. They have set me afloat to "Think or Swim," but it's just not the kind of thing anyone can totally teach herself. I'm the first person to do this work that didn't grow up with the development of the program, so they have never had the experience of teaching it to anyone from scratch.

I had a lot of pain last week, but bounced back Saturday and felt quite good. Sunday was OK, but I had a stuffy head Monday and yesterday, but no pain! Is this progress? I felt pretty good this morning, so don't think it is a full-blown cold.

Last Friday Keith's brother had cancer surgery. I was pretty bummed out over it and didn't sleep well the night before. My boss Rick came by my desk just after I had talked to Keith when the surgery was over and I had tears in my eyes. Rick said, "Now, Lois, you mustn't get discouraged." I thought that was pretty nice of him. He's a very compassionate person, although yesterday he was undone by the deadline pressure and pretty upset with me.

So this deadline is over. I hope the next one (and the ones after that) will go better. I certainly want to get my work done before the last minute.

Aug. 5, 1992

Little did I know when I last wrote here that I would be told, "I'm not happy with your performance." Rick is angry with himself for letting the situation develop as it has. I think I defended myself pretty well. We had another chat on Friday and I told him that it never occurred to me that it was up to me to decide how I should be taught to do this work. He and Karen don't realize how difficult it is to learn, since they invented it. The carpet section was supposed to be perfect by Friday, but I'm still working on it and I don't think I can make it perfect. This whole business is humiliating for me, who thrives on being a quick-study, thorough Scholar, Ms. Perfect! I'm getting very tired of it. There must be lessons and growth here somewhere. Would I be better off if I had stayed where I was? Don't know yet. Discouraged? Yes!

Last night I got the Short Form carpet spec to work in review, which is a way to test if the program is working. I was excited, showed it to Rick, but he found more problems. Only perfection is good enough and I just can't produce that yet. Paula and I went to lunch and I was fighting back the tears. "I think I may be losing my job," I told her. She used to work for Rick and reassured me that he would never fire me. Paula has become such a good friend. She makes me laugh with her off-the-wall humor, but is very advanced and interested in new age ideas. She can't believe I'm her mother's age.

I'm pretty troubled about this job situation and am having trouble applying my ideals to it. Instead, I find myself lapsing into the drama, stress and upsets. "Mature-soul-itis." A re-evaluation process is definitely going on. One nice thing happened when I called one of my best friends who lives in Ohio. When I told her how much trouble I was having in learning this work, she said, "Well, if it's hard for you to learn, it must really be hard." Thank you, Peggy!

Aug. 9, 1992 Sunday

Well, I've bounced back again. Had a tense day Thursday, but found and fixed all the problems I could—there are over 500 updates to the section! It's a new record and I'm not proud of it. Friday I waited all day for Rick to review it, but he never did. Thursday night I did a bentonite bath and Saturday afternoon the MAP process, the first one in a while. I have really felt great all weekend. All the painful physical manifestations have retreated, thank Goddess.

Intellectually I know that I did the best I could under the circumstances and I know I should detach emotionally. But I still let Rick down and that is really hard for me to deal with. Keith has been very helpful and supportive. He says, "It's just another spec." Yes, I know, but I still want to do it right. Mostly I want to break the cycle of physically manifesting these emotional excesses. What else do I need? More psychotherapy? More bodywork? More meditation? A cave?

Aug. 12, 1992

Karen, Jeff, Sandra and I spent all day yesterday attacking the carpet section in the conference room. We did the updates, then started testing about 5 PM. Finally quit at 7, I left about 7:20. This morning there were still problems, and by 5 PM I found some things that are worse now than the way I had it before. Unbelievable. I wonder how many subscribers will try to use it in the first month. I've decided that I'm not the only one who is learning lessons from this experience. The amazing thing is, physically I'm feeling good!

Aug. 15, 1992 3:30 AM

Misha woke me up chasing a shrew around the living room. Now I can hear the thumping of music and lovemaking next door. Several other things are keeping me awake: Joya's visit, I need Ayurvedic herbs, I need to recycle, Work, Trip to San Francisco, Work. I'm already concerned about the next big deadline, nine weeks away. I need to do: Carpet (ever and always!), two or three short form/preliminaries, enhance Wall and Corner Guards Section, and Updates. Well, maybe that is enough time, an average of two weeks for each task. I can do it, of course I can!

Sept. 1, 1992

It was a wonderful week with Joya. She is so much fun to be with, full of light and joy. Truly beautiful. She's moving away from many lifetimes of karma completion of sixth level into the freedom of seventh level Old. Tuesday night Joya, Diane, Wendy and I went to a Japanese restaurant for dinner. It was so special. I felt the "love surge" while we were sitting there talking. Diane said she did, too. My left wrist hurt that night and the next. I think I was having trouble letting Joya go. I hugged her and felt very sad Wednesday night when we said good-bye.

Keith and I have made plans for our vacation: four days in San Francisco and three in Monterey.

During Diane's channeling, Michael said I was feeling a little hurt because I don't get to see her as much now that Hobie is in the picture. Well, it is true, but I would never have said anything. I told her, "You need to do that if I'm going to have grandchildren." We have made plans to get together next week.

Michael told me that Rick and I are doing a teacher-student monad and I am the teacher!! He's a Priest in discrimination, so he's alert to details, but his attitude is cynic, so he tends to expect worst-case scenarios. When Michael said, "Be open to change," I replied rather forcibly, "I just changed jobs!" They repeated that I should take change in stride, just say, "Lah-de-Dah"! They also recommended that I see a bodyworker for about four sessions to help move some of this stress out of my body.

Sept. 2, 1992 Wednesday

Felt the old panic rising today when Sandra discovered another problem with the carpet section. Well, I found the glitch and fixed it. Went back down to work tonight after dinner for a while. Rick's been in DC all week. He will be very unhappy if there are still big problems when he returns. I got it to run, but it still needs refining. Will test it tomorrow. Please, God, please, Higher Self, let it be OK. Please, me!

I did MAP healings Sunday night and last night. I'm going to try reducing Trilisate to one twice a day instead of two twice a day. I got a "footsie roller," as Duane recommended, about a month ago. My feet were tender when I first started using it, but now I can do it quite hard with no tenderness.

Sept. 6, 1992

Survived the deadline in great shape. I now feel energy streaming from my feet!

Just before Keith and I went to San Francisco, Hobie called me to ask my permission to ask Diane to marry him. They were going to Charleston for the weekend and he wanted to ask her then—thought it would be nice for anniversaries! I was so touched, we both cried a little. He is so sweet and thoughtful. I know he will be a wonderful son-in-law and I am thrilled.

Sept. 28, 1992

This is really hard for me to admit, much less understand, but I think my "perfect job" has gone sour. Rick really gave me a hard time about taking the vacation time to go to San Francisco. Had I really been there long enough to take a week's vacation? (yes), had I signed the vacation sheet? (a month ago). Then on Friday he came by at 4:15 to see what I was doing. I had asked Karen early that morning to help me at 10:30 am, but she never came around. I was rather irritated with them both—they reminded me of dysfunctional parents. Have I recreated my family here?

Diane called Friday night to tell us that she had said "yes" to Hobie. She's so sweet and excited and so am I. It is such a blessing that we are living in the same city and can share these experiences. And I will be in the same town as my grandchildren!

Keith and I flew to San Francisco Saturday. On Sunday we took a Gray Line Tour of San Francisco, then late in the afternoon we drove to Palo Alto to see one of my college friends. Had a great time visiting and went out for excellent Chinese dinner but my hands started hurting like they did in June. As we were driving back to the hotel, I was in agony. I told Keith, "I am so disappointed that my job is not working out." I felt confused, guilty, angry and overwhelmed. That picky, detailed work isn't fun and I am having trouble making sense of this situation and why I am in it. That night I was unable to sleep for hours. It was miserable, like having my hands in that hot vise again, just unrelenting pain. Finally at 3 AM Keith gave me two Tylenol with codeine tablets and I was able to sleep. In the morning I slept in and felt a little better and thought I might be up to some sightseeing. So we drove to Muir Woods, the Marin County Buildings by Frank Lloyd Wright, Tiburon and Sausalito. My hands were on fire again by lunch. We went back to the hotel and I rested for a couple of hours, but was still miserable. We went out for a quick dinner. Later I ran cold water over my hands and that seemed to help. The pain finally released and I slept well. I think it was pain was self-punishment and the inflammation was anger and resentment and my need to release, let go, forgive. I guess there's not much doubt about what to do next.

We drove to Carmel down the famous Highway 1 that I've heard so much about, which is truly spectacular. We decided on the spur of the moment to stop at an old lighthouse at Pigeon Point. There was a flock of pelicans flying by and I was very moved by the beauty and ruggedness of the scenery. When the tears started, I knew I was having one of my past life memories. I think I must have been there with Father Junipero Serra, the priest who founded all the missions that evolved into the cities of California. I remembered that my high school term paper subject was the early history of California, which was basically the building of the missions. I always thought it was a strange topic for a Midwestern girl, but that was my choice and now I think I know why.

We loved Carmel, a spectacular setting with many, many well-designed buildings and lots of architectural regulations to keep it beautiful. Spent one day driving to Big Sur and another to Salinas where we did a little John Steinbeck pilgrimage. Saw his house, the cemetery, the library. We had our last dinner of the vacation at the exquisitely designed Highlands Inn high on the hillside, looking out to a gorgeous Pacific sunset. The food and view were fabulous. We flew home on Saturday.

Diane and Hobie came for lunch Sunday and afterwards she and I talked wedding for two hours. She tried on my 1958 wedding dress, but there's no way she could wear it, we are built so differently. The big date is March 6, 1993. She's so organized—has a pink notebook going already.

I dreaded going to work today and it was awful. I didn't sleep well last night (surprise!) and was tired and hung over. Rick said two words to me all day: "Welcome back." I don't think he meant it.

Lynn says I'll be out of there in October or November. She said that big planetary stuff is going on and Rick is learning major lessons. Pluto is transiting past my natal Mars in Scorpio and bringing me to my knees, one reason my knees have been hurting!! This makes me feel out of control and unable to manifest, at odds with everything. Aaargghhh! What to do next?? God, I hate to change jobs again! Well, one day at a time. Hope to sleep well tonight.

When I talked to Michael about my hand problem in San Francisco, they said, "You wanted to punch him in the nose," meaning Rick. I guess I had a lot of feelings building up that I am only beginning to admit, which certainly "charged up" my hands. I'm disappointed in myself, too. How, why did I manifest this job, this mess?

Oct. 9, 1992 2 AM Friday

This is feeling like the downward spiral of 1981 when I left Jack—and here I thought I was heading for an upward turn! I haven't been able to do my work well at all because feelings of not measuring up tend to immobilize me. Rick thinks if he pressures me it will help, but all it does is bring up my old performance anxiety which immobilizes me. Yesterday after one of our little critiques, I didn't know what to do. I was depressed and unable to concentrate. So I went up to see the personnel director who did my initial interview last spring. She just happened to be in her office. I closed the door, sat down and started to cry. I talked and cried for 30-40 minutes. She was really shocked that it wasn't working out. I told her that the ad had been for a Specification Writer, but that the position was not about writing specs, it was computer programming, which is quite another thing and something I'm apparently not cut out to do. She was very sympathetic and responsive to my distress and said she would talk to Rick and was sure we could work it out. After talking to her, I came home without going back to my desk.

I went to bed early, but woke up after three hours and can't seem to go back to sleep. I am having trouble seeing myself going in there in the morning. I don't think I can face it. In fact, I can't imagine ever going back in there except to pack up. This is not what I want to be doing and they are not who I want to be doing it with. This is some perfect job!

Oct. 11, 1992 Sunday

I called in sick Friday morning. Paula called me shortly after that and said that Rick had called and asked her to come to his office. Before she went to see him she wanted to know what she should tell him. I said, "Tell him the truth as you see it. The truth cannot hurt me." I had lunch with a friend from the big hospital project which felt good and by late afternoon I felt pretty normal, like I was going to survive.

Saturday I went to the Discovery Expo. While I was there, Paula called and told Keith that I was not fired. I didn't think I was! At the Expo, I went to a seminar on "Holistic Career Transition" and really liked the presenter who will be giving a workshop on November 7. I think I'll go, since I seem to be in a career transition mode—again! Had a massage treatment on my right hand and a Reiki treatment, which felt very soothing. I bought some amber jewelry, which Michael says is good for mental clarity. Had an aura photo taken: Lots of white (intellect—surprise!); green (healing, which they said will work its way up higher); red, faintly in the corners (current stress, but I'm keeping it out there, not letting it get too close and am handling it well). That was good to hear. They also said I would be a good teacher (!) and that spherical stones are good for me.

I drew a card from a Voyager Tarot deck, the Ace of Wands: Illumination. It said on the back that light symbolizes illumination and insight. The hand symbolizes touching on the truth and seeing beyond appearances. Illumination can represent the torch of revolution and purification which means changes and the destruction of old patterns. I think that fits! What a feast that Expo was! I loved every minute of it. It all felt <u>wonderful</u> to me.

Keith and I keep talking. We have some real differences in perceptions of what is going on and he admitted that my quitting the job scares him a little, since he's not working, either, except on the Keowee house. I keep telling him to just love me and support me emotionally.

Oct. 22, 1992

Resolution!! Win-win! Relief! When I went in today, I noticed the carpet section printout was missing from my desk. Sure enough, Rick called me into his office at 9. Both he and Karen were in there. I could not believe how many problems there still were! They very carefully and patiently started to go over it with me. After a few minutes I asked Karen to leave and I said, "Rick, why don't you just let me go?" He said, "I just don't understand it!" I said, "Some things we're not supposed to understand," etc., etc. He went into his Priestly compassion and asked how he could help me. I said, "Give me a good reference," which he readily agreed to do. After all, I was a perfect employee except for being unable to learn how to pull off the programming! We agreed that I will stay on for a couple of weeks doing the things I do know how to do while I look for another position. I felt <u>so</u> much better. Rick shook my hand and was very pleasant and kind. He's got to be relieved, too. And Karen finished the carpet section!

I called Keith and asked him to meet me downtown for lunch. I told him what had happened. He seems to be pretty much OK with it, although the money part bothers him. I KNOW this is right! I almost feel like saying, "I will be available for my next job on March 15!" I would like to just do the holidays and the wedding and then decide what I want to do professionally. I signed up for the career transition seminar on November 7.

There will be no lack of activity in my life, work or no work. The engagement party will be Oct. 31 because Jack will be in town then and I'm getting ideas for that. It's time to do Christmas shopping, too. I think a little rest from working will be a good thing for me.

Nov. 1, 1992

Yesterday we had the engagement party with Hobie's family and it was fun. Diane and Hobie are adorable together. I like his mother. We all drank a toast to the female condom!

Later I broke a corner off the crown of tooth #15. Michael says teeth represent decisions. Am I having trouble making a decision? Not anymore! Keith is still a bit uneasy, but he's letting me go with it. I will get a month's severance pay and a year's free subscription to the spec writing system and that helps a lot. We were out for dinner tonight and Rick came into the restaurant alone. What a coincidence! He joined us and drank a beer while we had ice cream for dessert. Keith was pleasantly sociable, but I was a little tense. I was glad everyone was friendly—win-win!

Nov. 3, 1992

While meditating tonight it came to me that it may be time to start Grant/Weiland Architects. Ever since Keith and I met, we have talked about this dream all architects have, but I have hesitated. I think we could work together; I think we can have a good marriage. I'm just not sure we can do both at the same time. But now that we have been married seven years, it might work. It's exciting and scary, but it would be wonderful to be independent and our own bosses. Can we create this win-win thing?

Nov. 13, 1992 Friday

A nine day (closure, according to numerology)! I felt rather exhilarated during my last day in this job. I packed up and realized that no one but Rick and Karen knew I was leaving today. So I went around and told them, saying that Keith and I wanted to give Grant/Weiland Architects a try. They took me to lunch and the conversation was great: UFO's, conspiracies, near-death experiences, quantum physics, creation, etc. I got in a few good "weird stuff" comments.

When it was time to leave, I went around and said good-bye. Even Karen hugged me. The last thing Rick said was that they would have me do some consulting and send work our way. I could tell he was just amazed at how positive I was and that I wasn't angry with him or depressed that I had "failed." I felt great about it all and came home very satisfied. A monad completed. More change. Lah-de-dah!

So, what did I teach Rick? I think it was about making him aware of his nit-picky perfection and its effect on others. I stood up to him without anger or resentment and turned a potentially bitter and disappointing experience into positive growth with grace.

Now, what's next???

The Holistic Career Transition Workshop was good. At the end of the day we each summarized what we had learned. My conclusion was that the best thing I can do for myself is to be a peace with being unemployed and to work on manifesting my next perfect job/situation on March 15. On to the holidays. And the wedding.

Nov. 21, 1992 Saturday

End of week one. I was a little overwhelmed by where to start, what to do first because there were so many choices. On Sunday Keith and I did a survey of things we want to do to the condo and then we went through the alphabet: A for architecture, C for Christmas, etc. It helped us to focus on what we want to accomplish. There is no shortage of things to do!! And we want to give Grant/Weiland Architects a go.

I was busy every day this week with lunches, dentist, CPA appointment, AIA environment committee meeting, etc. On Thursday I went back to the building, turned in my parking card and saw Paula. She's such a good friend and so much fun, she always gives me a lift. We agreed that one reason I took this crazy job was to meet her. I also think there were some lessons for Rick, Karen and myself to learn. Another possibility was that it pushed Keith and me into Grant/Weiland Architects.

On Friday Keith and I went to the Gem and Mineral show where we did some Christmas shopping and got some goodies. On the way home we picked up the wedding invitations. They are so beautiful that I choked up in the store while proofing them.

Only disappointment is that I've been a bit achy, so I started the sesame oil rub again. Seems better after only two days. Can that be?

My right heel Achilles tendon sheath was really swollen and sore, but I've been sleeping quite well. Keith has been very understanding and supportive and I think we've gotten along quite well for being together all the time.

Dec. 2, 1992

Thanksgiving was a fun day. Diane, Hobie, Scott, Sue, Mark, seven people! Not bad for our little expatriate group. We toasted Michigan.

The client who had the property on Lake Keowee is moving to New Jersey, so that project is over. But Amoco has asked Keith to do an addition to a quality control laboratory building in Decatur, Alabama, and it's moving along. Then yesterday we went to an epoxy paint seminar and another one of my former co-workers was there. He got so excited when we told him about starting our firm! His wife is also an architect I have worked with and she is now with the Board of Regents. She called me today and we had a nice visit. She said the Board of Regents is very interested in hiring women-owned firms for architectural work! So maybe Grant/Weiland Architects is the next step. Have I found where I belong?

Dec. 5, 1992

Yesterday morning I went to see Maya, who bills herself as a "Body Psychotherapist." Paula has been to her twice and from what she described, it sounded like something that might help me and be what Michael recommended. Well, it was wonderful. I laid down on a foam mat. She put her hands under my neck and pressed along my collarbones. Then she put her hand on my heart—what did I see? I saw my heart. What did it say? It said that I have been through a lot and that I am OK just the way I am. That I am good enough. That I don't have to work so hard. Then I saw a Valentine heart with gold around it, then blue light and love flowing down and washing over me, love, all the love I need. It was beautiful and inspiring. She had me talk to my hands, to love and accept them the way they are. By wanting them to be different, I am giving them the same judgmental message I always got from my mother. So I should love my hands and feet just the way they are. It was a bit of a new way to apply this idea. I liked her a lot and will go back next week.

Dec. 10, 1992

My second session with Maya today was even more powerful than the first. I told her about making up a new song: "I love my self just the way I am" (also hands and feet). She said she could see why Michael said I only needed four sessions, since I had gotten so much out of the first one.

She held my neck, then went to my lower back. What did I see or feel? I saw a tree like the ones in the Wizard of Oz, sort of scary. I looked inside and it was hollow and dark. Could I go inside the tree? What if I took someone with me? My sister Linda, of course! We were little girls again with our Dutch-bob haircuts, wearing red and white striped ticking dresses with puffed sleeves and sashes. We held on to each other. Did we need another ally? Maya asked if we had had a dog No, but we had Sparky, our 15-pound orange angora cat whose full name was Sparky Twistle Ginger Jingles Toddles Ulysses Sampson Grant. Suddenly he was there, about six feet tall with his huge fluffy tail and a red heart with all his initials on his chest. He held out a paw for each of us and the three of us went down the steps into the tree. The farther we went, the lighter and less scary it became. Then it opened up to a meadow and a cute little house with a white picket fence, gardens with flowers, like hollyhocks, in all the colors, and lots of birds. The house had a blue roof and a chimney with a red heart on it. We went into the house and all my guides and friends were there—Keith and Diane and Jack's mother and Herman and Misha, a good chunk of my support group. We all hugged each other. Then we went out into the backyard and had a tea party.

I wondered if my mother might be there some place. Well, she was over in the woods looking like the witch and we threw water on her and she disappeared. She has no power anymore. We had given her that power when we were little because we just didn't know any better. I cried and cried. Then the party was over and we hugged and said good-bye. Everyone there told me I could have all the love I wanted, I always could have had it if I had only known, but I didn't know it. How do we leave, do we have to go back through the tree? No, there's another path and it leads to Atlanta and it looks just like OZ!

POWERFUL! I am still feeling the effects! Maya is so good, although she said I did it. If I weren't ready to feel and move through it, nothing would happen. WOW! It was every bit as powerful as a

Hellerwork session. Maya works completely from her intuition. Last week she sensed there was pain in my heart; today she felt there was a block in my lower back.

Jody and Jan are now the parents of twins born on Christmas Eve. Quite a houseful with the dogs!

Right before Christmas I got a job offer to work on a new medical office building. I told them I would like to start on March 15, but they said, "We'd like you to start next Wednesday!" Once again I denied my true feelings. I didn't really want to go back to working in an office again, but my ego liked being asked to work on a new medical project. So I accepted. (See Chapter Eleven.)

Jan 11, 1993 Monday
What a comedown! I've just experienced the worst flare-up of arthritis <u>ever</u>. Started medical office building job on Wednesday, Dec. 30, the same day that Kenny started. I worked half a day New Year's Eve, then four days the next week. I felt the stress of starting a new job, adjusting to a new parking deck with a walk through not-such-a-nice area and it was cold, rainy and damp most of those days. I'm spoiled from working at home on the lab project and disappointed about putting on hold what I really want to do: Grant/Weiland Architects. I was trying to address wedding invitations and was not pleased with the way they looked. This is not the time or place to learn calligraphy and the arthritis has eroded much of my fine motor control. Then Thursday I talked to a family member in Michigan who made a crack about all of us not being with them for Christmas. It bugged me. I went to bed, but my hands started aching like they did in San Francisco. I went upstairs to try and sleep. Took two Tylenol with codeine, finally slept about three hours. When the drugs wore off, my hands hurt just as bad as before. I got up, did the sesame rub-down and went to see Maya at 8 AM. I was a mess. Cried from beginning to end. She put cold towels on my hands, which seemed to help. I saw a brick wall. Sparky the big cat came to help knock it down with big gloves. Maya talked a lot about growing up with mean people and how I was so little and didn't know better. She said it's OK to feel sad when I'm hurting and I mustn't feel like I've failed.

Before I left Maya's office, I called in sick and called Keith to tell him I was coming home. I spent the day in bed with plastic bags of ice on my hands. I called Dr. M.'s office, but the gastroenterologist was on call. (He had performed my first liver biopsy and I didn't care for him because he seemed to be rather cold and uncaring, plus he had kept me waiting in the hospital until 5 PM for a 2 o'clock biopsy appointment.) I told him I needed a shot of cortisone, but he said they don't like to do that. I should take more Trilisate and call him Saturday if not better. I knew that wouldn't help. Had an awful sleepless night— saw every hour on the clock, although my feet quit hurting about 4 AM, which gave me hope. In the morning Diane and Hobie came by to get the invitation envelopes so she could have them addressed. I showered and rested with ice on my hands all afternoon. Tried to watch "The Magic Flute," but couldn't even enjoy that. The pendulum (which I'd been learning to use to access higher wisdom) kept saying that the pain would stop, so I didn't call the doctor back. We went out for dinner with friends from North Carolina, me with a bag of ice in a Saks shopping bag. We came home and I tried to rest, but it was impossible. The pain and heat were so unrelenting, just constant agony, just like the night before. By 2 AM I was crazy, hysterical. I was so exhausted, being in my third sleepless night in a row, I just couldn't stop crying. Keith took me to the emergency room. Besides 60 mg. of cortisone, they gave me Decadron (for pain), Toradol (for pain and inflammation), Demerol (sedative) and Phenergan (antihistamine which acts like a sedative). Around 5 AM I was no longer in pain and was dozing. We came home and I slept till 11, then rested all afternoon. Diane came by and that's always good medicine!

Today I spent a lot of time on the phone. Talked to Dr. M.'s nurse and also his former nurse who used to give me methotrexate shots and is now doing home care. I called another rheumatologist in the same office to make an appointment for a second opinion, but she never called me back. Dr. M.'s former nurse said the other doctor and Dr. M. are two of a kind and both would want me to do methotrexate. She said that two of their patients have died while taking it. Well, I knew it wasn't health food! I studied the phone book and found a rheumatologist, Dr. G., who can see me tomorrow at 2:30! I talked to the Ayurvedic Dr. He recommended more herbs and I have an appointment with him on Feb. 10, but I had the feeling he was just looking it up in a book and didn't really have much experience with it. Also will see my chiropractor tomorrow. Nothing like covering the waterfront!

Got a short psychic reading from Lynn—lots of planetary stuff was going on last Thursday! She said that the symbolic focus for the flare-up was giving up control. She saw a rabbit and said I need to find a rabbit-shaped basket, actually put my hands in the basket and release all my fears to the rabbit. She said that in two months I will be independent, not need as much medication. After the wedding!

I'm planning to work tomorrow till 2, then see Dr. G.

I hope I have completed whatever lesson I am supposed to learn by having this flare-up.

Jan. 15, 1993 Friday

I liked Dr. G. very much. She is an attractive black woman and very warm. She was quite amazed that I could wear regular shoes with my feet. When I told her that I think methotrexate is poison, she agreed. She instructed me on how to take cortisone after getting the injection at the emergency room: I need to taper off the dosage over two or three weeks to avoid serious side effects. She is recommending that I take Plaquenil, an anti-malarial which seems to help rheumatoid arthritis. I will consider it. Hey! If someone told me to jump off a roof because it would help my arthritis, I would consider it! I'm desperate enough to try everything, including conventional Western medicine. Only problem with Plaquenil (every drug has a problem) is that it can cause eye damage. I went to an eye doctor for a baseline visual field test and color vision evaluation. My color vision was pronounced flawless.

Jan. 16, 1993

Much different from a week ago—much better. Of course, I'm taking 60 mg. of cortisone a day! Can't sleep with so many things on my mind. The wedding: So much to do. Arthritis: What to keep doing, what to drop. Work situation: Not good money, but they want my life. I think Grant/Weiland Architects is going to get more work in North Carolina and I would much rather do that! Keith: Elbow bursa is swollen. He snores and thrashes, so we sleep separately most of the time. Cortisone: Not good for me, too many side effects.

During this time I was working with my old buddy Kenny (see Chapter Eleven) and answering his questions about life, etc. I now know that the reason I took the medical office building job was because he and I had important spiritual work to do together and Spirit was once again "encouraging" us to get on with it.

I ordered the tape of Michael's "State of the Planet Address 1993" and was astounded. According to Michael, each year has its own overleaves and this year has Higher Intellectual energy which started coming into the planet in December. This type of energy comes along only every thirty years or so and is very stressful because it is so much more intense than normal. It pushes everyone on the planet into being more aware of the truth and what is right, making it harder to be in denial. A lot of healing of society's problems will be initiated which will continue during the next several years. The downside is that the higher centered energies are hard on the bodies of those of us who have weak constitutions and are strongly impacted by weather. This is the time of year when we want to be hibernating, not starting new cycles. Adding this to everything else that was going on in my life helps to explain why I had the flare-up.

March 4, 1993 10:30 PM Two days to The Wedding!
        What a day, what a week! Tuesday saw Dr. G. who said I'm doing great. My knee was hurting, but she said it was bursitis, "not your rheumatoid," and she treated it with ultrasound and heat. Wednesday I saw Maya and had a clarifying session. I'm pretty much overflowing with love. She said, "You're so <u>clear</u>!" which felt good. Joy, joy, joy!
        Keith was pretty bummed out because his van was broken into and the TV and video player were stolen, right outside the condo.

The wedding was wonderful. Everyone from out of town arrived on schedule, including my cousin from Sweden. I asked for 63 degrees and it was 58 and sunny. Close enough! Everything went perfectly. Diane was a gorgeous bride and Hobie is so sweet and sincere. The reception was great fun and the Lucas House was beautiful. I asked Paula to be my "lady-in-waiting" and it was so comforting to have her there to take care of any details and to be available for moral support. Afterwards, she and her boyfriend David packed things up in the van, like 25 plates of leftover wedding cake, the leftover champagne, and other food. A week later we knew we had picked the right date when the Storm of the Century dropped eight inches of snow on Atlanta and completely shut down the city, the airport, everything! We were without power for 37 hours. On Sunday evening, our trip to the airport (where 30,000 people had spent Saturday night) to pick up the honeymooners became a real adventure. Their plane was delayed and it took two hours to get their luggage. We arrived home at 1 AM!

A friend told me last summer about Howard, a "Kahuna Healer," who lives in Columbia, South Carolina, and that I must go see him. Kahuna healing is based on ancient Hawaiian healing wisdom and the legendary Kahuna teachings. My friend's brother had been wounded in Viet Nam and had suffered a lot of pain, both mental and physical, for about twenty years. Howard worked on the brother for about a week, at the end of which his pain was gone. Not only was Howard a miraculous healer, she said he was "drop-dead gorgeous" and he didn't charge for his treatments, except for expenses and whatever you wanted to give him. I asked Michael about Howard and they said, yes, the sooner I went to see him, the better. I had been very interested in planning a visit to Columbia in the fall, but when Diane got engaged, I pretty much forgot about anything but the wedding.

Two weeks after the wedding, Keith and I drove over to Columbia for a weekend. We called Howard when we got into town, about 8 PM on Friday evening. He came over to the motel. When I first saw him, the words "drop-dead gorgeous" jumped into my mind. He is indeed very handsome, with dark, deep-set eyes and an easy smile. We visited for a little while and he asked us some questions about our respective ailments, Keith's back and elbow and my arthritis. I'm sure he was "reading" us. Then we went to a nearby chiropractic office where Howard began working on Keith, as I sat and watched. He does bodywork, a very deep massage with special oil. As he works, Howard talks in his soft Carolina drawl, telling us stories of people he has healed, asking us questions, etc. He looked at me often with a twinkle as Keith would answer his questions. While the bodywork is sometimes painful, it is very energizing. When Keith's session was over, he was standing up straighter that usual and feeling very lively. We agreed to meet the next morning, when he worked on Keith again. During that time I was told to write down: All the grievous wrongs that have been committed against me, all the grievous wrongs I have committed against others, all the grievous wrongs that I have committed against the earth and the life of the earth, and all the grievous wrongs I have committed against myself. A tall order!

Howard invited his friend Ruby to join us for lunch. She is an fascinating, intelligent person and we hit it off right away. Ruby said something that day that I have remembered and quoted often: "Coincidence is a word we use when we think God isn't paying attention."

After lunch, Howard and I sat outside on the grass for the Kala ritual for emotional healing. We took the lists I had made that morning and I talked about every one of the things I had written down. I wish now we had recorded it, because Howard gave me much good wisdom and advice. We burned the paper and prayed. He said words over me. Then we finished it with water and more prayers. Then it was my turn for bodywork. It was pretty painful, but I knew that it was helping rid my body of a lot of the old stuff I have been carrying around for many years. Then I think he worked on Keith again, briefly. We were physically and emotionally exhausted and could barely drag ourselves out to eat some dinner and back to the motel.

Sunday morning Howard worked on us both in turn and then we left Columbia to return home. When I told Kenny about Howard the next day at work, I was surprised at how interested he was. (See Chapter Eleven.) On Tuesday, Howard called me at the office. He said I needed to call my mother and get her to tell me I am a good person and that I also needed to go see her and get her to tell me that in person. I was very quiet. "That's not going to be easy," I said. He agreed, but said I really needed to do it. After we hung up, I stood up because I needed to take a break and think about what he had said. I noticed a little pain in my knees. The problem wasn't really in the knee joints, but was a stiffness in the tendons above and below my knees. While it was a fairly mild level of pain, it still made walking difficult.

Thus began a very frustrating period of pain and self-examination. After about a week, I called Howard told him, "I cannot deal with going to my mother in person. Is there some other way I can do this?" He apologized for setting me back and proceeded to tell me how to call my mother's Higher Self to me by saying her name out loud three times, then talk to her and tell her what I want and what my feelings are. Which I did. Amazingly, within a week I got a note from my Mother telling me what a great job I had done raising Diane. This was high praise since she always took credit for anything Linda and I did right. It was magical to receive this, but my knees were still stiff and continued to be a problem until I decided to take the Plaquenil. After several weeks the Plaquenil took effect and I could once again walk comfortably.

Another thing that Howard taught us was deep breathing. Kahuna healing recommends breathing in to the count of eight, holding it to the count of eight, then blowing it out to the count of eight. This creates Mana, a form of healing energy which can be directed to any part of the body. It makes me light-headed and can be useful as a distraction, sort of like deep breathing during labor. Here is a prayer that Howard channeled for me:

I have made peace and opened my entire being to the light, love and power of Life and of God. I join myself with this seen and unseen Presence in respect and humility. I have great reverence for All That Is. In this new station and position in my life, I now reach outward and I reach inward to claim for myself a perfect, happy, healthy, normal body, mind and spirit. And, as I live my life, I am returning to complete, natural health, unbound and free of all past illnesses and problems in this or any other lifetime. I live free, I live healthy, I live!

Joya came for a week in June. She wanted to see Howard, so I arranged for him to come to Atlanta for the weekend. This was when Kenny saw Howard (which is described in Chapter Eleven). It was the week of my birthday and also June 6, my parents' anniversary. My mother has always had a huge thing about their anniversary, probably because it was the most important day of her entire life and she has built her whole lifetime around being Mrs. Grant. When my first husband Jack remarried on June 6, 1986, she said "Why did they choose our day?" It is very important for Linda and me to observe their anniversary. I got a phone call on the 5th from my mother: "Did you send us flowers?" "No, I sent a card." "Well, it's the least you could do." "Oh, you want flowers? O.K." So I called their favorite florist and ordered flowers. I decided to put automatic flower delivery into effect for several occasions during the year and have the florist just charge my credit card. It has worked very well. But I struggled with that old feeling of not having measured up. Keith can't understand why it is so important for Linda and me to have to remember it. He said he never even knew when his parents' anniversary was! And why isn't my dad sending her flowers?

Late that summer Grant/Weiland Architects was appointed by the Board of Regents to do some work at Georgia Southern University in Statesboro, Georgia. We were thrilled to receive this assignment and I was delighted to have reason to leave the medical office building job, but the work had to be done very quickly. In six weeks we made four trips to Statesboro. As with any project, we worked long hours and became very tired. Toward the end, Keith and I were strained and it was hard to be both working and living together. Keith tends to become critical and hard to please when stressed, which makes me defensive and angry, a familiar pattern. But when the project was completed, we were very proud of what we produced. We had good comments from both the Board of Regents and Georgia Southern and they paid us well.

When I stopped working in a downtown office I had to find a new hairdresser because I had been going to the shop in the building. So I found a young man in a solo practice and as time progressed, we became good friends. Alan was only 28, but I could tell by his attitudes that he was a fairly old soul. I naturally began chatting with him about Michael and even told him about Kenny and the angels. He was mildly interested. One day when I arrived for my appointment, he was very concerned because his salivary gland was swollen. This gave me a good opportunity to repeat some of the "spiritual causes of physical pain" ideas. At one point I took off my shoes to show him my feet. "This is what strong emotion can do," I declared. It wasn't too much later that he was diagnosed with lymphoma. It was a shock to me that such a young man could have such a serious disease, so I took his picture and talked to

Michael about it. I was right about him: fourth level old Artisan. Then Michael said that Alan and I had been cousins during a lifetime in China. I was a girl and Keith was my mother who enforced the foot-binding custom which deformed my feet and caused me much pain. Alan later had daughters, but because of my experience did not allow their feet to be bound. I thought this was extremely interesting in light of the fact that I had shown him my feet. It also answered Duane's question about previous Chinese lifetimes.

About this time Kenny began to channel the angels for me (see Chapter eleven). I felt—and still feel—very fortunate to have this incredible resource to facilitate my life and healing and began asking questions on a fairly regular basis. About two weeks after I stubbed my toe I asked: Why is my little toe still hurting?

Ariel: There are many painful areas left in your body. Your life experiences are allowing you to peel away layer after layer of the protection you have accumulated during this lifetime. You are getting closer and closer to the core of your being.

Visualize your body like an onion with layer upon layer. Your little toe is shining through like the core of the onion, but you did a messy job removing some of the other layers. See your little toe partially exposed, a pristine orb with its veining showing through, wanting to be free from the other layers,.

As you let yourself feel these emotions, you should feel stinging and burning in your eyes. Let the tears cleanse your eyes. Remember pearl onions. A pearl is a painful irritant covered over with layer after layer of beautiful nacreous coatings. Visualize white light surrounding you, then see the pearl slowly dissolving until only a grain of sand is left. Recognize it, bless it, see it for what it is: a tiny, insignificant speck which brought about the creation of a pearl. The grain of sand is good. The pearl is an object of wondrous beauty created to mask pain, to make it bearable. When you see the grain of sand, you can throw it back into the sea. It's gone. History. Cherish the pearl for its beauty, but rejoice in your freedom from what it represents.

Sept. 10, 1993

Kenny: Michael, I have some questions from Lois. May I ask you for answers and direction?

Archangel Michael: Yes.

Kenny: Thank you. Is Ariel giving answers as well?

Archangel Michael: Yes, for now we are folded together.

Kenny: Thank you. What is Ariel's color?

Archangel Michael: Ariel's color is red. Red is the color of the root of Lois' (anyone's) being. For now, as Lois seeks out these answers, red is the color. (Red is the color of the root chakra!)

Kenny: What is Ariel's favorite music?

Archangel Michael: Vivaldi and Mozart. Mozart especially. Lois has ties, as she has told you, to Mozart. His music can awaken in her some long buried areas that require work. She needs to explore Mozart and study some more about his life and times and listen to his music with her heart without counting the beats. She must be the pupil, not the teacher. These are some keys to her heart.

Kenny: What does it mean to be sprightly?

Archangel Michael: Sprightly means lighter than air, lighter than your surroundings, your circumstances. The spiritual side of life is beyond the weight of the physical, beyond the hurt and pain. In walking with a sprightly gait, Lois is demonstrating and living out her healing. She needs to start walking around her area, concentrating on lifting herself beyond the here and now. The pep in her step will help lift her beyond her intellectual nature, to see more of what is in store for her.

During my meditations, I started working at opening "the doors to my heart." I saw lots of little doors in my heart and when I started opening them, old, sticky stuff like phlegm started running out. So I visualized an angel with a fire hose washing it away and then closing each door.

I bought a book called *Ask Your Angels* by Alma Daniel, Tim Wyllie, and Andy Ramer, which outlines a process for getting in touch with your personal angel. One of my favorite parts says that there are three steps to getting the angels to help: First, to make your request. Second, be aware when they have responded. Last, say, "Thank you." It's so simple! Another chapter is called "The Angel Oracle" and it tells how to make a deck of cards with various messages. I had fun putting together three colors of 3 x 5 cards to create my Oracle deck. The book also has excellent meditations and visualization exercises.

On October 1, 1993, Kenny channeled these answers to my questions:

> Lois: What did it mean specifically when they said I did a messy job of peeling away layers?

> *Archangel Michael: As you have recently been delving into your heart, you have done a thorough job of looking at each area that is unfolded or exposed. Some of what you find is very painful for you to deal with emotionally. Your great desire for haste in your growth has led you to gloss over some areas and go on to the next layer. In doing so, part of the layer gets removed, but not dealt with emotionally. Your lifetimes of experience have given you much wisdom and intellectual understanding, but your emotions are the deepest parts of your heart and because of your intellectual makeup, they are difficult to reach. Try this:*

> *As I face the morning of a new day,*
> *Shine the light of your love*
>   *deep into my heart, my being.*
> *Wash over me, cleanse me, energize me.*
> *Connect me with the powers of the Universe.*
> *I open myself to your leading.*
> *I walk where you lead me.*
> *My life, my heart, my hands, my feet,*
>   *these are for you to use.*
> *Thank you for love, for all that I am.*

Lois: Should Keith and I continue to work together?
Archangel Michael: Yes.
Kenny: Is there more to this question?
Archangel Michael: Yes, but Lois has not asked it yet.
Lois: Am I making progress in opening the doors of my heart?
Archangel Michael: You are making great strides in opening these doors. Your angel Ariel is a powerful help in your progress. She opens doors for you, she shows you parts of you that you weren't aware of or were not dealing with in a healing way.

Remember, Ariel's voice is small. It probably is not what you expect to hear. Think back over your life to very special times of great joy, of help, of powerful confirmation that God was looking out for you. Remember a common thread and I think you will begin to hear her voice. Each person has a different way of communicating with her companion angel. Your way is not like Kenny's way.

Ariel: Lois, I care very deeply about you. Gentle thoughts, sweet fragrances, small sighs, these are ways that I reach out to you. Be still. Know that I am beside you every step of the way. Look closely at your heart. Turn off the scholar and just experience. Open wide the door. I am sitting right inside the door, waiting to share with you. You have reached a very crucial stage in your walk. Open the door. Do not be afraid.

Kenny then wrote: "Lois, I don't know what that meant exactly. My hand was shaking, my whole body was trembling. Those words seem simple, but they were profoundly delivered."

On October 21, I asked the following:

Lois: Are Keith and I doing the right thing by practicing architecture together?

Archangel Michael: Yes, as long as you remind yourself to go with his flow. Keith has a great need to lead and you have a strong desire to follow. You fight against this desire to be the follower in your professional relationship. Do not fight this, as you are where you are supposed to be.

Lois: Are there changes in the direction of our practice we should pursue?

Archangel Michael: Yes. As you both add years to this lifetime, seek less stressful ventures. Your qualifications are excellent. Pursue joint ventures where you can assume an advisory role. Lots of money, less liability. Sell your expertise. Look beyond the confines of traditional architectural practice. Insist on a practice that assures leisure time. What you are now doing is where you are supposed to be, but look beyond. Read want ads, follow up on AIA leads. Call firms advertising for positions and explore the idea of consulting on a regular basis. Offer your expertise for a price.

The next day Kenny asked Archangel Michael, "Do you have any thoughts for me?"

> *Archangel Michael: Call Lois today. Discuss with her the trip she plans to make to see her mother. Give her this:*
>
> *When you see your mother in your imagination, replace her face with that of an angel. An image will come to you. As you imagine that face as your mother, envelop her in love. Then turn away and say, "My love I give unto you. All my love. I am worthy of all the love in the Universe. I am wonderful."*

Linda and I visited our parents to celebrate our mother's 80th birthday. Before going, I practiced the above exercise. It was a little tricky at first to see my mother with the face of an angel, but soon became easy and made me feel good about myself. During the visit I was actually able see the angel's face while talking to her in person. Because I expected absolutely nothing in the way of emotional support or response from my mother, I was able to view her with real detachment for the first time. Something inside me had healed and I no longer needed or expected her approval. It was a watershed visit because of this victory and I felt very strong and empowered when I came home.

Grant/Weiland Architects was taking off! Keith did two more small projects for Amoco and we were the local architect for several Remington stores. Then Scott's office brought Keith in to solve some problems that Delta Air Lines was having with the ticket and gate counters at their new terminal in Cincinnati. Scott had called Keith several times to ask questions about millwork and counters and when these hour-long conversations were over, I would say, "They need an architect." Scott's boss finally asked him how he was doing with this work and Scott said, "When I have a problem I just call my dad," so they decided to bring us on board. Keith is so happy to again be doing the work he loves so much. I began to do Michael's Meditation for Prosperity (see the Appendix) and the work just kept flowing in. Strangely enough, the water stopped flowing into the condo. St. Germaine said it represented unexpressed emotion. I believe that since Keith was happy working again, this outward symbol of distress was no longer being created.

We worked with a graphic designer on a logo for our stationery and business cards. Keith liked the double eagle and I wanted a triangle, so we decided to have "his and hers" logos. There was still a little residual uncertainty about how long the work might last. We both knew that making a go of an architectural practice was not a simple matter. Keith would often say, "We can't afford to..." or "Can we afford this?" One day I had a realization and I told him, "Whenever you say, 'We can't afford it,' you are creating that and we won't be able to afford it. If you want something, say, 'Soon I will be able to afford this,' and you will create the ability to afford it." It is so simple to think this way, but no one I know has been taught how to do it. Millions of people in this country are in debt over their heads because they want things but deep down don't believe they deserve them and don't know how to manifest the capacity to afford them. Michael calls this "havingness" and there are exercises in *Tao to Earth* by José Stevens to help develop this aspect of life. Sanaya Roman, Deepak Chopra, Louise Hay, Arnold Patent and Wayne Dyer all have useful ideas and there are new prosperity books and tapes coming out all the time.

Shortly after the visit to see my folks, I asked Kenny to channel answers to several questions.
Nov. 9, 1993

Lois: How am I progressing with the doors to my heart?

Archangel Michael/Ariel: You are progressing beautifully. You must release much of what you carried with you all your lifetime now that you have settled your feelings with your mother. Be careful not to confuse your love for your mother with the guilt she piled on (with your willing cooperation—but that's OK, too— over all these years). It is wonderful and right that you love your mother. In fact, for your healing to continue flowing, you must love your mother.

Continue to tell her and show her your love. Gifts, letters, flowers and an occasional visit will be welcomed. As you visualize your mother in your meditations, continue to substitute the face of an angel for her face. She has an angel, too. Her spiritual progress is between her and the Creator. Do not confuse your opinions about who and what she might appear to be with your need to love her, to hold her in your heart.

Ariel: Lois, our journey together is becoming more and more delightful. The next time you listen to Mozart, be aware of the little notes and innuendoes in the music. Let the feelings these trigger flow. Listen carefully for me. Read this, file it in your brain, and let me do the rest.

Lois: What is my percent complete in opening the doors and releasing pain?

Ariel: 73.9%. As you have noticed, you experience varying rates of change and growth. As you go through what seems like a rapid rate, look very deeply into your heart. Deal very honestly with your feelings as you release things. When you feel stuck, just say so. Release the stuck feeling. Be honest. Truth is stark, unvarnished, even black and white. These are bytes of information you have logged away, just like in your computer. Even when you reach 100% in your "housecleaning" mode, you will still have today and tomorrow to deal with. This process is part of the necessary, ongoing maintenance of your system.

Love yourself. You are so wonderful. Reach out. Listen to your urgings. I, your guardian angel Ariel, am right inside your heart at all times.

As you meditate, visualize your heart with me standing inside the open door. Ask to enter and then come inside. Let your feelings flow over you fully and deeply. Feel the flow, like in a raft in the River of Life. The flow takes you past many rough areas and the water cushions the shock. This will speed you on your journey.

You have been told much. Treasure it. Love it. Love yourself. Enjoy! In many ways the ride is just beginning. Over and out for Ariel.

Kenny: Thank you.

Lois: I feel that I reached a new level of detachment in dealing with my mother. Do I have more work to do on that?

Archangel Michael: Your observation is quite accurate. Your understanding of your relationship to your mother is greatly increased. Your understanding of how to break the emotional lock between you and her has been achieved. This is a vital link in the cleansing and healing of your heart. You are probably beginning to notice unknown or unfamiliar spaces within your heart which have been exposed during the cleansing process. As they are exposed, fill them with love. The River of Life flows constantly and keeps your heart refreshed. You have more work to do to maintain the relationship with your mother, but you now have the key to do this.

As Grant/Weiland Architects was becoming a viable entity, it was taking up more and more space in our little condo. Architecture is very bulky—we need drafting boards and computers and copiers and files and catalogs and samples and code books and reference books, etc. We were running out of space and things were just piled up in stacks, giving us a claustrophobic feeling and making it harder to work efficiently. Our accountant advised us to buy a larger home to work out of rather than to rent office space, so we started looking. I asked Lynn what she saw for us. She said, "A modern two-story house with a porch across the front and a driveway off to the left with room for parking. There are trees all around and a deck or patio in back." It sounded good to me!

We really liked the first house we looked at, on Kingswood Lane, even though it didn't quite fit Lynn's description. We decided to make an offer, but were disappointed to find it was already under contract. We hoped that the contract would fall through and we could buy it.

Nov. 11, 1993

Lois: Keith and I both want the house on Kingswood Lane. Will we get it? If not, where else should we look?

Archangel Michael: This is a right house for you. Much can be done with the house and both of you can nurture each other there. You will get it if you follow your leading very carefully, but continue to look, as this will sharpen your focus. Make sure that Keith and Lois are on similar spiritual wavelengths here. Remember, you make the choices, you make the decisions. Make the search for the house a spiritual journey and keep looking in the same general area.

Lois: My shoulders have been hurting. Any advice?

Archangel Michael: You have been under stress as you are working through emotional areas and this is causing you to hold back your shoulders, symbolic of your shying away from confronting what you find in your heart.

Study your posture. Become aware of how you hold yourself as you walk and sit. Do some conscious relaxations of your neck and shoulders. Keith might give a great neck and back rub. Think about how many decisions/thoughts you are carrying now. Are you carrying the whole load? Can you share some of it? Do you want to give up all of it? You still make the choices. You are still creating your lifetime here, but remember you are not alone.

Keith and I kept looking at houses and found another one that we liked all on one floor with low (Frank Lloyd) Wrightian lines and a roof overhang. We decided to go back to look at it on the Friday before Thanksgiving. Thursday night my hands started hurting and I was fearful they might get hot like they were in January, but they didn't, thank Goddess. The next morning we went to the house. While we were sketching and measuring and Keith was using the video camera, the tenant came in, very upset, saying that her privacy was being invaded. She was pretty nasty, but I tried to tell myself it was OK, she was choosing to have a bad day. We went to lunch with the realtor and signed the offer. By the time we got home, my knees were hurting. The whole thing was very complex because the owner lives in North Carolina, her agent was out of town and according to our realtor, he was a very unpleasant and unethical fellow. Our offer was good until 12 noon Saturday. That morning Keith went on some errands and drove by the house. The next door neighbor was out in his yard raking leaves, so Keith stopped and chatted with him about the sewer line and things like that. The neighbor told Keith the name of the architect who designed the house and when he came home, he looked up the architect, Jim K., in the phone book and called him. Jim did not remember the house very well, but said he would check on Keith's questions. Then he mentioned, "I've got another house for sale on a lake," and gave Keith the address. We heard nothing from the realtors until 3 PM with a counter-offer consisting only of a roof allowance. We decided to make a counter-counter-offer, take it or leave it, good until 5 PM Sunday. During that night my hands were still painful. If this was the right house for us, why was everything about it feeling so difficult? Mostly, I wondered, why was I in pain? I decided that we were not going to buy that house.

Sunday morning I felt better when I woke up and by 11 AM the pain
was gone. It was a bright, sunny day and we drove out to the house on
the lake. There aren't many lakes in Atlanta so we were very curious.
We found the street. There were two houses on small lakes next to each
other. The one for sale was big and beautiful with all the architectural
features we liked in the house we had made the offer on, but in much
better condition. It was surrounded by trees, had large glass doors and
multiple decks across the front. And the driveway was on the left. We
picked up the information sheet from the mailbox and looked at the price
which was quite a bit more than we had been talking about. I looked up
to the carport and said, "I don't think anyone is living there." So we
drove up the long driveway (to the left of the house) and saw that the
carport was high enough for the van and there was room for parking. It
was obvious the house was vacant, so we parked and got out. The back
yard was nearly all natural woods. We walked around the back of the
house past a patio and down the side yard to the lower deck. We peeked
inside the glass doors to see a spacious room with one wall of stone
which housed a fireplace. "There's your new office, Lois," Keith said.
Tears leaped to my eyes! I was thrilled because it was the first
confirming emotional reaction I had experienced since we started house
hunting and I had been wanting some such indication from Spirit. Even
the house on Kingswood didn't move me like this! We reveled in the
beauty of this place, looking out over the lake. I knew in my heart at
that moment that this was to be our home. On our way back to the van,
we discovered a pet door! The only house we had looked at that had
one! Another sign. As soon as we returned to the condo, I called Jim
and we arranged to meet at the house on Monday to see the inside. A
second unresponsive counter offer on the other house was received from
our realtor that evening, well past the deadline. We said, "Forget it."

On Monday afternoon Jim arrived with plans for both houses. As we
walked through the house we tried to restrain ourselves. It was perfect!
Jim had designed and built it for his mother who lived to be 92 and had
passed away a year earlier. It had vaulted ceilings, triangular clerestory
windows and many thoughtful and unique architectural features. He had
put in new carpet, new vinyl flooring and painted everything inside and
out, so it was ready to be lived in. Plus it was built like a fortress. We
loved it. We made some feeble attempts to get the price down and said

we would call. That night we struggled with the practicalities of owning that house with its lake. Basically, we decided that we did want it, that it was the only magical house and setting we had seen. Somehow we would find a way to make this forward leap from our small condo which we were "never going to leave" to this special, very beautiful home. On Tuesday Keith went to Cincinnati for the Delta project so I called Jim. "We are very interested in the house, but Keith is out of town today and Wednesday we are going to Gatlinburg for a family Thanksgiving. Would you give us a week? We would like to look at it one more time before making an offer. If anyone else is interested, would you please give us first right of refusal?" He said he would. And then he told me there was a combination lock on the utility room door. I was astounded when he gave me the combination so we could get in! I thanked him, hung up the phone and burst into tears. Yes, yes, this is the house! I was overwhelmed and happy and scared and thrilled. As soon as I was able to talk, I called Linda and told her about it. I faxed her the information sheets and she called back reflecting my excitement and encouraging me to go for it. She even offered to help financially. The Monday after Thanksgiving we met Jim and signed a contract to purchase. We felt exhilarated and hopeful, telling ourselves that we could manage this with the help of Spirit and our resources on the planet—an unbeatable combination. On the way home we stopped at the house and let ourselves in. It was such a wonderful feeling to know that this beautiful place was our new home. It was perfect for us. As we stood in the living room looking out to the water, Keith hugged me and I was filled with exultation.

I asked Kenny and the angels for their input.
Nov. 29, 1993

Lois: Is buying this house what we are supposed to do?

Archangel Michael: Yes. This house can be a place where your Spirit will be nurtured. As you have learned much, so must you share. Your life journey is an inspiration and we want you to share it with many others. Ariel and I eagerly await your pouring out this story for publication.

Lois: Will we get the money?

Archangel Michael: Lois, as you are fond of saying, "I can afford it." You will get the money. Remember that this is a learning experience for you. All the doors that you have been opening have been preludes to this house. You will definitely encounter some learning experiences in your financing negotiations. Remain focused on your goal. Accept the challenges as learning times. Deal openly and honestly with your feelings as they relate to your bank account, your comfort and security. Come completely to terms with these feelings. Go with your heart.

Use this affirmation twice daily until you sign papers and close the deal:

> *My life, my heart, my total being*
> *I place in the hands of the Creator.*
> *I accept my role, chosen for me.*
> *I accept my place chosen by me.*
> *I accept the Love and Care of the Creator.*
> *My life, my heart, my total being*
> *All is in harmony. All is at rest.*

Keith and I were still bringing in the work. Early in December I did Michael's Meditation for Prosperity and within a couple of days we were asked to draw all the casework elevations for a hospital project. It was easy work and we were delighted to do it. The only problem was that the holidays were approaching and I told my friend Wendy, "I don't have time to make my German Christmas cookies." She suggested, "Maybe you need to do the Christmas cookie meditation."

On January 11, 1994, there was going to be a conjunction of seven planets in Capricorn. This is a pretty unusual event, occurring once every 400 years or so, and I wanted to take advantage of it. I asked the angels about it and was thrilled to receive this answer:

Archangel Michael: Lois, you are to continue your upward spiral. You are in a fantastic forward mode right now. Times of rapid growth alternate with times of assimilation. As you have said so many times, we choose experiences in order to grow. While you know the areas of growth you desire, you as a human do not know which part of the experience or your reactions will produce the growth. You are molding yourself to become the perfect creation who is able to fully experience oneness with the Universe.

The Universe, including the stars, planets, suns, moons and all the forces and energies, is a living, breathing organism. A conjunction of planets intensifies the energies, which affect every living creature in this galaxy. A person's response to this focused energy varies, depending on their spiritual level. You are at a level where these forces can accelerate your growth.

As you meditate, open your heart. See the doors that need to be opened, and visualize a shaft of light, many, many times brighter than normal. Each time the light grows brighter, say, "And unto me be doubled." When the light is as strong as you can bear (you will know), say the following:

> *As a child of the light, I fully open my heart.*
> *I praise the Creator For all the glorious fullness,*
> *For all the glorious Oneness, For all the glorious Joy,*
> *Peace and Love, which flow in increasing streams.*
> *Complete the cleansing of my heart.*
> *Bring to me the opening*
> *And then the closing of all these doors.*
> *My heart is open. It is full.*
> *My life is one of wholeness and joy.*

Then sit in the glory of the light. Relax. Get ready for a glorious new chapter of your life. Your wings are well-oiled. You are going to enjoy using them.

The first time I did this meditation, I felt a great surge of joy rising up and I was so grateful for the support and love of the angels.

On January 17, 1994, Keith and I moved into our beautiful new house on the lake, which I began to call "Dreams Come True." We were absolutely thrilled that such a beautifully designed and well-built place was really ours. We were concerned about our cat Misha's adjustment to a new home and I talked to him about it, telling him how much he was going to love it. Exactly a week after the move, Keith adapted the pet door so that Misha could come and go as he pleased. It was late in the day when we finished and showed him how to use it. Forgetting that we had planned to go to a college alum dinner, I cooked and remembered too late that we had intended to go out. We sat down afterwards, tired from our moving-in projects for the day. Misha jumped up, kneaded me, then went to sleep, curled up in my lap. Later he went over to Keith and Keith later recalled that he seemed especially loving. We vaguely remember that Misha sat at the top of the stairs for a time and then went down and out the new door. We went to bed knowing that he was probably still outside. I think we even called him. During the night we both got up and looked for Misha, but he was not in the house. I remember doing the "Bridge of Light" meditation, visualizing him coming back, but in the morning he had not returned.

We walked all over the neighborhood, calling him. I called Kenny and asked what to do. He called back and told me a little prayer for Misha: "This is your new home. You are loved. You are free." He gave me directions to a nearby street and told me to go there and visualize Misha and wait for him. I did, but nothing happened. I took flyers around to mailboxes in the neighborhood and a nearby school. Keith and I wept together and remembered how he had come to both of us that last night. We realized that he had been saying, "good-bye, thanks for everything, I love you, but I have to go now." We thought he might try to go back to the condo, but it was over ten miles away and there are lots of major roads between here and there. We tried to accept Misha's decision to leave, for whatever reason, if there was a reason. Later Kenny shared this with me:

Jan. 25, 1994

Kenny: I am confused about Lois' cat disappearing. When she asked the questions, I want to help, but I am afraid of asking such a specific question. Specific questions require specific answers.

Azriel: True. But to be truthful, the answers don't have to fit your preconceived notions. Lois needs to learn to trust the answers that lie beyond her reach. Kenny, you need to learn to trust my answers or Michael's answers. Our wisdom and knowledge are not bound by human dimensions. Through our eyes, you can gaze into the Universe. Angels are the key to spiritual understanding. Guardian angels can open so many doors of understanding. To live in your world in self-imposed darkness is unnecessary. Open the windows of your soul and look to the heavens.

Kenny: Is Misha really safe?

Azriel: Yes.

Kenny: What happens if he doesn't come home?

Azriel: You are getting into theology now! Remember that animals have the ability to make decisions. They have a less flexible set of values. Their communication skills are not up to human levels. Remember that no force in the Universe exists to meet anyone's beck and call. We facilitate the accomplishment of what lies within each human's chosen lifetime experiences and growth. Remember, goals were chosen. Growth patterns and areas were chosen. If you knew each situation, lifetimes would cease to hold any opportunities from which growth would occur.

The second week Misha was gone, I placed a lost animal ad in the newspaper. We got a call from a woman whose mother had been feeding a stray, friendly, black male cat for about a week. Excited, we drove to the woman's house. I was holding back the tears, hoping against hope that it would be Misha. When we drove in, a black cat came towards the van. I jumped out and collapsed on the steps, sobbing loudly with disappointment because he wasn't Misha. The woman came out and was so sweet. She had her own cat inside, so she had been keeping this one outside, locking him up in a closet at night. Keith picked him up and he started to purr. The woman said she was getting ready to go out of town and didn't know what she was going to do. "I've just be praying for someone to come and take this cat." I dried my tears and looked at Keith. "Shall we take him?" I asked. "He's a nice cat, he's purring," Keith replied. We agreed to take him home. "I don't know you, but I feel like giving you a hug," the woman said. "I've been calling him Midnight." We hugged and then I got into the van. Keith handed Midnight to me, who just settled down in my lap. As we drove home he explored the van, then sat looking out the window and twitching his tail.

Midnight adapted to his new home by sleeping for about three days and cleaning himself up. He never seemed to question that he belonged with us. He is a wonderful cat and we have come to dearly love him When I told my mother about him, she said, "You should call that cat Lucky 'cause any cat that you adopt is lucky!" (It was gratifying to have this compliment from my mother.) The funny thing was, Lucky seemed to like the name Lucky better than Midnight, too! And that's how we got

Lucky. I still missed Misha and was especially concerned for him when it was cold and rainy. So I asked the angels if he was still on the physical plane.

Feb. 10, 1994

Archangel Michael: Misha's leaving you is related to your having named him for the Michael entity. Your answers and guidance from the Michael entity are and were very important to you, but you experienced them on an intellectual level. Misha the cat was a physical manifestation with which you were comfortable. Part of your comfort arose from the fact that you were still in charge.

As you have opened to the angelic forces, your life experience is becoming more personal, more emotion-centered. You need and want this more immediate feeling, if you will. This is the direction your life is taking and you are much more comfortable now.

Lucky is more of an ordinary cat. Cats are wonderful and a true delight, but their roles vary. Just love and treasure Lucky. Misha is still on the planet and he is happy. His specific whereabouts are really unimportant. As your heart adjusts to the change in your feelings about the Michael entity and your intellectual vs. emotional transition, perhaps he will reappear. But for now, he must be gone. As you no doubt understand, his leaving was highly symbolic.

Remember this is not good or bad, it is growth, which is the primary reason for existence. You are on the threshold of some exciting events. Spend some time mourning this change, if that is what you need. Use this:

> *With my heart I accept my role in life, my love of*
> *life, my being in its totality.*
> *I am wonderful. My life is love. The door is*
> *open. I am ready.*
> *Love is the key. Love is the Heart. Love is my*
> *Center. I am Love.*

I have to say that on a conscious level I could not get in touch with the idea that I wanted to let Misha go. I missed him very much. But I had told Kenny that I felt I had moved to a higher level of understanding with the angels, although I still appreciated (the entity) Michael's approach to life. When I asked Michael why Misha left us, they asked whether any Indians had lived on the land (we don't know, but it was very likely). They said that it looked like there were some negative Indian energies on the land that Misha didn't want to deal with. Keith and I decided to accept Misha's decision and enjoyed getting to know Lucky.

April 1, 1994 More questions and answers:

Lois: How am I doing with the "doors of my heart"?

Ariel: You are doing well. You are almost through reviewing the doors. Others involved in your heart are not doing as well. (This was a reference to my mother and Keith, who both seemed to me to be stuck in their spiritual growth.) *Your wish to be free is being stifled by your wanting to effect changes in these people. Several keys are available to you to help you release yourself from your very good intentions and desire to help others. Sometimes we want to change others instead of ourselves and you are currently in this place. You are focusing your energies on others' good and welfare and forgetting about Lois.*

General key to your heart: When you meditate or when you feel anxious, visualize a pure beam of light emerging from the Creator, bouncing off your heart and focused on the object of your meditation or anxiety. Look at what you see. Let yourself see the details, but don't try to change anything. See what is there. You can adjust the light intensity if you feel a need to focus on something not clear to you. As you see what is there, say the following:

> *I am Lois. I am at the center of my being.*
> *I am one with the Universe.*
> *Show me what can happen as I release this thought.*
> *Convince me in my heart that all is well. My heart is open.*
> *The place of the Creator I accept.*

Call up as many thoughts, people, situations, as you feel led. Encounter them. See what is there. Turn around. Release all this thinking, all this anxiety. Let your mind go blank. Float in a pool of the light. When your heart tells you it is time, refocus on the object of your attention. Observe what you see. When you feel clear, say the following:

> *My life, All that I am; My being, All that I am;*
> *My love, All that I am, I release.*
> *Float my spirit. Wash me as I float unfettered.*
> *Bind up the hurts in my heart.*
> *Seal them with the love of the Creator.*
> *Close the doors which I cannot change.*
> *Heal the hurts with the balm of your love.*
> *Thank you for the Love of the Creator,*
> *For the Love of the Universe,*
> *For my Love for me.*
> *Awaken in my heart flowers of joy,*
> *Blossoms of eternal peace.*
> *I release the hurts and the healing.*

As you finish this meditation exercise, which will take several sittings, do the following visualization as a key to reinforce and sustain you as you complete the workings of your heart:

Approach the Center of your Universe. Visualize yourself ascending a path. Approach the gates that you see. Follow the directions on the sign. Open the gates. Walk through the gates. Sit down and rest in the peace of the Creator.

Because I was so grateful to be receiving angelic advice, I nearly always did the exercises and meditations they gave me. Of course, some resonated with me more deeply than others. Every so often they acknowledged my work and said it was time to go to the next level. I had the feeling that the angels, like Michael, only wanted to give me input that would make a difference in my life. On the other hand, they were careful not to give me too much information which might shortcut my lessons.

After our move, Keith and I made the necessary improvements to our condo: new paint and carpet, new kitchen flooring and white paint on the kitchen cabinets. Then we tried to sell it ourselves. There was pretty good response to the ads, but nothing really clicked. We began to get discouraged and were considering listing it with a realtor who lived in the neighborhood. This frustration kicked off another flare-up. Kenny asked these questions for me:

Lois: Why is it taking "so long" to sell the condo? Should I list it with a realtor?

Azriel: Lois, remember that you measure time in the years of this lifetime. The Universe looks at a much larger picture. (This was why I put "so long" in quotes!) You and Kenny share some financial concerns. You greatly desire to place your financial affairs in the "hands of the angels." Both of you want and need to learn more trust in the provision of the Universe. The length of time is directly proportional to your ability to truly let go. The Angels want to let you learn this measure of trust and ability to trust in forces larger than yourself.

Listing the condo with the realtor is the right thing for you to do. It removes you from the day-to-day stress and reinforces cooperation and trust. You are on the right track.

Lois: I have been somewhat discouraged about my flare-up this week. Guidance?

Ariel: The healing of your arthritis is keyed to your heart. You know this in your mind, intellectually. You know it in your heart, emotionally. What you don't know is how to put the fact and feeling together. Each human is a lot of facts and feelings. As you look in your heart you will see hurts. The hurt is a fact. Your feelings are real and also highly subjective.

Your healing is a gradual process. Many years have gone into the creation of your dis-ease. The healing will take time also. You have chosen to learn much from this. Slow steps are the best way for your growth to be accomplished. You are dealing with events from past lives as well as this lifetime. Some exploration of past lives will help, but the most growth will come from dealing with this lifetime. Renew your journal. Sit down and chart your progress. Chart milestones, graph your progress and look for linkages between your intellect and your emotions. You could be

healed instantly, but little learning would come from that approach.
You want so much to understand why you have created this illness.
The understanding will continue to come. Use this affirmation:

> *Show me the things I need to see.*
> *Open my heart, the windows of my soul.*
> *Let me see, Let me learn.*
> *Let me go to a new level of wholeness.*

One of the best of the many special features of our new home was a small room, designated as "Sewing Room" on the drawings. It became My Room. At last I have a dedicated space for my spiritual library and artwork, favorite family pictures, my meditation chair and my files on healing and metaphysical subjects. I have created an altar space with special angel figures, candles and natural objects such as a nautilus shell, a pine cone and crystals.

Keith and I gave an open house to show off "Dreams Come True" and about seventy people came. It was a beautiful spring evening and we loved entertaining our friends and business associates.

Soon after this, I resumed writing in a journal as instructed.

May 1, 1994.
      Josh gave me this blank book for Christmas. With the move and all its accompanying changes, I just haven't been writing. But the last time I did the Angel Oracle, it came out: Uriel (transformation), Information Angel, "Let the Angels Write through You," and the angels have also told me through Kenny to resume my journal. So here goes.
      I have finished reading everything that I can find that I wrote during the crisis years before my divorce. I burned five *Nothing Books* in Herman's fireplace on New Year's Eve of 1982. (A *Nothing Book* is a blank paperback book. When I was in architecture school and my marriage was coming to an end, I wrote in them, pouring out my heart and trying to make sense of my life. I kept them in a safety deposit box until my divorce and decided I didn't want anyone else to read them. Burning them was very symbolic of leaving that phase of my life behind.) I do have a series of poems and essays that I wrote during that

time. Reading them is like looking at an old movie. I remember having those feelings, but I have grown so much that I feel very detached. It's hard now to believe that it took me so <u>long</u> to leave Jack! It was seven years from when I realized that the marriage was over until I figured out how to end it. I was really miserable, but still fought and denied it. No wonder I got so sick. All I have to do is look at my feet and marvel at the strength of the emotions it took to create such pain and deformity.

I want so much—in this lifetime—to heal this body completely. If this lifetime is about finally dealing with stuff I have refused to deal with in many lifetimes past, then, let's <u>do</u> it! Learn from it, fix it, get over it.

I made a chart of the development of my arthritis. In reviewing it I can see the direct correlation between emotional stress and arthritic pain. I had forgotten about the "attacks." I used to have them mostly on Monday nights when I was living alone. They don't happen like they used to. I would gradually get achy all over until all I could do was lie on the bed, depressed, discouraged, unwilling to move. I would think about things I needed to do, like feed the cats, go to the bathroom, make a phone call. I would then plan exactly how to do them with the least amount of motion possible. If I had to walk any distance at all, I would count the steps. One time I was talking to my friend Merry and I had to tell her that it hurt to hold the phone. And once I told Linda that I felt like a prisoner of war, that I never had a nice day. Well, I've come a long way from feeling like that! Thank Goddess.

When I feel good, it's hard to remember the bad times and I tend to think I'm on an upward trajectory, that perfect health is mine now. When I hurt, like last week after listing the condo, I feel depressed and discouraged. I actually quit writing in my journal because it was so depressing to go back and read about this pain and that pain after all the Hellerwork, Ayurveda, MAP, Chiropractic, Howard, etc., and none of it seems to be a permanent "fix." I still want a <u>complete</u> healing. One hundred percent off <u>all</u> medicine. Heal the deformities. But it's hard and I really don't know who to listen to. Actually, I don't feel there is anyone I can trust with one hundred percent of my efforts, who knows everything I'm doing and who can tell me what (more) to do. I'm not sure I know if there's more or less I should be doing and if so, what? I always come back to the opinion that <u>I</u> am the only one who knows all I'm doing and while I can ask others what to do, <u>I</u> am the only one who can make the decision, that I know better than anyone else what is right for me and this body.

June 29, 1994

Ouch! I'm feeling the effects from our trip to San Francisco for the CSI (Construction Specifications Institute) convention. It was an interesting exercise from start to finish. It started before we left the ground with a seven-hour delay complete with change of "equipment," so we were zonked by the time we arrived at 4:30 AM Atlanta time! Friday and Saturday we attended the convention, mainly the exhibits. It was hard work, but worthwhile. At the banquet on Saturday a young architect from Philadelphia sat next to me. He started telling me about his children, then about his headaches. I shared a little of my story and ended up telling him that headaches could be caused by self-criticism. He thought about it for a minute and then said, "You, know, that's right!" I talked about self-love and forgiveness and he really seemed to take it in. He was so grateful. When he rose to leave, he shook my hand and then suddenly leaned over and kissed me on the cheek. "God ordained for me to sit next to you tonight," he said. I love to touch people's lives that way.

Sunday and Monday we did the tourist thing and saw friends. Both nights my hands were a bit achy and I think I was in fear of a flare-up like the one I had in San Francisco in September of '92. Well, Michael said this would be a heavy processing month for scholars and I always feel these things. It's incredible how many layers one onion can have! I process and grow, feel great, think I'm done, coast, and then, whoops, there's more. I'm learning the pattern.

July 1, 1994

Angel Oracle today: Uriel, Your Companion Angel, Visit a Healer. My only question, "Which one?" Maybe it is time to see Kenny's healer, Patsy.

My hairdresser Alan is really struggling with his lymphoma. He did radiation and it didn't help. He did chemotherapy and it didn't help. He called me last week and told me he is closing his salon while he works on getting better. I was so sorry to hear this. I wished him well in his search and said he could call me anytime he needed to talk. I have tried a couple of times to call him and recommend a book and a healing place I learned about at my health food store, but there was no answer and I could only leave a message.

July 1, 1994

Lois: How am I doing with the doors of my heart?

Azriel: You are doing well, but, you have been pushing too hard. A good analogy is a tender wound that is not allowed to heal on its own. You are making progress in visualizing the opening and closing of the doors and releasing years of pent-up feelings, growing and maturing into the wonderful person that you are and always have been. But you need to back off a little. Step aside, be calm and let the angels do their part. A visualization can help you.

You have chosen the beautiful place where you now live. It is a sea of tranquillity in an area in the midst of upheavals of change. This choice was made by you on a much deeper level than what you might have thought. Ancestral forces are at work in your being where you are. Use this:

The Affirmation of Steadfastness and Healing:

I, Lois M. Grant, am one with the Universe, with all the angelic beings of Light, with all the healing forces in the Universe. I, Lois M. Grant, am wonderful. My heart is full of love and peace. Any doors concealing hurts are being healed. I am free to move on in this lifetime. My heart is in the gentle hands of the Master of all healing. My hands are open and receiving all that is good and wonderful. My back is strong and straight, supporting me in the march toward time and space. My feet are soft and true, marching me forward, holding me calm and serene. I, Lois M. Grant, am free to be me. I accept myself and I move on in this life with the understanding that total healing is mine.

Lois: While working on a proposal, I kept hearing Mozart on the radio, but we didn't get the project. Was the music significant? If so, what does it signify?

Azriel: As we have mentioned several times, Ariel manifests in ways other than a "voice" or direct thought. You respond to Mozart and similar music on several levels. One is that music is Ariel's communication with you. As the music especially moves you, respond by opening your heart. "Listen" for a message. Be mindful of the thoughts that come to you during these times.

Regarding Mozart's significance to you, your personal impact in his lifetime was significant, therefore your soul "remembers" his music as it was originally written and performed. Music comes to you as a trigger which releases thoughts which are often the answers you seek. The music is confirmation of what you are doing, where you are headed.

As far as the proposal goes, you did many things properly. You learned a lot about the process. Use what you learned as a tool for the next time. Many people are listening and acting on their guidance. You are growing and moving in the right direction. You are nearing a big turning point in your life and still have some hurdles to maneuver over, around or through.

Your heart is mending. Listen for the music in your heart. Act on the thoughts. Grow in love and grace.

Your Angels

Kenny then continued beyond what I had asked:

Kenny: Is there further information for Lois?
Azriel: Yes
Kenny: What is the deepest need of her heart?
Azriel: The need to feel truly loved and wanted by her mother.
Kenny: Can Lois produce this feeling?
Azriel: <u>No</u>. It can only come from her mother and her mother does not know where that feeling lies within her own soul. This is a door that Lois must close and let Spirit do the healing. There is nothing wrong in feeling hurt about this, but the hurt will damage Lois if it is not released.

I lost a crown from a tooth before we went to San Francisco and the repair failed, so I knew I was in for some major dental work.

July 9, 1994

I had lunch with Kenny on Thursday. I told him about my "Angel Oracle" which was: Uriel, Your Companion Angel, Visit a Healer. My only question is, "Which healer, Patsy, Howard? Someone else?" He said, "Patsy came to mind."

Late that same afternoon I got achy all over and my hands started hurting. Keith wanted to go out for dinner and to the bookstore.

We had an excellent Italian dinner, but my hands were getting progressively worse. I was getting scared that it was going to be a full-blown flare, but I hid it from Keith because he would want to know what caused it and I wasn't sure. I think I was just so tired of pain and illness that talking to him about it would make it "real" and then I would have to deal with it—again. After dinner we went to the bookstore, but I was so uncomfortable by this time I just couldn't stay in the store. I told Keith I would wait in the van where I started crying and praying. When Keith joined me, I had to tell him what was happening. We drove home and I called Dr. G. She told me to take two of the ten mg. cortisone tablets for inflammation and Darvocet for pain. She said the weather had been terrible for arthritis and other patients had also been calling. Great! Let's blame the weather! An hour later I was up to eating some watermelon which had a cooling effect. I greased up my hands with the Ayurvedic oil mixture and listened to my Super Immunity tape (a subliminal cassette tape to boost the immune system). Slept pretty well, only got up once for another pain pill and felt great in the morning. Keith wanted to know what had triggered it. I said, "I think I don't want to go to the dentist." I truly was not upset with him or work.

When I went to the dentist he told me I needed a bridge or an implant, but before I needed to decide, the root needed to be extracted. He is pretty advanced and his new assistant was surprised when he pulled out his pendulum to ask which dental surgeon I should go to. When I brought mine out, her eyes were really wide!

There was an article in the *Aquarius*, Atlanta's New Age newspaper, about burning candles with intention. Yesterday I bought some meditation candles and used two last night, a big orange one for health and vitality and a white one for the purity of my intent. Lit a red one upside down to release any resistance to healing. New moon yesterday, too, so it is the beginning of the "bring time." (Release time is between full moon and new moon.) The candles are fun, colorful and add a new dimension to my meditations.

Saturday I received this incredible fax from Kenny and the angels:

Lois, this is a Gift from the Angels:

Lois, your observations about things you have done and learned in response to your arthritis are very insightful. Your Angel Oracle is very appropriate for your pursuit of your healing.

Your arthritis is the result of many lifetimes because of what you have subjected yourself to in terms of relationships and choices. You have wisely chosen a partner for this lifetime who will allow you to grow and much growth has taken place. We think you are ready to move beyond your arthritis into a glorious state of wellness.

Document what you know about your disease. Recognize the reality of your arthritis. Be willing to look beyond this current reality to a freer state, a place where your body matches your soul/spirit in openness and wellness.

A healer can unlock some of the spiritual and past life blocks which have made this transition difficult. Recognize that you are ready to move, ready for your body to match your spirit. Recognize your fears and deal with them. Examine them honestly. Release them, and let yourself move on.

(Kenny wrote here: Lois, I felt a really powerful presence here. It seemed to be of really great importance.)

Azriel/Archangel Michael: Our desire for you is to be whole—full of life, joy, and to know a deeply transcendent peace. Your angels are all around you. Your loved ones are being moved to growth by your example. You are much loved and cherished in the Universe. There are many hands reaching to you to aid you in your crossover as your ascendant journey is reaching its climax. As you read this, open your mind. See whatever comes. Don't feel a need to visualize. Just be. The love of the Universe is all around you.

The Angels.

"Ready for your body to match your spirit..." Oh, yes! This message was extremely heartening and I was thrilled to have such a positive prediction that my complete healing is not only possible, it is really going to happen! This is the most welcome thing that could possibly be said to me. I was overjoyed.

In my journal I continued to analyze my arthritis and how it was engendered by my thoughts and attitudes:

July 10, 1994

On Thursday one of the things I had talked to Kenny about was the "gifts" of my arthritis, how it allowed me to stop doing housework, yard work, and backpacking. I needed a "real reason," not just that I didn't enjoy these things and didn't want to do them. That would never have been accepted. As one friend said, "It let you say, 'no.'" He was right. It also gave me a "real reason" to start counseling and to begin exploring my inner world.

In addition, the arthritis was symbolic of my not moving forward in my life, of staying in the marriage, in spite of incredible emotional pain and the fact that we had completed our karma. (Of course, I didn't let this become conscious at the time.) The inflammation was a manifestation of my anger and resentment over feeling unloved by my mother. The pain was self-punishment. According to Ayurveda, it was a Pitta aggravation. According to Michael, it was a slide from Impatience to Martyrdom. Given the way my life was (not) going and who I was at that time, I believe that the arthritis was probably inevitable. Next April it will be 20 years. Is that significant? Are 20 years enough for me to learn all these lessons, release all these fears, all that anger and resentment, to truly love myself and let myself be loved, to forgive?????

After the flare-up last week and seeing how easily the cortisone handled it, I now know I need have no more fear of a flare-up like January of '93, a possibility I had been dreading. (Did I create it by dreading it? Somebody said, "What you resist persists.") Because of the drug, the flare didn't fully develop, so I was able to sleep and survive it with ease. Thanks to Western medicine for that!

July 11, 1994

Interesting. I read the "Gift from the Angels" to Linda and Diane. Linda's reaction was the same as mine (only less intense). She said, "It feels right," and I was somewhat surprised that she accepted it as "authentic." Diane accepted it, but cautioned me that "you are ready to move into a glorious state of wellness" might not mean that the arthritis is going away right now or right away, or as soon as I want it to, which is right now! I don't know how this message could be interpreted any other way! She didn't get nearly as excited as I thought she might or hoped she would! I guess it is the MD urging caution and suggesting that I recognize the reality of my arthritis now.

Assignment: "Document what you know about your dis-ease." What do I know about the big RA?

It's Psychogenic: One of the first books I ever read when I got the arthritis, *Psychosomatics*, stated that the typical rheumatoid arthritis patient was: Over 35, Female with a domineering mother and repressed anger; onset usually occurs after a dramatic change in the life. I thought it fit me pretty well. (I don't know who wrote this book because I can't find my copy and it is now out of print.)

Stress: Affects the immune system. Rheumatoid Arthritis is the immune system gone haywire, the body attacking itself. When a person is continually in the "fight or flight" response, the adrenal glands become weakened from overuse. I remember that when I was in high school and college I wore underarm shields because I perspired so heavily, a very real symptom of stress. I tended to get headaches when I sang in choral concerts. When I took singing lessons at the age of 30, the teacher could hear the tension in my voice and she figured out that I had been putting all my nervous tensions into my jaw (where my mother couldn't see them) and singing with tight jaw muscles for all those years. She taught me how to consciously relax those muscles. Now when I realize I am walking around with a slack jaw, I am pleased and congratulate myself. I was stressed early and often by my mother's constant criticism ("Why are you moving your leg like that, are you nervous?") and later by my first husband. She picked him out for me, just as she picked out my china and silver patterns. Both of them are Scorpios, have the goal of Discrimination, were demanding, faultfinding and impossible to please; they both had a way of making me feel like everything was my fault, that I was the crazy one, and I didn't know enough to think otherwise. Linda has read that people from dysfunctional families have trouble sleeping because they become hyper-vigilant from never knowing when the next attack might be coming, which creates more stress.

Medical: Sometimes called "symmetrical synovitis," which means inflammation of the synovial fluid which surrounds the joints. Causes deterioration of joints. Destroys cartilage. Painful. Systemic because it affects the entire body, not just the bones and joints. Chronic and supposedly incurable, although spontaneous remissions occur.

Treatment consists of analgesics for symptomatic pain relief and anti-inflammatory drugs to reduce inflammation. The most powerful arthritis drugs actually suppress the immune system to keep the body from attacking itself. Drugs I have taken include: Bufferin, Motrin, Gold injections, Penicillamine, the drug with the name I can now not remember that was killing people in England (but seemed to help and was "only" one pill a day), methotrexate orally, methotrexate injections, Plaquenil, cortisone. I have taken Darvocet and Tylenol with codeine for pain.

Metaphysical: It's a physical manifestation of spiritual and emotional problems such as anger, resentment, feeling unloved. Joints represent motion; I resisted moving forward in my life. Inflammation and fever are manifestations of anger. Deformities are the result of intellectual stress and constriction. Pain is guilt which is seeks punishment.

Lois: My pattern is that achiness will begin to come on during the afternoon or early evening. I try to repeat affirmations and figure out what might have caused it, whether emotional upset, stress, the weather, etc. It usually gets worse during the evening. I take extra drugs to sleep and it's usually OK by morning. Sometimes stubborn pain will last a couple of days or so and that can make me very unhappy and fearful that it will get worse instead of better.

Michael says that rheumatoid arthritis comes from repeatedly refusing to deal with an issue over many lifetimes. J.P. Van Hulle channeled Michael regarding "The Spiritual Causes of Physical Pain":

The oldest issues we have are stored in our teeth and bones because they are the densest parts of the body and thus have the greatest capacity for storage. When you are still carrying something around and have not allowed yourself to work on or handle whatever it is, you tend to give yourself a lot of joint pain. People who get intense arthritis have run up against something they haven't handled in a lot of lifetimes and they don't want to start handling it now. Once you get arthritis it's very difficult to have it go away, but you can get release and have it not get worse if you start working on the problem.

Emily Baumbach is another Michael channel who has researched this subject. She writes:

In both animals and humans, arthritic joints are often places where we store our stoicism and stubbornness. Healthy joints normally bend with flexibility and spontaneity. When part of us wants to be flexible and another part holds back in stubbornness, we unconsciously contract whatever body part has symbolic meaning for us... If we want to cry out with emotional center expression but hold back stoically, the conflict can end up in an immobile joint.

Some arthritis patients offer devoted server-like submission to others, then resent their sacrifice, because an equal amount of recognition doesn't come back their way.

Rheumatoid arthritis is an inherited auto-immune condition, an inappropriate self-attack against our own bodies as if they're our enemies. We need to see where we self-punish, where we self-hate and where we're afraid to make mistakes. One benefit of arthritis is the payoff of martyrdom, where people rush to help us get in and out, up and down. However, arthritic people with a goal of dominance often resent this help, thinking it makes them look "weak." Their anger covers their fear that they can't be physically dominant and competent. (I have a goal of dominance.)

Problems: Do you hold back or "clutch" your normal healthy aggression and self-expression? Do your emotions get trapped in your joints? Have you gotten "stuck" in life and is it hard to "move" easily. Do you punish yourself instead of punishing others?

July 12, 1994 Tuesday

I called Kenny's friend Patsy, but felt that her office was not conveniently located and she referred me to Sue Ellen Renn who also practices Inner Nature's Integration (see the Appendix). I phoned Sue Ellen yesterday and we had a great conversation. When I told her about the arthritis, she said, "You need to forgive someone." Hello! She uses Applied Kinesiology to "remove the blocks, so the body will heal itself." I'm looking forward to seeing her on Monday. I have sent her a copy of my chapter in *Take Two* (see Recommended Reading) and some of my writings.

July 21, 1994

I saw Sue Ellen on Monday. She is a small, radiantly beautiful woman with white hair and perfect teeth. She said to me, "What a lovely lady." (She later told me that when I showed her my feet that day, she wanted to cry. She sensed how much emotion was crushed into them.) As I lie on a massage table, she taps on my midsection, pulling on my arm for muscle testing/kinesiology to see where I go weak and what needs to be looked at. By putting my fingers together in various numerical combinations she finds what the number of the issue is. Then she looks the numbers up in her books to find out what they mean, clears it or provides a remedy, then "taps it in" to my forehead, and "saves it to the biocomputer" by tapping up my body. I don't begin to claim understanding of how it works. It is very esoteric and mysterious. I don't remember everything that came up, but I do remember this: First thing, a biggie: lack of bonding at birth! Inability to receive, which was put in my DNA 21 generations ago on my father's side. She put acupressure dots on two bladder meridian points behind my knees. These are little steel balls on a small circle of tape; I am to massage them whenever I think about it. The main thing I need to do is bless my body. She put me into timed processing which means my body will gradually assimilate and respond to the changes that were made and issues that were cleared during the session.

She read all the stuff I had sent and seemed thrilled to get a copy of *The World According to Michael*. I also took in a copy of the graph of progress which I drew in response to the angels' suggestion and my overleaf chart.

Talked to Lynn today and asked about the significance of Jupiter and the comet impacts (Shoemaker-Levy 9). She said this is the time to plant the seeds for what you want. Well, I have been doing that! I want a complete healing and I want the kind of architectural work we are doing now to continue. I also want grandchildren.

Aug. 3, 1994

I had lunch with Kenny yesterday. That night my right thumb hurt and I took Tylenol with codeine at 10 PM and 2 AM. This morning I was really groggy, even after meditating. After breakfast I rested a bit, then tried to get dressed for a meeting, but just couldn't manage it. I lost my breakfast! Very unusual. I went back to bed till 11:30 AM. Keith made me some soup for lunch and then I rested and listened to my Super Immunity tape. Feel somewhat better this afternoon, but am tired and weak. Have been reading and listening to Mozart while Keith works. I'm really not sure what is going on.

I called Kenny for the angel angle on my strange illness this morning, but didn't tell him anything about my symptoms. He faxed this to me:

Lois: What happened? Why was I sick and what does it mean?

Azriel: *Your sickness is a combination of factors. First, you are processing the healings which took place during your visit to Sue Ellen. Your body is a wondrously complex system and some deep-rooted areas are being dealt with as a result of your session.*

You also are continuing to open and close doors in your heart as you continue your growth and moving upward. Your body is playing "catch-up," if you will. You also are sick because you needed to take some time to rest. Your body knows what your inner self needs and responds accordingly. The symptoms you feel, the lightheadedness, nausea and pain, are physical manifestations of what is going on at the spiritual level. You feel slightly helpless to control your surroundings. You want to cast all your cares to the wind and float freely with the stars, but you are still earthbound for the time being. You are being presented with a challenge to test your wings a bit more.

Use this affirmation. It should help you feel better:

> *My life, My surroundings, My Oneness, My All.*
> *I release my bonds to All that is mine.*
> *I receive from Spirit All that is mine.*
> *I bless my Oneness. I bless my Wholeness.*
> *I bless my life, I bless my All.*

Well, Sue Ellen told me it would take about two weeks from the time I saw her for my body to process the clearing and other work she did. It took two weeks and two days! So I guess it's time to go back. According to the theory, once the body has processed the work, whatever was cleared and released is forever taken care of. I don't quite understand how this works, but it certainly seems to be worth pursuing.

Aug. 21, 1994

The weeks fly by. We finally got an offer on the condo, made a counter-offer and they accepted it! What a relief. We had a busy weekend, all good, but I was exhausted. It was rainy due to tropical depression Beryl and I was achy all week till Friday. Let's blame the weather again. Wednesday night Lynn came over to do a reading and ended up talking more about Kenny than me. (This reading is given in detail in Chapter Eleven.) This is such an incredible time.

Angel Oracle: Uriel (again!), An Attunement Angel, Visit a Wise Person. OK, which one?

It was time to deal with my broken tooth. I saw the oral surgeon and he counseled me that I could have either a permanent implant or a bridge, which would involve replacing the perfect crown of an adjacent tooth with a new crown. He showed me the literature about implants which means drilling into the jaw, inserting a titanium base into the hole and literally bolting a new crown onto the base. It made me weak to look at the drawings of this metal thing implanted in the jawbone, but I said I would think about it. The root had to be pulled in any case and I made the appointment for that for the next Friday. I lit candles and asked all week during my meditations for the extraction to go smoothly.

September 2, 1994 Friday

When I arrived for the appointment, I heard Mozart's music in the office. After all the preparations, the doctor pulled the root. He said, "You must have prayed a lot this week—it came out so easily." I was elated, full of joy and gratitude. And I said, "Mozart and the angels helped." Everyone smiled benevolently. I was very high and happy the rest of the day, very relieved. The next day I had very little pain from the extraction, just a little tenderness. Keith and I went to the grocery store which made me tired, but I rested when we came home. During the evening, my left hand began to hurt and by bedtime my right hand was also warm and painful. I hated to do it, but I took five mg. of cortisone about 10 PM, then another five mg. at midnight. Had trouble going to sleep until about 2 AM. Had I overdone? Was I too cocky on Friday?

The next morning I thought I'd treat myself to soft-boiled eggs (comfort food) and burned my right index finger. Then while I was making the bed, I jammed my left foot into the bed frame and tore away a little triangle of skin from my toe, which protested by bleeding quite freely. I am somewhat chagrined and mystified about why I have done these things to myself after my seeming victory in the dental operatory. The rest of the day has been OK. I've tried to dial back and rest.

I was confused. When the extraction went so well, I felt very strong, as if my efforts and requests had been perfectly manifested. I didn't understand why I subsequently experienced a flare-up and the injuries. So I made a list of questions for Kenny to ask the angels.

Lois: What about my tooth? Should I have the titanium implant?

Azriel: You should not have the titanium implant. Energies in your body would be blocked from their healing flow and would make your spiritual progress in your healing more difficult. Remember that your body is the temple of your soul. Treat it lovingly.

Lois: What is happening to me? Am I punishing myself?

Azriel: Many things are happening to you. You have been instrumental in bringing to the Light a forerunner. (This is Kenny!) There are forces in the Universe who would prefer continued discord and they are causing the inner turmoil which you are experiencing. Also, some rewiring of your body is being done by the Angels to better equip you for your healing. Remember, you must receive your healing. It comes from the Spirit, but is received in your heart. Look deeply into yourself and consider what you will do when you are fully healed.

You will not be able to conceal your wholeness from anyone. Your radiance will be an attraction for all and you will share it freely. This is a big undertaking with lots of responsibility and your body is not quite sure it is ready to move on. This conflict is also contributing to the flare-ups and accidents.

The changes you are experiencing are difficult. Try to avoid the "just one last hill" syndrome. Your journey is a long one and each step involves choices. All paths lead to your goal, but your choices affect the aspects of the journey.

Continue working in your journal. Use favorite meditations and prayers. See yourself in a lovely, light-filled garden, surrounded with plants and flowers and hearing Mozart's music.

September 3, 1994

It's been cool and cloudy all day. Funny how fall always arrives on Labor Day! Friday I saw Sue Ellen. Things that came up: A miasm. Problem with speech going back 30 generations on my dad's side. We decided it had to do with inability to express feelings. Biggest issue was with Guess Who: Power trip from my mother. Remedy is the Seven Dragons meaning seven dots on acupressure points on my head. Supposedly, stimulating them will fix this particular power trip once and for all. Bringing up these issues made me cry and I could feel the negative energy flowing out of my feet. I was lightheaded for about an hour afterwards and wasn't even sure which way to go on I-285 when I drove home, but fortunately made the right choice.

I've been lighting a red candle upside down since Tuesday (the full moon was Monday) for the release of all resistance to a complete healing, all anger, resentment and negativity, all that is unlike love in my life.

September 9, 1994

It's Friday already and I have been so busy with work, etc., I haven't written here since Monday. Did not sleep well Wednesday night because Keith had to get up at 4:30 AM to go to Cincinnati and I never went back to sleep so felt hung over all day. I became frustrated when I had to wait an hour for an appointment downtown. Had lunch with Kenny, came home, then drove back downtown in the cold, rainy evening for a Women in Architecture meeting. It was held in the AIA office in the back of the bookstore, but the store was locked and I had to bang on the door for ten minutes before someone came to let me in. I was angry about such a stupid, non-working set-up! Came home with my left wrist hurting. I still feel somewhat inflamed today, have low-grade fever, achy hands, less than two weeks since the last flare. Is it coincidental that this has happened more than once after lunch with Kenny?? Is it rewiring? Maybe it's processing my visit to Sue Ellen last week, plus the weather, being tired and getting angry twice.

I hope I'm learning what I am supposed to learn from these detours on the road to healing. No fun. I realize I get impatient about wanting to be healed, but the pain puts me on edge, especially when I can't sleep in spite of exhaustion. Well, it is depressing.

Let's try this assignment from the angels:

What Will I Do When I Am Fully Healed?

I will weep with joy.

I will praise Father/Mother/God and proclaim to all who will listen: "This is what the Creator's love can do."

I will have Diane write it up for a medical audience.

I will go see Dr. M. For lunch.

I will buy a piano.

I will buy all new shoes.

I will finish and publish my book.

I will speak to groups, like at the Inner Space.

I will be filled with Light, Peace, Love and Joy.

I will know that this is but another step on my journey and will be ready for the next lesson.

I will know how truly wonderful life can be.

I will have to deal with people who will not believe what has happened. It will be their problem and I will say to them, "Goddess Bless You."

I will have the joy of sharing the wonderful news with all my friends, family and support group.

We will have a party of thanksgiving and play the *Exultate Jubilate* by Mozart!! There will be much joy and celebration.

I will wear rings on more fingers.

I am certain there will be many other things for me to do that I cannot even imagine at this time.

Most of all, I will simply be more than grateful to my guides, my angels, my healers, and to my earthly family and friends for all their love and support.

September 10, 1994

Much better today, but I still took two cortisone tablets last evening and had trouble going to sleep. I feel sleepy now after meditating. Angel Oracle: Michael, A Dream-Worker Angel, Just Have Fun. Sounds good! I am trying something else new. I lit five big orange seven-day candles for good health and vitality, one each day for five days and will just let them burn themselves out.

September 11, 1994 Sunday

Michael (the entity) said this would be a month of emotion. Boy, I feel it! Keith and I have been at odds off and on all day

Went to a psychic fair and had my aura photographed. It's completely different from the one I had taken two years ago. Today it's a big white circle with violet on top and blue coming down all around. One guy said, "You look like an angel." Neat! Guess it rubs off!

September 16, 1994

What a week! I've been drawing on CADD (computer aided drafting/design), mostly for Delta Air Lines counters. It's very draining because of the continuous concentration on the computer screen, and I put in a full forty hours of it.

All of my seven-day orange candles burned out on schedule this week. They were beautiful in the fireplace and it felt magical to walk by and see them sending my prayers out. Hope it helps. I felt really good all week, but was taking five mg. of cortisone daily until Tuesday. I did the Attunement Exercise from the *Ask Your Angels* book which Kenny recommended. It made me light-headed and very tingly all over.

Kenny has been procrastinating about asking Howard to be his teacher. When I offered to call Howard and Kenny said to go ahead. Howard said, "Send him over!"

September 17, 1994

Dear God, Ariel, et. al.,

I am so discouraged today—again. Last night my left hand, especially the ring finger (feminine, unions/grief) started aching, so I took two Tylenol PM, hoping I could get to sleep by 10. No way. So at 11 PM I took Tylenol with codeine. Another hour, no relief. At midnight I took another Tylenol with codeine and watched another sleepless hour go by. Finally, I took 20 mg. of cortisone. At 3, figuring the 11 PM codeine had worn off, I took another. Yikes!! I can't live like this—it's enough to make me consider checking out, walking out— or <u>something</u>. Methotrexate can't be any worse for me than living on codeine and cortisone. Can it?

Do I need to rethink everything? Again?? I've lit dozens of candles and prayed and meditated a million times for healing and spent thousands of dollars on healers and doctors and drugs and vitamins and organic food. It probably is my emotions and the stress of hard work and drawing on the computer. Can I live without emotions and work? Not in my current setup! HELP!

What am I doing that I should stop? What am I not doing that I should do??????????? Whom can I turn to? Does anybody really know? And why do I use the word "should" so much?

September 18, 1994

I listened to my Super Immunity tape this morning. Tried to call Sue Ellen at home and Kenny at work. Neither is available. Hmmm.

What is really hard for me is that I have been told I will be healed. Is this imminent? A year away? Five? Ten? Will the angels tell me? Does anyone know? It's probably up to me some way. I think I'm making progress and then—BOOM. Suddenly I feel like I am back to square one. I certainly have more questions than answers.

September 19, 1994

Keith and I went to an overnight party at Lake Lanier. I wasn't sure I would be up to it because of flaring the night before, but decided to go anyway. The drive was pleasant. We walked around exploring the area, then went down to the boat for drinks while motoring to the Yacht Club for dinner, then came back to the hotel for the night. We had a very loving time and I felt relaxed and happy. Enjoyed socializing with the people we've been working with and especially with Scott and Sue.

Wendy was house and cat sitting for us and was here when we came home. She had been to see Sue Ellen and wanted to share her experience with me. I told her I first needed make my *de rigeur* Sunday phone call to my mother. While I was on the phone, Wendy left the room. She said my energy changed, becoming so different and so negative, she couldn't sit there. Interesting!

After the phone call we sat out on the deck and Wendy shared some of her session with Sue Ellen, which was profound for her. She also confided that, for some reason she didn't fully understand, she was not comfortable sleeping in the guest room downstairs and so had spent the night in the living room. I'm not sure what to do about it.

After Wendy left, I called Sue Ellen and started crying when I told her how discouraged I was about having had yet another flare-up on Friday. Suddenly there was a whole flock of little birds in the trees and on the deck outside my room. We decided it was a sign that I should not be discouraged, that Spirit is with me. She could see me right away, so I went over to her house and we worked for 1½ hours. All very deep stuff. Issues that came up: Integrity of the Vessel, No Role Model, An Animal Force was taking me over, the Black Bear. I need to make a list of what I want and what I don't want. (That will be easy!) Need to spiritually ask my family to pray for me. When it was over, she said my eyes were clear. She was looking for something just before I left and a piece of paper fell out onto her desk. It said, "'You're not that Body, You're pure Spirit Soul. To taste Love of God is Life's ultimate Goal.' Dasaratha." What a stunning message! I copied it and put it up on the shelf above my desk when I got home. It truly inspires me to keep on keeping on.

Monday I faxed Kenny a list of questions about all the drugs and supplements I have been taking and all the things I have been doing to get a read on whether the angels think I should be taking and doing them. I was quite discouraged and a bit frantic because of all the flare-ups and seeming lack of progress. Thursday I received the following:

September 19, 1994

Azriel: Kenny, when you answer Lois' questions, use your left eye. Visualize Lois with us behind her and let the light from your eye shine into her. As the answers come to you, see them radiating through her. She will begin to feel the answers as you receive them.

This is the prelude to Lois' healing being fully manifested. The timing is completely up to her. The healing is done. Her belief manifests the healing in her body. Her healing is manifested as she accepts it. This does not mean "Oh, if only I had enough faith," or "I'm not worthy because I can't believe enough." It means complete and total surrender to the forces of Spirit in her life, believing in her heart that she accepts it. The simple statement, "I believe and accept my healing," is sufficient. It can be made with her mind and intellect swirling in doubt. It can be made with her hands in total, excruciating pain. The secret is that it is made. It can be made over and over. The power of the spoken word is enormous, very powerful.

The reason Sue Ellen is important to Lois' healing is that the arthritis goes back many generations in her family and there are also linkages to past lifetimes. Sue Ellen can remove those blocks with her healing technique.

Remember what was said about Lois' being prepared to accept the consequences of her healing. Much is required to whom much is given. Her total healing will be a wonderful manifestation of Spirit in this world.

September 20, 1994

Azriel: Kenny, today visualize Lois before the angels over and over. See her bathed in a glorious warm light. The light is healing her spirit. As her blocks are released, much energy can flow back and forth, cleansing and renewing. What Lois experiences will spill over into her mother's heart because the old blocks are no longer there to impede the flow of energy.

Lois: Should I go back on methotrexate? Can it be any worse for me than codeine and cortisone? Is there anything else I can do to counteract the pain in my hands when these flare-ups occur? If I could sleep, I wouldn't get so desperate.

Azriel: The methotrexate is a personal decision. You are waiting very impatiently for your healing. Your impatience is the cause of these flare-ups. You recognize the cycle. You grow impatient. Then you feel unworthy and you punish yourself with a flare-up. Some of this is on a conscious level. Some stems from your past. What Sue Ellen is doing in you is releasing blocks which are generations old. Only what is healed through the methods that she is using can truly open you to function as you were created. Look at your healing as a whole mind, soul and body event. Your illness is but a symptom of what has been at work in your life. The healings which are coming through Sue Ellen's gifts are complex and because of their longevity, take time to process. Every step of the clearing and healing involves choices on your part. When you are on the path to wholeness, these choices are easily made. In your case, as an intellectual scholar, you have chosen to try and figure all this out. When you arrive at your cleansed state, you will still not know exactly what happened. You do not need to know for the healing to occur.

If you feel that the methotrexate would calm you as your soul and body are working through this, take it. Do not feel guilty. Be thankful that it exists and can help you. Do not believe that it is a giving up. Ask Sue Ellen to confirm all the medications, vitamins and supplements that you are taking for effectiveness and purity. Bless everything that goes into your body.

Lois: If I am to be healed, and if I might be permitted to know this, I would like to know generally when this might occur. Is it a matter of months or years? I want it so very much and I realize this is probably part of my impatience lesson. It would help me to not be so disappointed when these setbacks happen. It is hard to feel that progress is being made at such times.

Azriel: Months. But part of the lesson you have asked to be taught is patience. You have wrapped these lessons into a common experience. You recognize the need to accelerate your growth here and the time is now.

Learn patience by allowing yourself to be in situations which you find disturbing and unpleasant. In these situations, do not be a doormat, but also do not be a closed door. Open up and allow your warmth to come through and receive from the situation. Let things flow and you will develop patience. Patience will not be just dropped into your heart. The quality of patience comes from making the choice to serve others and to surrender your will.

Lois: Which brings me to my last question: Is progress being made?

Azriel: Progress is being made. You are doing right things. Undoing lifetimes of blocks takes time.

Kenny added: Lois, This is from me. Thank you for all the many gifts of learning that you have shared with me. Your gifts have made such a wonderful difference in my life.

I am feeling that I need to use the power in my hands to speed your healing. This frightens me, but I think that it is part of my teaching. As you know, one does not sign up for Shaman 101, so I guess you are my guinea pig. Lucky you. Let me know how that feels and we will work on it.

Much love as we continue our journey. Kenny

One of the items that I asked the angels about was meditation, which I have been doing for 20 minutes twice a day. They said "Longer," so I have started doing 30 minutes twice a day. I am using the prayers the angels have given me, some visualizations from *Ask Your Angels*, and the Infusion of Golden Light from *Ascending Times*. Any time that is left I just relax or do Transcendental Meditation.

Keith's nephew Jody called and said he and his wife and their two toddlers want to come here for Christmas. My main reservation was that they always bring their two very active, noisy dogs and I asked Keith, "Do they have to bring the dogs?" He did not reply.

September 25, 1994

Angel Oracle this morning: Uriel, A Healing Angel, Create a Sacred Space and Create Your Own Ritual. I looked up Bear in the Medicine Cards because black bear had come up with Sue Ellen: Bear signifies Introspection.

Interesting item in the newspaper: A doctor has devised a new legal abortion method. He first gives a woman an ulcer medication, then a day or two later a dose of methotrexate. This causes termination of the pregnancy. Does this tell us anything about methotrexate?

Oct. 1, 1994

What a month September was! Lots of emotion, activity, cash flow and completion. Michael predicted that new Higher Moving energy would start coming in now and continue until March of '96. It feels like a new year to me.

Wendy gave us a Feng Shui evaluation of our house as a housewarming present and it was wonderful. ("Foong Shway" is the Chinese art of placement which facilitates the movement of *chi* or energy in buildings for optimal health and prosperity.) Karmelah, the practitioner, spent about two hours observing our house, making comments and recording it all on tape. Most of it was very positive. One interesting thing that she asked was, "Have you been real healthy since you moved in here?" I had to reluctantly say "no." She suggested smudging to clear out old vibrations, especially from the original owner. They were not strong, but still needed to be removed. (Smudging is a process from Native American tradition which uses smoke from sage, herbs and grasses to cleanse a space and remove negative influences.)

She made several recommendations and today Keith and I shopped for things she suggested, like a shelf in our closet which is in the partnership corner of our house. On the shelf we put a Hopi wedding vase, some flowers and an affirmation. I hung shiny copper jello molds over the stove to reflect the light from cooking and to alert me if someone comes into the room. I tied a tiny angel and some small bells on the back door so I can hear when it opens. Bought a pair of angel earrings for a dollar and placed them in the bark of the trees on each side of the opening where our property backs up to the neighbors. Got some streamers that are for "just married" cars and put them in the wealth corner, both upstairs and down. We have been storing baskets and vases in that corner, so I found candy coins and play money to put in these containers. In the basement we cleaned out the wealth corner and placed a table there. I put a green candle on the table with a gold cornucopia and then I wrote a bunch of big checks to us from sweepstakes, the lottery (even though we don't play the lottery), etc. It was fun and I was thrilled that Keith was so open to these ideas! Of course, he has seen how I have been able to manifest things we want and how our lives are working better with my "weird stuff," so he figures it can't hurt anything at the very least.

I have felt very good for the past two weeks. Have not even taken any Tylenol! Last night I was a tiny bit achy, but took a warm bubble bath and slept well. I have been asking the angels for sound sleep and that works better than anything, even the "Sound Sleep" tape! I'm amazed, although I guess I shouldn't be. It's also been beautiful fall weather. Acorns and pine cones are falling like mad. Must be why they call it fall. It's a verb, not a noun!

I heard lots of Mozart this week on the radio. That always reassures me that I'm doing the right thing. Also some Vivaldi. Work has been very busy and good and we'll have another big invoice for September. We're doing work we enjoy and are being well-paid to do it! The cash is flowing! But best of all, Keith is so happy when he is doing architectural work. Angel Oracle: Gabriel, A Nature Angel, Create a Sacred Space and Create your Own Ritual (second time in a row for that one!).

Oct. 4, 1994 Tuesday
I felt a tiny bit achy Sunday night, but didn't flare. Thank You! Yesterday I saw Sue Ellen. Things that came up: My eagle is chained. My Inner and Outer selves and my male and female aspects are unable to

function properly. (No wonder I am having problems!!) Then she found: There's an entanglement on me—it's a death wish—from guess who—my mother! Sue Ellen was more shocked by this than I was. It was confirmation to me, since Linda's psychiatrist has always said that she wanted to destroy us. The remedy for this was for me to stand up and wait until I felt an urge to move. I literally felt myself pushed to take a step forward (probably by my higher self), symbolizing moving out of my old Self.

Oct. 5, 1994

Did the smudging this morning. It took a long time to get the smoke to go into every corner of every room! I placed a little cross of rocks in my closet, which is the approximate center of the house, and loudly pronounced, "This is MY house!" to Mrs. K. (the former owner) and anyone else who needs to hear it. I felt a little groggy all day. The pendulum said I am processing Sue Ellen's work and being rewired. And that the smudging was the ritual I was to create. The cross of rocks is the sacred space. So that feels good.

Oct. 9, 1994

Thursday I flared again after feeling a bit dumpy most of the week. This time I took two cortisone at 8 PM, two Tylenol with codeine at 10 PM. Still could not sleep because of the pain in my hands, but for a change, I was calm. At 4 AM took another cortisone. Friday morning we drove—well, Keith drove—to Jekyll Island for the Georgia Architects Conference. I rested in the back of the van till about noon. Then we had to stop so I could throw up. Had a little lunch about 1:30 and then I felt much better. Took another cortisone late that afternoon. I rested when we arrived and we took it pretty easy for the whole weekend. I was processing my visit to Sue Ellen after only five days and not blaming myself, for once.

Oct. 22, 1994

I got Sue Ellen's overleaves: She's a fifth to sixth level Old Priest with King Essence Twin. Joya wrote a note, which she rarely does with overleaf orders, saying that Sue Ellen is an "incredible woman, healer, power source, a fabulous find!" Pretty exciting! Sue Ellen was thrilled when I called to tell her about it. She has recommended that I see Dr. L., the chiropractor in her office, so I made an appointment with him for Monday morning. I am eager to continue working with Sue Ellen and have no intention of stopping. I would like for Dr. L. to find a way other than cortisone to ease the pain and flare-ups which seem to follow each visit to her.

Angel Oracle says: Gabriel, Your Companion Angel, Let the Angels Write Through You. Wow! OK!

I am ready!
Ready to let the angels write through me.
Ready to move on in this lifetime,
Ready for my healing, For once and for all.
I know that all the loving and healing forces are with me as I take this next step.
There is nothing to fear. I am safe. Even if I must endure more pain, I want to proceed.
Whatever it takes, I will prevail.
I want this more than I have ever wanted anything, probably in many other lifetimes as well as this one.
It's time to break that cycle at long last, to learn this lesson and move on to something new.
It is time to let the true Light of Healing into my heart—to forgive, to release, to know only Peace, Love and Joy.
To witness to all the world the magnificent Power and Love of Spirit, of all the Angelic Beings of Light, of the Unconditional Love of the Father/Mother/God, God/Goddess/All That Is.
I Surrender to Spirit. I trust the Healing Powers. I give my All over to Them for this Great Gift.
I am ready to receive It. I believe and accept my healing!

Oct. 29, 1994

Monday I saw Dr. L. He's the first medical person I ever went to who was wearing jeans! I liked him. He's from Poland and is very mild-mannered. He said I'm doing very well, that I am already doing most of the things he recommends, such as diet and supplements. He felt I might be suffering from poor protein digestion and having the flare-ups because of toxic byproducts, so he gave me protease enzyme tablets and an herbal supplement to support my liver. He was very interested in everything I am doing and said, "Oh yes, W.S. That's what we say for 'weird stuff.'"

Sue Ellen was in her office when I went by. We chatted and she was available, so she worked on me for nearly 1-1/2 hours. Some of the things that came up: Integrity as a Receiver, again! Geopathic stress. I need to counteract this some way. (And we just did the Feng Shui!) My condition is result of criticism from parents (this is not news). My 16th previous lifetime in Japan around 1200 was important. She also corrected two basic misbeliefs: "I Cannot Do This By Myself" and "I Can't Believe What I Know Is True." She cleared all this stuff. I have felt lighter and brighter ever since.

Thursday night the 4th knuckle on the right hand started hurting. It kept me awake till 2:30 or so. But it didn't get hot and it was basically <u>just the one joint</u>! I called Sue Ellen in the morning to tell her, and when I said, "That's progress," I got chills. She said, "Praise God!".

Friday I was tired and a little achy. In the evening I took a bath with Dead Sea Salts and listened to a Mozart tape. Then I listened to my Super Immunity tape. Slept well. I feel strong and invigorated today. No pain!

Saw my dentist Wednesday. I have opted not to have the implant, so he's making me a partial to replace my lost tooth. It will be made mostly of titanium, but I don't have to wear it all the time.

Oct. 30, 1994

I saw this quote from Eleanor Roosevelt: "You must do the thing you think you cannot do."

Linda called after visiting our parents. She thinks our mother is really deteriorating—her ankles are swollen and she's almost frail. She's no longer the powerful queen.

Wednesday, Nov. 16, 1994

Saw Sue Ellen today for a comparatively short session. My body just shut down after an hour. It's hard to remember the specifics, but had to do with being female. She asked if I ever felt trapped in a female body. I responded that I think it's been more a case of having been limited by being in a female body.

Talked to Joya last night for nearly an hour. She suggested adding two pints of hydrogen peroxide to my bath after seeing Sue

Ellen. I just finished doing that and listening to Mozart. During the bath when I shut my eyes I saw beautiful, intense colors—red to fuschia to violet. It was gorgeous! Happened three times!

I'm planning to have a celebration of 12:12. December 12th at sunrise, at 12 minutes past noon and at sunset is predicted to be a significant time on the planet, when there will be an acceleration of energy and an increase in the amount of light coming into the planet in preparation for the coming millennium. *Ascending Times* calls it "The Gateway to Freedom" and says it is at least as important to the planet as the Harmonic Convergence in 1987. The spirit guides want 144,000 people to observe 12:12 and to plant the seeds of a new awareness in the earth's population.

Yesterday had lunch with Jenny, a woman I met on a project, and she is another sponge, open and receptive. I gave her a copy of *The World According to Michael* and some 12:12 information. She is eager to send for her overleaves. I felt so energized and happy afterwards. I love enlightening people! I was especially tickled when she said, "What about Jesus?" (According to Michael, Jesus was a manifestation of the Infinite Soul, a soul so big, encompassing so much, it is just a hair away from merging with the Tao, God/Goddess, the Universe. Lao Tsu, Buddha and Krishna were other Infinite Souls.)

Plans for Christmas are shaping up. Jody, Jan and their two new sons *and* the two dogs are coming. Lah-de-dah. My son Mark is coming, too, but will stay with Diane. I will spend Christmas Eve with them.

Dec. 8, 1994

Nearly a month since my last entry! We've been busy. Too busy, really. Work, Christmas, house, etc. We decorated for Christmas and it looks magical. Our new ten-foot-high tree is covered with angels and hundreds of lights. We put a four-foot diameter wreath on the stone fireplace wall and it's gorgeous! This is such a great house to work with. It already looks fabulous and we are just enhancing it.

Did our annual marketing submittal for the Board of Regents—what a chore. Then I had pain Monday night. Took 25 mg. of cortisone at 2 AM, but never slept. I was exhausted in the morning, but relieved when Sue Ellen answered her phone. She's always there when I am desperate for help. I went to see her and we worked for three hours. Felt

<u>much</u> better afterwards. I can't remember much of what came up because it was pretty deep, abstract stuff. It felt really good to have it all cleared out. Geopathic stress came up again.

I called Karmelah about the geopathic stress. She suggested I use the pendulum over the plan of the house to find out where it is coming from. When I did, it immediately started swinging on the diagonal, from the north corner of the bedroom through the bathroom! Truly amazing. It makes sense because pain usually gets worse after I go to bed! When I told Karmelah about this, she said perhaps driving a rod into the ground outside that corner would be a remedy to diffuse or deflect the negative, stressful energy. She's going to come over and check it out. Sue Ellen showed me how to make flat spirals of copper wire to counteract geopathic stress, so I made three of them. Put one under my bed, one up on top of the cabinet in the north corner of the bedroom and one in the same corner of the lower level.

I took Dr. G. a copy of Sue Ellen's explanation of Inner Nature's Integration. She was quite receptive (and was wearing a nice necklace of crystals). She said that when I start to flare, I should take the cortisone earlier instead of hoping it will stop.

I told her about the plans for Christmas and she said, "Tell them not to bring the dogs." I said, "Would you write a prescription for that?" So she did. When I showed it to Keith, he said, "She's practicing veterinary medicine without a license." Then the other night his son Curt called to ask if we had room for him, his wife Laurie and their son to come for Christmas?? Curt and Jody have always been close. Of course we said, yes, come on down. Wow! Seven people and two big dogs! Well, we do have room. It will be interesting, and fun, I hope. Scott, Sue and Mark will go to Michigan, as they normally do.

12:12 is shaping up. I'm hoping to have 12 people.

Dec. 11, 1994

Had a great weekend. I baked German Christmas cookies, finished shopping, ran lots of errands. Sunday we helped Diane and Hobie trim their tree. And I got ready for 12:12. Copied some prayers from the *Rainbow Bridge*, tied ribbons on white candles. Wendy is very excited. I am too. I'm planning to get up a little early to experience sunrise. Dare I hope for healing? Keith has a noon appointment with his doctor regarding his knee. Interesting that he won't be here.

I had an inner urging to send a 12:12 invitation to Candace, the owner of my favorite metaphysical bookstore, The Phoenix and the Dragon, because there was nothing in their newsletter about 12:12. She called during business hours to tell me that there would be an event at the Inner Space on the evening of the 12th, but it didn't get into the newsletter. We talked a little about Joya's coming visit. Then she said, "Did you say 'architect' when you answered the phone?" "Yes." "Do you do commercial?" "Yes, we do everything." She proceeded to tell me that she wants to expand the store and is looking for an architect. I kept having chills the whole time we were talking! Later I sent her a letter and our brochure. I was glad I followed my inner prompting!

Dec. 12, 1994 Monday

Eleven people came, 12 counting me! We lit candles, read the *Rainbow Bridge* prayers. Wendy had a reading about Isis, Tom played his guitar and sang, Jenny read an affirmation. I read some things from *Ascending Times* magazine. Then we had a circle, held hands and affirmed our guardianship over the planet. Then lunch. It was very pleasant. Sue Ellen stayed to help me clean up. Bless her!

Kenny called later and said he liked it, but was hoping for something "more overt," like my healing. (So was I!) On Wednesday, he got a message about it from the angels, which I sent out to all who participated. I am so glad that I arranged the celebration.

Words for people who attended the 12:12 Ceremony at Lois Grant's from Archangel Michael through Kenny:

Light is entering the world at a new rate. See yourself in this light.
Look deep within your heart. Imagine opening wide double doors,
  Both arms outstretched. Receive this light.
Let the light burn deeply into the core of your being.
  This light is cleansing and healing.
See yourself living in this light.
By coming together on 12/12, you are opening yourself to growth
  and the assumption of your place in the new age, which is
  opening in its fullness and wonder.
Continue to share the light with those you meet, love, and with
  whom you are commonly linked. Listen to what is said with

your heart. Your instincts are the urgings of Spirit. Follow your leading.

A couple of weeks later I sent this out to the 12:12 crowd:

Dear 12:12 Friend,

Enclosed are two things I want to share with you as follow-ups to 12:12. The first is a transcription of part of a channeling I had with the entity Michael through Joya Pope. The second is a meditation from *Ascending Times*. I was struck by the similarity in the two visualizations.

Here's to a great year! I send you Peace, Love, and Light.

12:12 From Michael (the entity) as channeled by Joya Pope

Lois: I'm interested in the Michael angle on 12:12.

Michael: What we are seeing happen very, very strongly since July of this year are huge shifts of energy. One of those days when a lot of things shifted was on 12:12, although it actually started on 12:11.

We don't see that 36 Ascended Masters joined hands and held a ritual on 12:12, but Infinite Soul energy is definitely coming into the planet with lots of Transcendental Soul energy. Energy is shifting within the earth itself plus extraterrestrial energy from the impacts on Jupiter (the Shoemaker-Levy 9 comet) which also left marks on the earth. These cause the Earth's energy to shift and magnetic and electrical fields to change. And then, with 1994's being a Higher Emotionally Centered year and the next one (1995) a Higher Moving Centered year, there's a lot of upgrading of the light for you to use.

A really wonderful thing about the 12:12 literature is the idea to make agreements with the planet and all the new energies: "Yes, I will channel this light in and I will ground it. I'm committed to holding this new vibration." These are very useful concepts for people who are interested, and will help them as they get used to consciously holding more energy in the body. As the vibration increases, you have the opportunity to hold more and more light and glory and wonderfulness and angels.

Lois: Is there an exercise we could do?

Michael: Are you going outside to take a walk every day? Just five or ten minutes would be a really healthy idea, to get out, to have the air and the sunlight and the movement. Do a little bit of this 12:12 visualization: Open all your chakras in a big funnel from the third chakra, the power chakra (solar plexus), upwards and an inverted funnel down from the third chakra, like an hourglass. Bring the light in at the top of your head, pull it into the solar plexus, then send it out through your feet. Feel like the center of the earth is coming up to take on the light that you're bringing in. Consciously grounding the new light and giving it to the earth looks really useful.

A GIFT OF GOLDEN-WHITE ENERGY INFUSION
FROM THE CREATOR

Center your consciousness about one foot above your head and feel the pulsations of Christed energy begin to build and surge around you until it completely enfolds you. Envision it as a sparkling, golden white light as you feel this energy begin to gradually flow down through your crown center or chakra. Hold it there for a moment and feel its power increase until it permeates your head, the pineal gland, the pituitary gland, all of your brain cells and your third eye chakra. Allow it to build and swell until you feel a fullness or completion and then let it flow into your throat, energizing and activating this area so that as you learn and live the wisdom of Light and love, you will also be able to communicate it clearly and truly with discernment. Now allow the energy to permeate your heart center—healing, clearing, washing away old residual pain and anguish, leaving a pure, pulsating vastness of Christed love energy. Feel the fullness in you chest area and be aware that you are building your spiritual armor through which no negative energy can ever penetrate if you hold fast to this perfect infusion of God's Love.

Feel the energy cleansing and purifying your emotional center, the solar plexus chakra, balancing and releasing any impacted memories of aloneness, hurt and suffering. Remember, it is the emotional center that is of primary importance at this time, for it is the emotional body that must be brought into complete balance and under control if you are going to be given the gifts of Mastership. A Master is at all times in complete control of all the energy centers and no disruptive vacillation is permitted. We understand that this is a most difficult area for you to conquer, but as long as you begin to make a concerted effort, we will direct and help you in every way possible so that this can be accomplished with the greatest ease and the least amount of stress.

Now, let this precious energy drift down through the rest of your body and being, energizing and purifying, and allow the excess to flow from your fingertips and feet down into the earth...a gift of loving infusion from you to your dear planet to assist her in the release of stress and pain as she goes through her transition.

It may seem to you that we should focus on the remaining chakras also and not stop at the solar plexus, but we say to you that if you feel a connection to our energy and feel the validation of truth in our message, then you have surely shifted your consciousness to the soul level of your being (in the higher chakras), away from the ego and the purely physical (in the lower chakras). Your body and all its parts will benefit and be balanced by the infusion of energy to the higher transmuting centers of your being. And even though you must exist and function in the material world, you are focusing on your Light Body, not your physical body. Your physical being can then only follow in your path to perfection.

If possible, take time to do this exercise morning and night. It need not take but a few minutes and will be of momentous benefit. It will open the pathways for us to be in direct contact with you and to be able to advise and guard you at all times. You see, your devotion and loving emanations enhance and empower us also, even as it does your brothers and sisters in the physical.

We will close now, but we do not leave you unattended. You are surrounded and protected and, as always, you are dearly loved by the Spiritual hierarchy and the Masters of Light. I, Lord Michael, bring you these truths

From *Wings of Light* by Ronna Herman, Copyright 1995. Reprinted with permission. First published in *Ascending Times*, December 1994.

Dec. 15, 1994

Troubling news yesterday. I went to the eye doctor for my regular Plaquenil check-up and I was unable to see the numbers on the color vision test. The doctor was very concerned—me too! I was also upset and impatient for having had to wait a long time and for not being scheduled for the visual field test, which is the main reason for the appointment. I cried when I got home and told Keith. Later I ran an errand. Got into the car and the top clip of my seat belt came off in my hand. Then as I was leaving the drug store, I dropped my keys and the remote unlocking device broke off my key ring! My negative energy seemd to be impacting things around me—I felt like a poltergeist! I think these incidents may have been the effect of my strong feelings—at least I was taking it out on things other than my body! Both thumbs (worry!) were hurting by evening, so I took a bath in peroxide and baking soda and slept <u>really well</u>. I did not flare! I think it's the first time that I did not get worse once a flare started. Dr. G. returned my call and said to stop the Plaquenil, which I had already decided to do. So I'm not really taking any heavy hitters right now.

Karmelah was here on Tuesday and used a dowsing rod to detect the geopathic stress coming into the bedroom. The copper spirals are 80% effective against it! She recommended hanging wind chimes in the magnolia tree just outside, then putting red and gold ribbons around the sewage pump/grinder cap, in the ground right at the corner of the house. She used Kaballah cards and drew "Honor to Kingdom" and "Victory to Kingdom," both of which are very positive She's such a gifted person— she does Feng Shui, psychological counseling and she also does past-life regressions. I have read Brian Weiss' books *Many Lives, Many Masters* and *Through Time into Healing* and I told her that I was very interested in pursuing past-life regression with her. We agreed to discuss it after the holidays.

Grant/Weiland has billed out a nice sum for November, so I'm not going to work much till next year. We are really manifesting work we enjoy doing and people who will pay us to do it. It feels so powerful! I am feeling good about everything I've accomplished in preparation for Christmas. It should be fun. Still quite a bit to do, but I'm on schedule.

Dec. 18, 1994

On Friday I went for the visual field test and it was fine! Also, my color vision was normal. Hmmm, so what happened? Was this just a way to get me off the Plaquenil? Kenny said maybe it was a wake-up call.

Called Candace at the bookstore because I hadn't heard from her in a while. She was waiting to hear from the bank, etc. The whole time we were talking I was having chills, like our first conversation. It looks like the project is a go. I feel it is a real gift to have this opportunity to design a building for new age and metaphysical books, gifts and events!

Dec. 22, 1994

We are really on schedule for Christmas! Baked more cookies, got all presents wrapped, etc. Did grocery shopping, ordered turkey dinner (Keith's idea so I don't have to cook), etc. I am feeling good. Saw Dr. L. on Monday. He gave me a new homeopathic remedy and said it might make me might flare, but it hasn't so far. He thinks I'm doing really well.

I am looking forward to Christmas, even though it may be stressful. I just want to go with the flow, maybe leave if I need to, or accept the chaos. I want to enjoy it. Weather looks good for driving.

Dec. 26, 1994

Well, out of 57 Christmases, this has been the most unpleasant. Mark arrived Thursday evening, so Diane and I went to the airport and picked him up. When I came home about 10 PM, I thought Keith's family might be there, but they weren't. I asked Keith what time they were arriving. He said, "About 2 AM." "What? How come so late?" Because Curt and his family left from Michigan in the morning and met Jody's family in Louisville where they transferred everything and everybody to a big rented van so they could all ride together the rest of the way. This was the first I'd heard of these arrangements. I went to bed, but was pretty excited about everything and couldn't go to sleep. By 2 AM they hadn't arrived and it began to make me angry. Then I got angry with myself for getting angry and not being able to detach from it and get some rest. Jody called from the car about 2:30 because he had left the directions at home. They arrived at 3:30, so it was about 4:30 when we finally got to sleep. I was really exhausted the next day (Christmas Eve), even though we slept till about 9.

We spent the morning visiting and getting to know the kids who are very cute although they were pretty wired coming off the long drive and being in a strange place. I thought Jan and Jody were awfully strict about some things. Making a two-year old say "excuse me" when he burps seems like a lot to ask of a little guy and they tend to yell at the kids the same way they do at the dogs, "Sit!" One of the dogs wasn't feeling good and refused to drink water until I got the idea to put some bouillon in it, which worked. (This was the same dog that had a bladder infection the time before when they came down. I wondered if she was "pissed off" at having to ride in the car for so long and might rather stay home.) After lunch I listened to my Super Immunity tape and napped for about an hour, which helped me to feel a little better, but I was still groggy from losing so much sleep the night before. Keith and I went to pick up the turkey and fixings we had ordered for Christmas dinner and then it was time to go out for early dinner to celebrate the twins' birthday. They were pretty wild and made a big mess, but the restaurant wasn't busy, so it was OK. Again, I think it's a lot to ask of two-year-olds that they sit quietly while waiting for food. They need things to play with to keep them occupied. When we came home, I noticed my hands were a little achy, but ignored it, changed my clothes and left for Diane's. I should have taken cortisone right then. I asked Diane for some Tylenol, but it didn't help.

By the time I returned home, about 10:30, I knew I was in for a rough night in my own personal torture chamber. I started the cortisone and Darvocet, but did not sleep all night. I took 30 mg. of cortisone at midnight, ten more at 2 AM, ten at 4 and twenty at 8 with no relief. Christmas morning I talked to Dr. G.'s back-up who said I might need a shot of cortisone. Everyone was opening presents, but there was no way I could participate. The living room was full of toys and wrapping paper and the dogs and kids were all over the place. It was really chaotic. When I went out to the kitchen to eat some breakfast, I caught Jody's eye and felt some intensity there. Maybe it's karma—he's a sixth level Young Warrior. Laurie joined me in the kitchen and was very sympathetic. She hugged me and wanted to know what it was like and if she could do anything to help. I really appreciated that. But neither Jody nor his wife expressed one word of concern or understanding to me during the entire visit.

After lunch Mark drove me to the ER. The doctor thought I had already taken enough cortisone, so gave me a shot of Demerol which was supposed to knock me out, kill the pain and let me sleep. It didn't help. I tried to rest when we got back, but the pain continued and I couldn't even lie still, much less sleep. About 4 PM, I called the hospital and they suggested that I might need to come back. Keith took me at 7:30 PM and this time I got the injection of cortisone. I was able to go to sleep around 1 AM for about 7-1/2 hours. It was a blessed relief.

Needless to say, I am extremely unhappy to have had so much agony <u>again</u>. It was 30 hours of intense, unrelieved, unrelenting pain and heat in my hands. The hot vise again. Even though I get very exhausted, the pain will not let me sleep which makes me get desperate and miserable. My mother always said, "The difference between hope and despair is a good night's sleep." I try not to put that much importance on it, but at times like this, I think she's right. It's hard not to slip into martyrdom and discouragement. I keep thinking I've made progress, but then feel I have slid way back.

Dec. 29, 1994

Tuesday I saw Sue Ellen. Goddess Bless Her! First thing: "Your yang is strangled." How true. I did not assert myself. Then: "Denial of the Self". True again. I need to repeat an affirmation 20 times a day for three weeks and four days: "I believe and accept my healing," which the angels gave me. There was a block on my father's side from 29 generations ago. Then Sue Ellen said, "You must surrender your hands to God." So we held hands and prayed silently. I felt energy in my hands. She said when she opened her eyes there was white light all around my hands, not hers, just mine! I cried several times during the session because I was still so weak and tired. She also put tiny steel balls on six acupressure bladder points. As always, I felt much better afterwards. I can't imagine where I would be without her. She's a major key to my complete healing. I'm sure there are many healers and other kinds of healing that could help me, that if I hadn't found her, I would have been led to someone else. But I did find her and feel blessed.

The family left yesterday morning. The night before, Keith and I were sitting in our bedroom (there was no room to sit in the living room with all the toys, dogs, etc.) and he said, "I'll be glad when they leave." It was just too much confusion and noise, too many demands. I wanted to say something to Jody, but was just too weak. Maybe I will write him a letter. Spent the day doing laundry and moving stuff around, but nothing too strenuous. Found several places where the dogs had peed on the carpet, so have arranged for the carpet cleaners to come next week. One of the kids threw up on the loveseat and we cleaned that up.

Talked to Joya/Michael tonight. There is a minor karma between Jody and me. Also, all the 12:12 type energy coming into the planet is hard on old souls (who are more sensitive) and delicate bodies like mine especially when a sore spot or channel gets congested "when your life isn't exactly moving real elegantly forward. It's easy to see why your body, which is sensitive, will feel it." Well, that's one way to put it! They also said, "You have more ability to do the processing, to lift yourself up and hold a bigger vibration of light, but it can be difficult for the physical body to accomplish. It tends to put your negativity in your face and then you get to clear it. Also, '94 has been a difficult year for Scholars in general because it has been a higher Emotionally Centered year and Scholars like life to be more in the intellect where it is logical and makes sense." So that explained my latest flare-up from the planetary standpoint.

Michael said that the colors I saw in the tub are loving vibrations resulting from Sue Ellen's work which is clearing and focusing my system. Also, according to Michael, cortisone is not the only thing that works, but they didn't say what else to do or use or take. I'm greatly encouraged that they said I am still on a healing path. It's so easy to doubt myself and my progress when I feel imperfect. I enjoy these channelings so much. Joya said she loved me. It's wonderful to feel such warmth. She will come to Atlanta in April. What fun!!

I Believe And Accept My Healing!

Jan. 2, 1995

Angel Oracle: Raphael. An Angel of Peace. Turn to Another Oracle. Does this mean Karmelah again?

We had a little party on New Year's Day, low-key and pleasant. Candace and her partner came. We have our first meeting for the new Phoenix and Dragon bookstore tomorrow. I've got things pretty well cleaned up and put away from the holidays, except for the decorations. Have a little bit of a scratchy throat, hope it doesn't get any worse.

So here is another New Year! It will be interesting, to say the least, to see what it will bring.

Took a walk in the sunshine, which felt very healing and nurturing. I hope I can get my body to deal with the new light vibration, to grow stronger and to heal.

Sue told me that when Scott called here from Michigan on Christmas Day and Keith said I had flared, she cried out of empathy for my pain. Scott later told me, "My family was way out of line bringing all those people and dogs into your house like that." It's good to have a reality check and I really appreciate their support. Sue and I have become such good friends. We're both old Scholars and share a lot by having married into the same family.

Jan. 7, 1995

Scratchy throat has developed into a nice, loose cough. I just took a hot bath and saw the beautiful colors. Perhaps I am clear again. Dr. G. called me yesterday and said I need to come in and talk about what to do next about medication since I quit the Plaquenil and then proceeded to have that major flare-up. I'm still taking ten mg. of cortisone. Not sure what to do in the way of medication.

The Phoenix and the Dragon bookstore is moving along. Good visit to site with Candace on Tuesday. She's a Gemini, too! There are lots of questions about the site costs, etc., and probably not enough money for an exquisite project. But we're underway.

Kenny faxed me a message from Archangel Michael saying I need to trust my inner voice! The message to Kenny was fabulous, talks about his total healing! What about mine? I'm afraid to ask.

From Archangel Michael and Kenny:

Lois, much confusion surrounds you now as you search for relief from the pain of your arthritis. You have recognized that present and past life stresses and unresolved relationships are at the root of your illness.

Your arthritis dates back about 400 years. You have not fully dealt with the issues surrounding it in any lifetime to date. It also goes back many generations in your family. You have glimpses of the root causes of the illness and understand when you see them, but then you turn away out of fear. You fear the pain that you know you must endure to rid yourself of this deeply-held pattern. Sue Ellen's clearing work is a profoundly important process for you to complete. The meditation of light from Archangel Michael will allow you to bring your fear into consciousness so you can deal with it. Look for an image when you do this meditation. When you see it, call it by name, then release it to the Creation. As you see the light and energy pouring out through your fingertips and feet, know that the power of the fear is going out.

The reason that you flare after a session with Sue Ellen is that your fear recognizes that you are getting closer and closer to getting rid of it. This fear is buried so deeply and is so carefully hidden that even you are not always sure of the key. This is where your intuition development comes in. Start recording in your journal and acting on your first impulse. Think of a million other thoughts or ideas, but act on the first one! You will grow stronger.

Remember that you have a choice. You can function without doing any of this. You can wait until another lifetime. But the longer you wait, the harder it becomes. You want so deeply to be free and all of Spirit joins you in this. The entire force of the Universe is available to you, Lois Grant, one being in the midst of a vast Universe, cared for deeply by Spirit.

Postpone your appointment with your rheumatologist. Complete the cycle that Sue Ellen suggested before you begin a new program of medication. Know that all is working in a pattern for your good. Whatever you decide to take, bless it and let the healing life and light flow through you and bring you to your chosen place.

Jan. 10, 1995

Saw Sue Ellen this morning. Things that came up: An ancestral burden 30 generations back on my father's side, which she cleared. Toxic metal stress from a form of titanium. My new tooth is made of titanium!! (I've been wearing it most of the time, but will now do so just enough to prevent my teeth from drifting.) Then Sue Ellen felt Archangel Michael come in and heal my heart. Pretty wild.

Jan. 11, 1995

1:11! Is this significant? Interruption—a roach just appeared—I went to the kitchen to get the spray and there was another one in the foyer! Michael says cockroaches represent our fears. Well, I sent them both to Nirvana.

Saw Dr. L. and Sue Ellen today. He tested all my vitamins and supplements. Stopped two remedies and added one new one, and gave me more herbs for my liver. He has told me to come see him when I flare, but the problem is, I always flare at night. So he said to call him the morning after. He said I should try not to take the cortisone, but didn't give me an alternative. I wish I knew what else to take or do. Michael said that cortisone is not the only thing that works, but it works better than anything else I know at this time or have at hand. I would be happy to take or do something else if I knew what would help! I will see Dr. G. on Friday but will not take any prescription drugs until I see Dr. L. again in two weeks.

The angels have told me to follow my first impulse. I think this means sending the letter to Jody and Jan. Actually, my first impulse was to talk to them when they were here, but I was too weak at the time and was afraid Keith would jump in and make an even bigger mess.

Jan. 14, 1995 Saturday

Saw Dr. G. yesterday. I took her copies of Kenny/Michael's message of 1/8/95, the Michael information on 12:12, and the *Ascending Times* article. She read the angel message and said, "This is very interesting." She is recommending that I take one Plaquenil per day and five mg. of cortisone every other day. I'm not taking either right now and that may be part of the reason I was so vulnerable to a flare-up.

Got the Michael State of the Planet 1995 tape today. 1995 is a Warrior year with Dominance, Perseverance, Pragmatist, Greed and Arrogance. Higher Emotional energy till March, then Higher Moving energy coming in and peaking in September. A year of manifestation! Well, I can't wait to see what I'm going to manifest. First thing is that MARTA (Metropolitan Atlanta Rapid Transit Authority) wants me to do the specs for a bus garage for the Olympic buses. Should be interesting.

Jan. 29, 1995

I saw Sue Ellen last week. New layers: March 23, 1979, a sexual trauma (to do with a young man I met in architecture school). An important lifetime in Algeria, around 800 A.D. I had to bring back a part of myself through my feet. Another thing that came up was my need to "Declare Your Faith" in writing.

MY FAITH:

I am One with the Universe. My Angels and Guides are with me.

Love is the Answer to every question. I love mySelf fully, with or without the arthritis.

It is possible to cure my arthritis. Completely. It is up to me.

Spirit is with me and supports me in my quest. Everything is happening in Divine Right Order.

All power is in the present moment. I am safe. I am loved.

Meditation puts me in touch with Spirit, with my Higher Self, my guides, my Angels and The Creator.

Saw Dr. L. Wednesday. He said I am balanced and seem to be doing well. I will go back in three weeks. I do NOT want to take cortisone or Plaquenil, am trying to get along with the homeopathic remedies and supplements.

I've been told that I should follow my first impulse. These are the ones I have followed so far: I mailed the letter to Jody and Jan yesterday, basically asking them to get a room if they couldn't be here by 11 PM and to board the dogs. I offered to pay for both. I sent flowers to Wendy and a card to Kenny. I've agreed to do the MARTA work, although they are slow putting me in motion. I bought an angel for Sue Ellen.

Angel Oracle: Gabriel, A Transformation Angel, Expect Guidance from the Unexpected.

Feb. 4, 1995

Saw Sue Ellen yesterday. She put patches on nine acupressure points! There was an entanglement from my father, cranial pressure adjustment, a new affirmation to say daily for the next month: "I am love. I now choose to love and approve of myself." (This is the affirmation for arthritis from *Heal Your Body* by Louise Hay.) I am to take evening primrose oil. When I came home, I took a bath in peroxide, then slept great.

Met Candace at the bookstore site. We had a heart-to-heart about some things about me that had been bothering her. I was concerned, but not overly. She hugged me when we parted. I am pleased that I slept well last night despite this little confrontation.

Took the last of the homeopathic remedy tonight, so I'm not really taking anything for the arthritis now. I feel like I'm kind of just hanging out there, but I have been feeling really well. Both Linda and Sue Ellen say they can hear the peace in my voice. Is this a new plateau? A new level of wellness?

I will resume the MARTA spec job on Tuesday after Keith and I take a three-day cruise to the Bahamas.

We relaxed and enjoyed ourselves on the cruise. I wore a very sexy dress to the formal evening captain's party and Keith was thrilled by it. He later said that was the proudest day of his life. But the day we returned home, very tired (from being awakened at 5:30 AM to vacate the cabin only to sit and wait for US Customs to clear the ship for debarkation and then race for the airport), a major life shock was waiting in the mail: Jody and Jan's response to my letter. They turned my plea for help and understanding into a declaration of war. Took offense at everything I said, including my offer to pay for a motel room and boarding the dogs. I felt like I had been kicked in the stomach. I was so shocked and exhausted that I couldn't even read it all. In fact, it was such a diatribe I never did read some parts of it. I did not want to expose myself to it or put that kind of stuff into my emotional body. But I did read the concluding paragraph which said if I didn't tell Keith about it, they would. Well, I couldn't deal with it that night. I had to go in to MARTA the next day, as a preliminary project deadline was rapidly approaching. Keith came home with a cold, so I had a good reason to sleep alone in the guest room. For about half an hour thought I was going to flare. My hands hurt and felt like they might get hot. I repeated all my affirmations over and over and kept visualizing golden light coming in to my body. I took two pain pills and managed to sleep for about four hours.

When I woke up at 4 AM, I was very relieved that I hadn't flared. I went to MARTA for most of the day, then came home and told Keith about the letter. It was Valentine's Day and he had flowers and a card for me, but when I told him what I had done, he was very angry, as I knew he would be. I reminded him that he had refused to help me, so I felt I was on my own and had to handle it myself. He admitted, "I didn't know what to do." He can ream out any contractor or bad driver and criticize me at the drop of a hat, but cannot confront or disagree with any of his family. Later that evening he started in again. After a few minutes I said, "I think that's enough," and left the room. I decided that I needed to do something constructive and went to the office to call Jody to apologize. He said, rather gruffly, "Apology accepted." We chatted a little about the kids, I told him to please throw away and forget about the letter and to bring the kids and dogs anytime. Then I took a bath and went to bed downstairs. I had some aches and pains for about a week, but no flare. Also had sun poisoning blotches on my face from our day on the beach during the cruise, a perfect manifestation of my embarrassment. But it was now two months to the day since Christmas and six weeks without any cortisone! I was so pleased to be flare-free in spite of this stress. This is the best I had done since last summer. And furthermore, between times I feel better and better, clearer, happier, more relaxed and fulfilled. Thank You Very Much.

There aren't many things in this lifetime I really regret, but sending this letter is one of them. I should have known better than to tangle with a young warrior, especially when both Mars and Mercury were retrograde! But I felt I needed to express myself and that I do have the right to set some limits. However, I grossly overestimated my relationship with Jody and Jan. And even though I did call and apologize for causing the upset, they now know how I feel. The angels told me not to be a doormat.

On February 16, Kenny gave me these words from my heavenly advisors:

> Lois, You have taken important steps in freeing yourself from "other-imposed" stress and manipulation. Your letter to Keith's nephew was the correct way to approach the situation. You followed your instinct. To have gone through Keith would have diluted the impact of what you wanted to say and the release that you received from standing up for yourself.
>
> Lessons to be learned: 1) You are responsible for yourself and getting yourself on the right track. 2) You cannot control others' reactions to your actions. You can ask for guidance and influence, but everyone makes choices. 3) Say what you feel in love.

(I did, but it wasn't taken that way.)

Here's what was received for me a few days later:

Lois, you have grown so much and conquered so much. You are learning to connect the inner and the outer. You are becoming the real Lois. Allow yourself to develop. Do not feel any discomfort about where you are.

When you meditate, visualize the yourself as the person of your dreams. What would you show to the world if you did not have to put up any fronts. How is this Lois different from what the world sees? Would you like for this image to be your outer? If so, let yourself through the walls constructed around your inner. This is just another step in attaining your perfected state. Let yourself go when you do these visualizations. Just allow it to happen. Oneness and wonder await you as you continue your journey. Your triumphs are a tribute to the power of Spirit in a willing heart. Much has been accomplished. Many doors have been opened and cleared of the debris of so much hurt and unresolved feelings. Use this time to gather your book for publication. When you are ready, move on to your next level, to a new octave. The angels join with all of Creation in rejoicing with you.

Feb. 20, 1995

The weather has warmed up and it was beautiful and sunny today. Juggling the bookstore and MARTA work is challenging and keeping me busy, but I got caught up on some personal chores this weekend which helps me feel more in control. Still lots to do. Karmelah is coming Wednesday for my first past life regression. I'm really curious to see what that will be like. Keith and I are still at odds over the letter, but I have no inclination to back down any further. I apologized and they said they accepted it. Considering that stress, I'm doing great, feeling STRONG!

Saw Sue Ellen Saturday. It was mostly about the events of last week, basically a perceived loss of power. Saw Dr. L. on Friday. He said I'm doing well, gave me a thymus extract and said to come back in four weeks! I got his overleaves from Joya. He's a 7th Level Mature Server. Very sweet and nurturing.

I drove over to see Diane and Hobie yesterday and told them what has been going on. They are so adorable and loving, such an important part of my wonderful support group. Later I read my new book *Unconditional Love and Forgiveness* by Edith Stauffer and I realize that I can't expect to get unconditional love and forgiveness from Keith (or anyone else) unless I give it to him (them). Easier said than done.

Feb. 26, 1995

Karmelah came on Wednesday It was mostly instructional and practicing to see if I am a good subject for regression. When she said, "Now go up on the roof," she felt me go "Whoosh!" right up there! So I am a good subject! Then she regressed me back in this lifetime to my sixth birthday, since the angels said I was still angry with my mother about it. I saw that little Lois was very thrilled about having a birthday party. When my mother brought the cake out onto the porch, in my excitement I got in the way. She accidentally stepped on my foot and then scolded me because of course it was my fault. My foot hurt and I felt like a punctured balloon, embarrassed and disappointed that my birthday wasn't so happy anymore. I learned very early to go along with her blaming me for anything that went wrong. I'm beginning to see that I had a choice about how I responded, that there were other options. But as Maya told me, I was so little and my mother was so big and powerful that I just didn't know any better, so I accepted her blame and criticism as valid.

Karmelah is so sensitive and tuned-in and what she sees is very confirming. She made comments like, "I see you jumping up and down with excitement," and then, "She squelched you." After the birthday she took me back to when I was a new baby. Karmelah sensed coldness, that when I was born my mother gave me the unspoken message that although she had brought me into the world and would take care of me physically, I shouldn't expect any truly loving care or emotional support. Next time we'll go back to a different lifetime. When it was over, I was pretty spacey. It is so wonderful that Karmelah will come here for the sessions. She teaches kindergarten not far from here, so it is right on her way home. It's great to not have to get into my car afterwards!

Yesterday Keith and I met with Candace and her Civil Engineer. I was very nervous about it because of needing to tell her what it's going to cost for us to do the drawings, which I know is going to be more than she wants it to be. My throat got scratchy and after the meeting my right knee was swollen and stiff. When am I going to be able to just breathe through and release these stresses instead of stuffing them into my body?

Today have felt quite good. My knee is just a little stiff and cold/cough is minimal. Am I processing the regression!? Or the bookstore tensions? The knee pain is a lot like what I experienced in March of '93 when Howard told me to call my mother. Hmmm.

Joya's coming for the last week of April and I'm excited. I told Keith after Christmas that I felt I was entitled to 28 days of my friends and family coming to stay. (7 people x 4 days = 28 and that doesn't include the dogs!) So he is going to Michigan and Louisville that week, since he's not all that fond of Joya and all the Michael stuff. I got the idea today to have a brunch for her. People who just want to meet her can come and socialize without having to commit to a channeling.

It was a gorgeous day today. I planted flowers and fed the daffodils. Several Canada geese were here and turtles were sunning on the log.

Keith and I are still somewhat distant because of the St. Valentine's Day Massacre. What a toll this has taken on our relationship. But I can't have my yang strangled.

Lynn said Diane and Hobie would have a baby in '96. The little darling is waiting for the stars to be right. Well, I'm waiting to be a Grandma!

March 6, 1995

Today is Diane and Hobie's second anniversary. What wonderful memories. Diane confided in me that they are trying to conceive my grandchild! I am excited about it and also very pleased that she felt she could tell me they are trying.

Last Tuesday I had a good meeting with Candace and thought all was well, but my knees swelled up again and I needed three Tylenol with codeine to get to sleep. It was about 80% of a full flare, so the next morning I called Dr. L. and they worked me in. He said I'm doing well (!) and gave me some Chinese herbs to counteract "Damp Accumulation," which is one way the Chinese diagnose swelling.

Later in the week, Candace asked for drawings sooner than we had planned, so we worked all weekend. My knees were really bad both days. Thank you Goddess for Sue Ellen! She found: Stored emotions in my right hand and left foot. I need to do the unconditional love and forgiveness exercise from the book by that name for my mother today, just one time. Integrity as a receiver, again. Trauma in June of 1977 (the professor I worked for in architecture school). An ancestral issue 31 generations back on my mother's side which is a belief that females should be submissive to males. I need to call my spiritual name, "Lois," to center myself. I meant to ask if some of this was a result of the regression, but forgot. Oh well, as long as she can release and remove them, it doesn't really matter. The other interesting thing is that when she clears these issues and misconceptions from me, they are also cleared from my children and parents, the whole family tree. I can't believe how many ancestral burdens I have been lugging around all these years. It is rewarding, to say the least, to know that they will no longer be passed on to future generations! They've done enough damage and it's time to release them back to the Universe.

I'm seeing the colors often, not just when I'm in the tub. It is a very reassuring thing to be able to close my eyes and connect with this exquisite spiritual energy through one of my human senses.

Angel Oracle: Gabriel, A Connecting Angel, Connect Through A Book. I think this means I am to finish writing my book. Well, it will have to wait until all these deadlines are complete. Or might it mean to connect with my mother through the *Unconditional Love & Forgiveness* book?

March 6, 1995

Messages from the Angels for Lois M. Grant:

Lois, Your intuition has served you well. Your mother is the key to your recent flare-up and knee pain following your regression session. Many people would be satisfied to release a block such as yours on a spiritual level without necessarily knowing all the whys and wherefores. Your thirst for knowledge has led you to deal with your mother in a way that can have profound releasing power for both of you.

You must extend unconditional love to your mother. Use what you see in your regressions to help you visualize events which have clouded your relationship with her. As you see an event, catalog it, understand it and visualize another outcome based on your desire to be loved and accepted by your mother. Intellectually you have learned to live without this love; emotionally you still desperately want her love. Your visualization of these events and your alteration of "facts" will give you new emotional satisfaction and completion. Your mother, even in your visualizations, may be hard to deal with and may require some forceful redirection on your part. She cannot see beyond herself.

You can use regression to guide you to times and places. As you work through events, trust your intuition and you will recall events which can be altered by your visualizations. Do not do any of this with the desire to achieve a warm, loving relationship with your mother. She might respond and change, but that is her decision. You can do all that is necessary on your own without involving her, except for loving her unconditionally. This love expects nothing in response and is given freely. You will be blessed in this endeavor. Listen to your heart. You are learning well the lessons of this life.

Affirmation of Release: Say, "I release my anger." Let your thoughts arise. "Yes, that anger. I hold it no more." Replace the anger with calm serenity. Return to earth with a positive attitude.

This explained lot to me about my reaction in April of '93 when Howard told me to go to my mother and get her to tell me she loves me and thinks I am a good person. I knew deep down that it was not possible in this lifetime and put all that pain into my knees. I think about Louise Hay's affirmation for knees: "I am flexible and flowing, I am giving and forgiving; I bend and flow with ease and all is well." It's a tall order, but I am on my way!

March 9, 1995

A bad night last night. I had another minor flare like the one last week, about 80% of Christmas. I tried taking double doses of a homeopathic pain remedy. No help. At 1 and 2 AM I took my very last Darvocets. Some help. Finally at 3, I took 70 mg. of cortisone. I feel I have backslid again. I think this flare-up was the result of processing Sue Ellen's work on Monday which, on top of my knee problem, was just too much. If the only way out of this is through the thorns, I need some armor or chain mail. So I am considering going back on the Plaquenil with five mg. of cortisone every other day as Dr. G. suggested, temporarily, to help me get through this series of regressions.

March 14, 1995

Last Saturday was exhilarating! I got up and went straight outside to plant nine spruce tree seedlings along the wooded area at the street and do some other yard work. I was thrilled to find the trilliums that I transplanted from Diane's yard last year coming up.

Then I came in and showered. Diane called and asked if she could come for lunch. She is getting over a sinus infection, so I fixed chicken soup and it was very simple and nurturing. I think she is reacting to her new office location. We had lunch on the deck while mallards were mating in the lake (at least we hope that's what they were doing!). She told me that it's better to take ten mg. of cortisone every other day than five mg. every day. Apparently, the body needs days off for the adrenal glands to recover and not get dependent. I'm glad to know that. I took ten mg. Thursday night because I was achy all over. None Friday, five yesterday, none today. I can sure feel it on the off days.

People around me are manifesting new jobs. Linda is talking to *Fortune* magazine, then the *Los Angeles Times* called her! Scott wants to go into business for himself. Paula and David want to work in Oregon.

Yesterday I went to MARTA to turn in my time sheet and invoice. I had a good time seeing everyone there, but thank goodness they won't need me for a while, since we have lots of work to do for Delta! It was a warm sunny day and I enjoyed doing my recycling thing. Bought groceries, went to bookstore, bank and drugstore. I had a great time with everyone I encountered and even heard Mozart on the radio. It's a beautiful life! I was very high. Now to finish the Phoenix and Dragon drawings.

March 15, 1995

Regression No. 2: I was a servant in a kitchen in northern Africa (I later realized this was the lifetime in Algeria that Sue Ellen detected). I started crying hard immediately. She (my mother) was in charge of the kitchen and beat me often with a stick. She crippled my knees and caused brain damage, which made me retarded. An old man with a long beard (my father in this lifetime) was her father and he sat in a corner of the kitchen. Sometimes he would help me and make her stop beating me, but sometimes not. He could have stopped her, but he didn't, just as he could have stopped her emotional abuse in this lifetime. Diane was my lover. She took care of me and gave me unconditional love, even though I was lame and retarded, unable to respond the way I wanted to, and she stayed with me to the end. I died pretty young, crushed.

After the death, Karmelah took me up to the Pure Being State where I was surrounded by a healing pink mist. Diane was on my left and my father was three feet away. She was nine feet away. I had the stick, and could have beaten her with it, but I didn't. I didn't want to incur the karma. Karmelah told me to give the stick to Diane. When I did, it vaporized! Then they all were swirled away and a healing, spiraling green light whooshed all through and around me. After that a bright white light cleansed me. It was very profound. I cried a lot and felt a lot of energy flowing. Karmelah is fabulous! I trust her implicitly and she consistently confirms my reactions. She kept saying, "You're so brave!" Apparently some people back off from confronting such difficult situations, but I just kept feeling the feelings and letting them out. I've made a commitment to myself to heal this body in this lifetime and to complete and forgive these karmas.

Afterwards I was quite spacey. Heard Mozart on the radio, then sang while making dinner, which is somewhat unusual. I felt light and happy.

March 17, 1995

If seeing a cockroach means you have fears, does seeing three or four dead ones mean the fears are dead?

Had another great day, although I am still having trouble sleeping. Was it the Full Moon last night? Even a glass of wine with dinner didn't help.

Today we did our taxes—in one day, no trauma! I didn't get tense at all! Progress!

Lunch with Jenny yesterday—she said I looked different. When I asked in what way, she said, "Your eyes are level." I'm not sure exactly what she meant, but took it as positive. Then today I had lunch with Kenny and Wendy. I told about my regressions; Wendy and Kenny shared their recent growth experiences and it was all pretty exciting. Kenny held my hands and I could feel the healing vibrations. Then the vibrations stopped and it was over. On the way home I stopped to see

Paula. She's doing so great. I always love to be with her. I'll miss her if she moves to Holland or Oregon, potential places for new jobs for her.

Yesterday Keith and I cuddled and were very tender. We are beginning to recover from the February Fiasco.

March 18, 1995

I spent three hours with Sue Ellen this morning: My Inner Fire was out and I was paying attention to an outside authority instead of my Higher Self. I had to call my Inner Warrior. I am to say the affirmation from the angels ten times per day ("I believe and accept my healing") and repeat Howard's prayer once a day. She put patches on four acupressure points. Integrity as a receiver, which comes up almost every time. Ancestral/cultural burden three generations back on my father's side that women should submit to men. (This was also a burden on my mother's side recently.) Superstition: cockroaches mean fear, which agrees with what Michael says. And there was an aggressive matriarchal geopathic stress! It's great to know I am unloading all this garbage.

Came home and worked in the yard a little. Planted an evergreen tree I got for Christmas and some other flowers. Just now got out of peroxide bath.

March 29, 1995

Regression No. 3! I was a young lawyer named John Mayhew in England and she was my stepmother. She was wearing a big blue dress and wide-brimmed blue hat with lots of lace and frills and she was hitting me with a riding crop. She was angry because my father had died and she wanted his property. I had lost the case in court for her. It seemed I could never do anything right for her. I felt humiliated and was crawling under a big oak table trying to get away from her. Jack (my first husband in this lifetime) was the judge who decided that my uncle (my father in this lifetime) should get the property. When I was a child in that lifetime she had often smacked my hands on the knuckles with the crop. Later in the lifetime she had me committed to Bedlam, the insane asylum. That's when I started to cry. I was not insane, but she somehow put me in there. It was so mean and unfair. There was a beautiful woman/angel/deva there (we couldn't decide who it was) who gave me love and compassion. I died there young, very peacefully.

Karmelah said that the psychological and spiritual link between love and pain was very important and that my awareness of this will help me to help other healers and to even do healing myself. She seemed to think she was channeling this message for me. She felt that this English lifetime was very important to my healing and forgiveness process and that I would continue to learn from it over the next several days. I felt lots of energy moving through my hands and feet and some of it reminded me of sensations I had felt during the Hellerwork.

I'm very excited. We have bluebirds nesting in our new bluebird house that's been up only about a week! Dogwoods and azaleas are blooming now—Atlanta is so exuberant in the spring.

April 12, 1995

New psychic Tara came yesterday and gave me a fantastic reading. She bills herself as a business adviser and I wanted to chat with her to see if she would be good for Scott, Keith and me to see regarding the new business arrangement with Scott now that he is on his own. Immediately when she came in, she said, "You have a very lucky time coming up the first of next year." In February of '96 my life will change big time. I will be set free and will begin a whole new 12-year cycle. It will be magnetic, healing, clearing out my subconscious. Travel, money, luck, good business are all coming. Well, it sounds great to me!

She said Grant/Weiland has a big project, maybe two, coming up in the next six months. And that I may have as many as six grandchildren!

Wendy called this morning to tell me she heard a voice say, "Lois is pure gold." WOW!

Then Karmelah came again today. She had a dream about remembering our appointment and said that my healing will heal others.

Regression #4: I was a geisha in Japan and was very submissive, repressed and stoic. Everything felt very flat and level. I wore a mask of makeup and my only outlet was calligraphy and haiku. She was my daughter and she resented me because we were not accepted in society. I loved her and tried to please her, but was unable to reach her emotionally and our relationship was very stiff and formal like everything else in that lifetime. I committed suicide by drinking calligraphy ink, then went into the garden and collapsed. My angel came to take me to the other side where I reviewed the lifetime for the role of will and power. I had a box with inks, brushes and pens and after I died, my daughter rejected it and this was very painful for me in spirit. I felt absolutely no emotion while viewing this lifetime until Karmelah had me replay my death with my daughter accepting and loving and forgiving me. That is when I cried. It was very complex and relevant to this lifetime: I was so afraid to express any emotions, to be a real person, and resolved to change that in future lifetimes. (The future is now!) So different from the other lifetimes, but still quite powerful.

April 20, 1995

I was standing at my desk yesterday afternoon, trying to find something in a hurry. I stepped backwards, caught the heel of my shoe on the chair mat and fell to the floor, landing on my tailbone. It hurt, but I was pretty sure nothing was broken. Saw Dr. L. at 9:15 this morning. My shoulder, hip and knee were out of alignment so he adjusted me. Then I was able to see Sue Ellen. Another family burden was removed. Plus my mother subconsciously put a curse on me while she was pregnant with me. I need detox pills. Feel much better tonight.

This afternoon I got this message from the angels:

Lois, although all events can be used as learning devices and tools, do not attach too much symbolic influence to your accident. You fell because you were being told, "sit and be at rest." Rest in the knowledge and assurance of who and what you are. Take the time recommended to you as a time for rest and healing and carefully document your life and progress. You have learned so much and experienced such wonderful peace and joy. Take the time now to absorb and learn the lessons. Write these lessons and you will be amazed at what comes forth. Put your intellect in neutral and let your feelings come through your hands onto the written pages of your life story.

Part of your need to slow down your pace is to allow yourself to face and deal with the answers that have come through your many sources. You truly are on the brink of working through your relationship with your mother and your related illness. The messages and understandings you have received are right on the money. Just give them time to soak in. One more thing: As you rest your body, think of ways that you can worship. You have a very great need to worship the Creator and Sustainer of Life. The ways are not so critical, but the need for you is great and much healing of your Spirit can take place as you worship. Find a way, a place and people and renew this part of your life.

Kenny and the angels come through again! I will sit and assimilate.

TRIUMPH

April 14, 1995

When I called my parents last Sunday, my mother seemed to be depressed, which happens fairly often. Then I called her sister to wish her a happy 80th birthday. She's been having a rough time healthwise, plus needed a root canal. My mother had said to her, "Why are you having a root canal when you're going to be 80?" Such compassion. I think Mother was depressed because her younger sister is turning 80. Mother has always said, "When you get to be 80, you're really old," to which I say, "If that's what you believe." Another one of her favorite sayings is, "Old age is a shipwreck."

April 20, 1995

This is a significant day—the nearly completed week of Joya's visit. It has not been easy, but it has been wonderful. It was a stroke of brilliance to convince Keith to go to Michigan and Louisville because I truly would not have had the energy to deal with him, too. It's been like a job to manage her schedule, to be sure people show up and to get her to the right place at the right time. I end up visiting with everyone who comes to see her, which I enjoy, but it's strenuous. Tuesday I took Keith to the airport at 7 AM, had lunch with Diane, then picked Joya up at the airport late in the afternoon. I forgot to take my morning pills so that, combined with the excitement and stress of the day, made me quite stiff by evening, especially in my knees. Wednesday we had lunch with Candace at Café Sunflower. (She did not want to talk about the project and I didn't bring it up.) Joya thinks she is a Scholar.

Wednesday afternoon I had my channeling during which Michael recommended I get massage once or twice a week. They said my diet looks good and that I'm making progress.

Thursday Joya did a two-hour channeling for a dynamic woman, Joanne, who knows that in a past life she was a WWI German pilot who flew with the Red Baron. She had an incredible spontaneous past life recall while visiting an airplane museum in Rhinebeck, NY, which led her to explore her past lives. She actually has a picture of herself in that lifetime! Joya's program at the Inner Space that evening went very well, although not many people came. My knee hurt and I was very tired.

Friday Sue Ellen came here and worked on Joya in the morning. Sue Ellen had her channeling session after lunch and then she worked on me. Joya and I spent a pleasant evening going out for dinner; then Joya shopped while I browsed and read.

Yesterday eleven lovely friends came for brunch. At 12:37 there was a solar eclipse so we all made lists of what we want in our lives, stood around the grill where I placed my big white candle and we burned our lists. Wendy offered a prayer for the Oklahoma City bombing. Then Sue Ellen prayed for me and my healing. I was standing between Joya and Wendy and, of course, tears came up. When I opened my eyes and looked up, Diane was looking right at me. Our gaze held for several seconds. I was filled with warm and wonderful feelings. Everyone hugged. After everyone left, I lay on the couch with my feet up and overflowed with appreciation for all the terrific people I have brought into my life.

May 6, 1995

Sunday morning Linda called with the best news I've had in a long time. Our parents are moving to an assisted living facility! We are just amazed. And Linda and I are so very grateful that we won't have to force them into this transition. It is a great Miracle and Blessing. The only hint I've had that something was up was last week when my dad said, "You know, we're trying to decide whether to stay here. Would you like the player piano?" Of course I said, "Yes," but I had no idea what he really meant. It also explains why Mother was depressed. It's going to be a huge, stressful change for them to move into an apartment after their lovely custom-designed home of 30 years.

When Kenny had his channeling Sunday afternoon, Michael rather brusquely told him to just divorce Elena and get on with his life. He was pretty blown away by that, thought it was pretty harsh. We sat in the kitchen and talked afterwards. Regarding my folks, he said, "Maybe all the work you've been doing has helped your mother to be able to make this change." I thought that was an interesting idea. Later Wendy came for her channeling and while we were chatting she repeated Kenny's comment, almost word for word. Suddenly I got chills and tears of confirmation. So it must be true! It's wondrous to me how these subtle and profound energetic connections manifest themselves.

Joya had mentioned that there seemed to be some uncomfortable energy in the guest room, echoing Wendy's discomfort last fall, and that she had had some weird dreams since she arrived. So I called Karmelah, who said it sometimes it takes more than one Feng Shui "treatment" to fix everything a house needs. She came by with her dowsing rods and detected a deep underground waterway running under the floor slab, which she "diverted." Then she noticed a cold spot by the bed. When she consulted her cards, the death card came up and it felt like Indian times. I got excited and told her how after right after we moved in, Michael said our cat Misha left because there had been negative Indian activities on the land which he didn't want to deal with. (Some time later Sue Ellen told me that when she looked in the guest room she had "seen" Indians!) Karmelah cured it. We lit a lavender candle, put lights and silk flowers in the affected corner. We went out to look at the wind chimes I had put up to counteract the geopathic stress and they were tangled! So we straightened them out. When Joya came back that evening, she could tell right away that the energy felt light and clear, much improved. The next day I bought an angel to hang over the outside door.

Tuesday I was grateful I only had to make one trip to the airport since Joya's departure and Keith's arrival were within a half hour of each other. Keith was very glad to see me, but he came home with a bad cold which he caught from Jody's kids.

I saw Dr. G. for a follow-up visit. My right knee was stiff. She said, "It's not your rheumatoid, it's tendinitis." I told her I wasn't taking the Plaquenil and she just accepted it. I am now taking five mg. of cortisone every other day and one Trilisate twice a day. I had a copy of *Bringers of the Dawn* by Barbara Marciniak with me and she saw it.

"What are you reading?" she asked. She copied down the title! She suggested I use a capsaicin cream, so I bought some and that night put it on both knees. It started burning like mad. I called the pharmacist and he said I had probably put too much on. This body is so sensitive! I spent the next two hours cooling the chili pepper burn with ice and wet towels. Then my hands started to hurt. So I took 40 mg. of cortisone and Tylenol with codeine. The pain stopped and I slept well. We worked hard Thursday and finished Delta's San Diego counters. Then I started getting ready to entertain the Michigan delegation to the American Institute of Architects National Convention, which was being held in Atlanta all that week.

The party was a great success—about 30 people came. It was great fun for Keith to see his former compatriots. He was thrilled. And it is such a joy to have this spacious, lovely home for parties. The next day we went to the convention exhibits and the host chapter party where I saw my friend and colleague from the big hospital project, Vic, for the first time in months. He said I looked <u>great</u>, especially my eyes! I wondered later if it was the eye makeup I was wearing or is it all the inner work I've been doing?

May 7, 1995

Last night I received the most wonderful phone call from my former hairdresser Alan. I haven't heard from him since he closed his shop. He said that two months ago, after going through chemotherapy and radiation, nothing was helping his lymphoma, his weight was down to 100 pounds and the doctors told him he had two weeks to live. Then he had a Near Death Experience! He has gained thirty pounds back and is getting well. I was ecstatic to hear this. His voice sounded so happy and exultant. Michael had said Alan wasn't ready to check out and that this illness was for his growth. Michael was right! Alan and I will get together for lunch soon so he can tell me more.

May 9, 1995

Yesterday I didn't take any cortisone. I felt pretty good in the morning, but as the day wore on, my joints got increasingly stiff and achy, especially my right knee. Took a bath with Dead Sea salts, but I woke up at 2 AM really hurting and discouraged. After feeling the feelings and debating with myself, I took two Plaquenil tablets. When I got up this morning, I took ten mg. of the Big C (cortisone). I hope the Plaquenil will be temporary. I felt I had to do <u>something</u>—was this the right thing?

Sue Ellen saw me at 11. I was told to share my healing with someone.

My folks are moving the end of this month! It's happening very fast.

May 14, 1995

What an interesting week. Wednesday I had lunch with Kenny and he told me that he got the hepatitis B from having sex with men. (See Chapter Eleven, "Kenny.") This was a huge surprise which gave me a lot to think about. Saturday I felt somewhat swollen, but today have felt quite good. Took five mg. of cortisone. today, none yesterday. I'm trying to do five mg. every other day as Dr. G. recommended in January.

The angels recommended a little ritual to bless my mother: to burn a picture of her using each of seven colors of candles plus white. I found an old Polaroid photo of her and a candle in each color. I had to light the picture three times to burn it all. I said a heartfelt prayer asking for love and blessings to fill my mother's heart and for her to know on some level of my forgiveness. I felt a light sensation of release as I was doing this. St. Germaine told me that burning letters and pictures transmutes negative energy into positive vibrations. I did this after the full moon and it just happened to be Mother's Day! What a "coincidence!"

Merry called and it was really good to talk and laugh with her. It was the 13th anniversary of our first meeting. She said I need to let go of trying to be so perfect. I need her to tell me that again, more clearly!

Then an old college friend called. It was a little unusual because I never hear from her except at Christmas and we have never spoken by telephone. She has been having problems with her knees and wanted advice about arthritis. I told her about the low stress diet and some of what I am doing. She already meditates. It was very interesting to talk to her after so many years. Maybe she was the person I was supposed to share my healing with.

Speaking of healing, I had lunch with Alan to talk about his healing experience. "The doctors told me to find a hospice and start the morphine. I asked myself and my family, 'Do I have to do that?' I just didn't feel ready." He was already on methadone and was pretty spaced out, probably going in and out of his body and consciousness. About a week later, "Something happened. Someone intervened in my life. I feel different than I did before." His memory of the event is not very clear and it may have taken place over several days. When a friend gave him a copy of *Embraced by the Light*, certain sentences jumped out at him and felt like *déjà vu*. His liver and spleen became less swollen and the tumor began to shrink. The doctors were helpless to come up with a medical explanation and admitted it was "of a miraculous nature." His oncologist had never seen such a turnaround. Alan has grown tremendously in his understanding of life as a result of his experience and he shared this quote with me: "What you learn in the dark will help you in the light." It was wonderful to see him again and to know that he is on his way back to full health.

May 22, 1995

Angel Oracle: Michael, An Angel of Peace, Spend Time Alone in a Beautiful Space.

I had my first massage today with Bonnie—I liked her immensely. Gentle, but effective. I thought that her last name (Mah) might indicate nurturing. I'm going for two hours next week. She has told me to drink 100 ounces of water a day. I think I'm already doing that, but will concentrate on it a little more. Also had a brief reading with Lynn. She said, "I see you circling a mountain, but maybe it's not really a mountain. You are just seeing it as a mountain Allow the healing to come in." OK! She also recommended I get a tape of "Om Namaha Shivaya." It's a Sanskrit chant which means, "I honor the Divine within."

May 25, 1995

Saw Sue Ellen yesterday. When I took my peroxide bath afterwards, I did an exercise that she recommended. I lit a white candle and put it in the corner of the bathtub. Then I visualized myself surrounded with golden light and called in all the Ascended Masters, Buddha, Jesus, Hindu Masters, etc., to help me. I saw them all come into a long golden room. They were all up on a platform at a table with Buddha in the center and up above them all. I was seated cross-legged on the floor in front of the dais. I asked for special help to gain inner peace. I saw the mountain that Lynn talked about and it melted like so much ice cream. So I reduced my mountain to a molehill! I also chanted "Om Namaha Shivaya." It felt very good.

Today I received a big box of old framed pictures of Linda and me from my parents and had quite an emotional reaction. Taking down and shipping off all these portraits that have been hanging in their home for decades seems so final, so symbolic of a major change. It all feels very complete, like it's really over! Now tonight I am quite peaceful.

Had a thank you letter from Joya. She said, "You seem so emotionally healed." That means a lot coming from her, she's so perceptive.

June 1, 1995—In My Home Town

On Friday my parents moved into their new apartment. Sunday Linda called me because some of our parents' friends who were helping them move had called her, concerned that our parents were having problems making decisions and were doing some strange things. They thought that one of us needed to come out there. Linda and I resisted because we had been totally left out of the decisions and planning for this move and we felt that the last thing our parents want is for us to tell them what to do. After all, when we go back there, we are always treated like we're six years old again. After many phone calls back and forth, I called their doctor and left a message. He returned my call only 45 minutes later! I asked him, "Is there some physical problem causing my parents to make this change?" The answer: "Your father is in the beginning stages of Alzheimer's disease." After absorbing that confirmation, I called for plane reservations. Linda just started her new job at *Fortune* magazine and was under enough pressure with her first big deadline for them without adding a trip to the Midwest.

Before I left, Kenny faxed me the following from the angels:

May 20, 1995

Lois: Your parents are in the twilight stage of their lives. Their unsettled state is largely a result of their exposure to their own mortality. This has come about as you have released yourself from the role of the bitter daughter who was forever misunderstood and ignored. Your acceptance and release have opened the veil that allows them to look beyond. Of course, they don't understand what they are seeing, but they are being drawn to the Light. They knew it was time to put themselves in a place where they can let go of the physical plane realities of daily life and prepare to leave the planet. Their forgetfulness is their response to the Light. Even though they misunderstand, they can't look away because the pull is so strong. One doesn't always understand the Light, but the pull is unmistakably strong. They have opened to the point where they cannot resist.

Lift them up. Love them. Care for them. Do not worry about them. Know that the Light is calling them and that they are following. Their friends are there to ease their crossing. Continue to let them go. Deal honestly with your feelings for them and don't overanalyze them. Remember that they chose their life together.

This message was so profound and helpful that I read it over many times and faxed it to Linda. I feel incredibly fortunate to know what is truly going on at the spiritual level. What a Blessing to have Kenny and the Angels to guide me. Thank You!

Next morning I got on the plane and after renting a car and driving to a friend's home, called my mother to tell her I was in town. She didn't seem all that surprised, but sounded a little tired and dazed. When I showed up at their new home, the staff was sure glad to see me! They needed a contact person and for some reason did not have my name. I filled them in on some of the family background and explained why Linda and I had not been involved sooner—basically because we had been left totally out of the loop of their decision to move. I was pleased to discover that this is a very good facility. Not exactly beautiful by my architectural standards, but the staff is terrific. And there is a skilled nursing wing where care can be provided to the end.

I think my mother and father are very comfortable both with each other and their new living space. Mostly they are relieved that the move is over. It was interesting how they just accepted the fact that I showed up. Mother held my hand for a long time when I first arrived. Then we opened the champagne that Linda and I had sent last week. We had a relaxing time together. Dinner was pleasant. People are friendly and the hostess in the dining room makes a big fuss over everyone as they come in, which Mother loves. I feel certain that this is an important part of my healing and I'm glad I came.

June 9, 1995

On Friday I went shopping for a deluxe bath seat and hand-held shower head for Mother. Apparently, because of her knee she has had problems getting out of the tub even at the house and one time my dad was afraid he was going to have to call the fire department. They didn't even know such things as these tub seats existed; I explained that it is my business as an architect to know about them. We went over to the house where we packed up the piano rolls for the electric player piano they will be sending me and lots of pictures, clippings, and other mementos that were just sitting out in the attic. I also picked up some things that I had always liked that they would otherwise have sold. I was surprised at how few things they took with them. They are lightening up, just as the angels said.

Back at the new apartment I programmed their phones, installed long phone cords, did laundry, etc., just a myriad of little things. My dad was mystified because some of the outlets didn't work. When I turned them on at the wall switch, he was just amazed that I could figure that out! I labeled all their linens so they could get their laundry done, helped with little details that were boggling my dad, like how to do change of address cards, buy trash bags, etc. It really was the first time they had ever seen me as a competent adult and they were very grateful for everything I did.

They both had many lapses in memory while I was there and were confused by all the stress of moving and adjusting to this major life change, their first in over thirty years. But I just answered their questions as many times as was needed and was very loving and patient. I treated them like children. There is no use correcting them or becoming irritated with the repetitions. That would just make me feel bad and make them feel even worse.

Once when I was going to their new apartment, I went down the "wrong" corridor. The first door on that corridor had a beautiful angel on it, made from Battenburg lace. I showed it to my mother. Later I asked her if she would like me to find an ornament of some kind for their door. She said yes and when I asked what she might like, she said, "Oh, I like the angel." I tried to find one when I was shopping on

Friday, but everyone said, "It's the wrong time of year for angels." What a ridiculous idea! <u>My</u> angel works all year 'round! Well, I will find one in Atlanta or in a catalog.

When I left after four days, I hugged Mother and said, "I love you." For the first time ever (in this lifetime that I can recall), she said it back. I cried in the car. They both looked so helpless and vulnerable standing together on the porch as I drove away.

Although it was a fabulous trip on so many levels and I'm convinced it was healing for all of us, I was very worn out emotionally. Keith and I had a lovely reunion. Sunday I did little except talk on the phone. Diane and Hobie came by briefly to show us their new Volvo. They are manifesting.

Monday I was still tired and weepy and realized that I felt depressed because of these big life changes for us all. Tuesday I had another massage. Bonnie worked a long time on my toes and the tears were flowing out of my eyes. I said, "It feels like you are squeezing tears out of my toes." She said my body is very responsive and is ready to change. "All your hard work is going to pay off." That brought a few more tears. It was a good, gentle release.

Wednesday night was a reunion of the team that worked on the big hospital project. It was great fun to see everybody. Chris W. hugged me tight and said he loved me! Vic sat next to me and he said it was <u>not</u> eye makeup that made my eyes look different when he saw me in May, that my eyes are changed, more relaxed. This is great feedback from someone who knows me well.

Linda seems to be feeling the effects of my spiritual work. For the first time, she bought our parents an affectionate anniversary card. This is truly astounding. And she's calling our father "Daddy" again.

I will see Sue Ellen tomorrow. I want to get to the very innermost layer of that onion! Can't be too much longer, can it? Oops, there's that impatience again!

June 17, 1995

Wow! The weeks go by so fast. Saw Sue Ellen a week ago. First thing to come up: Family Burden (surprise!) Lots to do with sexuality attitudes on Mother's side. So I reviewed some of my mother's fixations, Linda's and my sex education, etc. Sue Ellen cleaned up "debris" from my lower chakras. She swept her hands down my aura (about a foot above my body) to gather all the unseen debris. Then she carefully scooped it up and literally threw it out the window! It took three trips to the window!!

On the way home I stopped at Michael's (!) craft store and bought a doll and angel outfit to make the angel for my parents' door. I finished her on Tuesday. When I hung her up to take her picture, I was very touched, she's so beautiful. I packed her up with some other goodies, then went to lunch with Kenny. I got the name of my family's angels. Mother's is Etheriel, Father's is Samuel and Linda's is Atheriel.

I called Mother and told her the angel was on the way and that her name was Etheriel. She asked in a rather childlike way, "What does it mean?" I answered, "Beautiful, spiritual, ethereal." "Well, I guess I have some of those traits." I agreed.

Another two-hour massage Tuesday. Didn't take a bath that night and had a lot of pain Wednesday It seems to be directly related to when I take cortisone. I'm trying to do ten mg. every other day. I don't think the Plaquenil is helping much, although it may not have "kicked in" yet. I was pretty achy again today. Also, I keep going in and out of depression. Tara the psychic said that I am grieving for my parents, grieving for my past and what might have been and what will never be, in this lifetime. Grieving and releasing are the best things I can do. Let it go, let it go. It should be complete in November of 1996.

Last night and this morning I made a beautiful book of all the family pictures I brought back. Plus I collected photos from the album Mother had made for me years ago and a bunch of framed pictures and combined everything into one big album. It looks really great and I am very proud of it. I think that this project has been another piece of my healing puzzle.

June 18, 1995

I had a wonderful conversation with my dad this morning. He thanked me for his Father's Day flowers, for everything I did for them while I was there and for the angel. Mother loves her new bath arrangement. After saying that I was pleased to be able to help, I said, "You were a wonderful father," and he replied, "Well, I'm just glad I was one." I said "I love you," as we hung up. Then I cried. Louise Hay's "I Can Do It!" calendar affirmation for today is: "My father is a beloved child of the Universe. Our relationship continues to grow in miraculous ways. I love my father." How perfect for this particular Father's Day.

Linda went to see them for Father's Day weekend. Our dad is pretty boggled by the house closing and she helped to explain things to him. Linda agrees with me that they are comfortable and that their friends were projecting their own fears and discomforts. It is wonderful that Linda's and my perceptions of these important parts of our lives are so compatible and we are thus able to support each other. We are both somewhat awed by the way our parents have just turned their backs on everything they spent this entire lifetime striving for—the accumulation of material things. None of that seems to matter anymore.

June 21, 1995

Today is the best non-cortisone day I've had in weeks. Had a two-hour massage yesterday and took Epsom Salts bath last night. I forgot the bath last week, which is maybe part of why I felt so lousy on Wednesday Or I might have been processing Sue Ellen's work. Bonnie's hands get very hot when she works on me. She said that the angle of my feet when I point my toes is ten degrees greater than when we started. More flexible life and feet!

June 30, 1995

Tuesday I worked at MARTA in the morning, had massage in the afternoon. Wednesday I got up early for a meeting at MARTA, then to a previously scheduled meeting with Candace at 10:30. Went back to MARTA for a couple of hours, then home. It was too much. I was aching all over. Came home and napped for two hours. Thursday I felt rested, much better. Finished some Delta work and also the Phoenix and Dragon drawings.

Yesterday I saw a Carolina wren on my deck and there was a great blue heron fishing the lake all afternoon. Today a bluebird flew right in front of my car and I saw a rabbit when I went to get the mail. Signs?

My dad called Wednesday He's used up all his change of address cards that we got when I was there and he couldn't remember where we had gotten them. So I explained it was the Post Office and exactly where in the Post Office. He doesn't seem to mind having to ask these questions when he can't remember something. Then I got an incredible thank-you note from my mother:

Hi! yuh, Honey, I cannot imagine how I would have survived without your plumbing fixtures—they are life-saving. Thank you again for all you did to make our move just splendid! And the angel is angelic! Thanks! If we can ever get all straightened up it will be nice. Anyway I must rush off now, but I wanted you to know how wonderful the plumbing is! Lovingly, as ever, Mother.

This from a woman who never ever said thank-you for anything—or "I love you." What a change! I catch myself thinking it's unbelievable and then smile at how affecting the work on myself has been. This is incredible progress and it feels rewarding.

Boxes with things from their house arrived. I was touched when opening them, even though they really don't have a lot of sentimental value. I'm not sure why I reacted emotionally, but think it must still be part of the releasing process and my response to all the changes. Hope I'm not overanalyzing.

July 1, 1995

We've had so many wonderful wildlife visitors this week: Great Blue Heron, Great White Egret (all day today), a rabbit on the driveway, a turtle laying eggs on the berm. This place is such a blessing and haven. I love it so.

July 2, 1995 Sunday

I did not take any cortisone yesterday, took five mg. this morning,. Have felt so good today. Is the Plaquenil is kicking after two months? Am I just better? Is it the massage? The changes with my parents? I guess I shouldn't be concerned, just relax and enjoy it. Thank you!

July 4, 1995

Today was scheduled to be a cortisone day, but I felt great this AM and didn't take any. Spent most of the morning cooking. I made grits, burgers, onions, fruit salad, corn on the cob. Scott, Sue and Mark came over and we had a great time. Scott set off his fireworks over the lake from the dock between rain showers. It was a very good day and my knees have been pain-free. The piano arrived yesterday It will be fun to play again, even if I can only use eight fingers properly.

July 5, 1995

I felt great again this morning and not just physically. Went to MARTA, then came home to finish the bookstore drawings. I have felt so happy. The little blue heron came by this morning!

July 7, 1995

Thursday started out good, but by noon I was really tired. After lunch I sat in the living room and thought, "I really would like to take a nap." I didn't and by late afternoon felt really dopey, almost like I had the flu. Keith and I talked about going out, but after meditating, I knew I wasn't up for it. I ate hot quinoa for dinner. (This is a grain that comes from the Aztecs that the entity Michael recommended to me. It is so pure and wholesome that I like to eat it when I'm feeling weak.) I went to bed and listened to meditation tapes while resting. Slept quite hard and felt good by morning. Had massage this afternoon and just took Epsom salts bath. Keith spent all day in bed resting his back. Guess we both are overdoing and need to dial back a little.

July 11, 1995 Tuesday

7-11! A lucky day, a wonderful day. I think it may truly be a turning point day. I put on my new white trapeze dress and new white shoes and went to see Sue Ellen. It turns out that my pain last Thursday was processing my previous visit to her after nearly four weeks!! Today only two things came up: First was that I needed to hold a certain posture for several minutes. Second thing was that I had two holes in my Astral Web (whatever that is!), one behind my head and one at my knees. The remedy was for us to pray together. While I was holding the position she put on a tape of the Mozart Elvira Madigan theme. I started responding emotionally to it, as this is my most favorite music and usually brings tears. So of course, when I started praying, I began to cry. Sue Ellen continued the prayer and she cried, too. It was extremely powerful and moving. I made the promise that when I got my healing I would spend the rest of this lifetime witnessing to the Power of Spirit. When we were finished, she said, "I felt a huge jolt in the room while you were praying." Then my body said that was it for the day. It's very unusual for me to have such a short session and I processed everything right then and did not need to go into timed processing, which is also very unusual.

It will be a year on Thursday that I first went to see Sue Ellen. I'm going to send her flowers. What a difference she and her esoteric work have made in my life—and the lives of my whole family!

In the afternoon I had massage which was much less painful than on Friday. I am going to start going twice a week for one hour. I asked Bonnie how many years she thought it would take. She said, "I don't think it will take a year." We're getting to be good friends.

July 13, 1995

Wendy called last night. Sue Ellen told her that my last session was one of the two most powerful she had ever experienced.

July 23, 1995

Yesterday Diane and Hobie came over. They brought me the music cabinet and a beautiful set of agate wind chimes that Hobie bought for me when he went to Sedona last week on business. I was so touched by his thoughtfulness. The chimes look perfect against the stone wall by our front door.

July 25, 1995

Both yesterday and today I went without cortisone—two days in a row! Can't remember the last time I was able to do that since the Christmas debacle, which is now seven months ago. Two hours of massage today had me a bit achy tonight, but Epsom salts bath seems to have really helped. Bonnie said that my hands and feet are much more "liquid" now. This is progress. She is moving joints that haven't budged in years! She got very excited about the way the bones were loosening up in my right wrist. Keith has started going, too, and she is really helping his back.

Paula came over and we had a delightful visit, as we always do. She's planning another job-hunting trip to Oregon. She and David will probably get married in the fall of '96. I was extremely touched and thrilled when she said she wants me to be her attendant, her matron of honor. She said, "I want to look over there and see you!"

Later Kenny faxed me these answers to questions I had given him about two weeks ago:

Lois: On Tuesday it felt as if a very significant event occurred during my session with Sue Ellen. Can you help me understand what happened?

Angels: When you were directed to consider how your past is to be carried forward into your future, you had a sense that "all is well." This feeling is the response of your heart to your unconditional love for your mother. When you released all the hurt and bitterness that you had been holding in your heart for so long, you freed yourself to love. That ability to love is spilling over into all of your life and is transforming you into the person that you have chosen to become. This gift of love was both from the Creator and from you to yourself, for you created it by giving up your right to your point of view and trusting Spirit to transform your gift into something glorious. This love will be a transforming power both in you and everyone whose life you touch. The love within you is so powerful that your body can no longer harbor the dis-ease habits that you have borne for so many lifetimes.

Lois: Is there anything I should be doing that I am not doing? How far am I from total healing?

Angels: You are ready to get serious about your book! You have put off wrapping up because you want to be totally healed before you finish it. Remember that most people who read your book will be in the midst of their own struggle and might relate more readily to a story of someone whose journey is not complete. Don't be afraid. "Perfect love casts out fear," as our Beloved Jesus so beautifully said. The letting go is the doorway for which you have searched. Picture those red double doors. One little clue: They open out!

Lois: Are the following signs from you/Spirit? Wrens, Bluebirds, Herons, Egrets, Wasps; Mozart and Vivaldi on the radio? Wendy also asked about Praying Mantises.

Angels: Wrens: Yes. Sign of Joy. Bluebirds: Yes. Sign of Happiness. Herons: Yes. Sign of Power and Cunning. Egrets: Yes. Sign of Overcoming. Praying Mantis: Yes. Sign of Submission. Mozart: Yes. Sign of Peace. Vivaldi: Yes. Sign of Confirmation. Wasps: Yes. Sign of the Pain of Change. All these signs are confirmation when you need it to help you grow. The goal is to live in the joy and comfort of perfect peace. The wondrous thing about perfect peace is that it anchors you against any thing, power, force, or obstacle that crosses your path. Learn to trust your heart. When you see a sign, become aware of the feeling in your heart at that very moment. That feeling is the <u>*real*</u> *sign. Overdependence on a visible manifestation will ultimately slow your growth.*

Sooo...now I must get this book finished! OK!

Aug. 8, 1995

Back from the weekend in my home town for my 40th year high school reunion. While I enjoyed seeing old friends, it was very superficial. I tried to tell two people what is really going on in my life but neither one knew about channeling, so that makes it pretty hard to describe. I visited my parents every day. They are looking somewhat better, but mentally I didn't see any improvement. My dad tends to get agitated and there is no way to appease him except by encouraging him to move or do something physical. There were two interesting moments with my mother. Once at dinner she told me to chew with my mouth closed. I said, "Oh, I thought I was! Thank you!" I was unruffled, bemused and did not get bogged down in self-criticism or anger. The other came after we had shared our breakfast table with some of the other residents. Mother said, "I think the ladies liked you." I had the funniest feeling because I knew they liked me. I didn't need her to tell me and if they didn't like me, that was OK, too. I just smiled and said, "What's not to like?" I don't need anyone else's approval anymore. I love myself and that is all that matters. This is an immense change from the way I would have responded to such remarks even a short time ago. More progress, more rewards.

I saw Sue Ellen this morning and as usual it was very interesting. There was a planetary interference on me from Mercury, a carryover from my most recent past lifetime. There was a virus in my biocomputer from Lucifer. Wild. After she fixed all that, it came up that I felt unprotected and wanted to be pristine and clean. Then I had radioactive metals fallout. My gait was disrupted. She put six acupressure patches on various meridian points. Sometimes it is hard to believe the stuff that comes up, but I'm feeling better and better, clearer and smoother with this amazing and powerful process. I thank the Creator every day for leading me to Sue Ellen.

Christmas is really shaping up. We are going to New York and Diane and Hobie are flying up, too! I have reserved four rooms at the New York Palace for three nights for Mark and Alice, Diane and Hobie, Keith and me and Linda and Josh. (Linda and Charlie are separating because of his alcoholism. Michael says their agreement is complete and Linda is ready to get on with her life, but Charlie has slipped into self-destruction.) We may be starting a wonderful new family tradition! I want it to be as different from last year as possible.

Aug. 12, 1995

On Wednesday I sat down to meditate. I started to recite my prayer from the angels. *"I, Lois M. Grant, am one with the Universe, with all the angelic beings of Light, with all the healing forces in the Universe. I, Lois M. Grant, am wonderful. My heart is full of love and peace. Any doors concealing hurts are being healed."* I thought, "These doors in my heart are open and healed!" I continued, *"I am free to move on in this lifetime."* Then I thought, "I have moved on in this lifetime!" Next, *"My heart is in the gentle hands of the Master of all healing."* I realized, the Master has healed my heart! *"My hands are open and receiving all that is good and wonderful. My back is strong and straight, supporting me in the march toward time and space. My feet are soft and true, marching me forward, holding me calm and serene."* These things are all true now! *"I, Lois M. Grant, am free to be me. I accept myself and I move on in this life with the understanding that total healing is mine."* I am me! I do accept myself! Total healing is mine! I wept in joy and gratitude.

Last week I went for three days in a row without taking any cortisone! I was very pleased and have decided to take it only when I feel I need it. It has been easy to go without for two days most of the time lately. This is real progress!

Linda called and asked me to come to New York to help support her when she has surgery on her finger.

Aug. 17, 1995

I've been so busy working on the book, I haven't been writing in my journal. The biggest task is to transcribe four volumes of journal, which is a bit tedious. Paula is going to help with one volume. She's in Oregon this week and has five interviews scheduled. I've been called twice as a reference, which is pretty exciting. Before she left, she called me and said that she wanted to just quit her job so she could stay out there and hunt for apartments, etc. I said, "Do it! (The entity) Michael says that when you remove something from your life that isn't working, you create space for the new to come in!" She said, "That's right! It's like my friend who won't get rid of her crummy boyfriend and so she doesn't get a nice new one." It was great the way she just got what I was saying. She's so quick. Of course, she's Gemini, too.

I mailed a check to Kenny for the latest transmission and I forgot to seal the envelope. When I realized I had done this, I asked the angels to keep it safe. When I called him the next evening, he said it had arrived safely. Thank you, Ariel and Michael and whoever else.

Aug. 25, 1995

Today I received this message:

Archangel Michael: Lois is truly on the verge of a major breakthrough in her life. Paula's experience in creating her new job is very important to Lois' wholeness and wellness. Share all of this with her, along with this new meditation:

> *As I enter the light, I let it shine from within.*
> *I turn my eyes inward as I look down life's pathway.*
> *In my heart I know that All Is One;*
> *In my spirit I know that All is Now;*
> *In my life, I know that All is Beauty.*
> *I rest in the Oneness of All That Is. Peace.*

For Lois: When you are in New York with your sister, listen with your heart. You will hear the truth of Linda's feelings this way. Love her unconditionally while you are with her. Rest in the knowledge that your path is clear and that you know your direction. While you are away, you will feel freedom unknown to you before. Listen and look for the signs of the presence of Spirit and know that they are the manifestation of all that is good and wonderful in your life.

Well, I'm ready for this breakthrough, whatever it is. I teased Keith, asking if he was ready for another one of my breakthroughs! He laughed.

Aug. 27, 1995 Rye, NY Sunday

It's been an incredible week. <u>Another</u> incredible week! Paula got four job offers from five interviews, including the one she really wanted, which will pay her $10,000 more per year. She did what I advised and manifested the whole thing, which gives me a great feeling of pleasure and power. Friday afternoon she came over and we hugged and laughed and cried. I will really miss her. She said that as she came up the driveway, she thought about how I had made this house happen and now in the same way she has manifested this change for herself. When she exclaimed, "We have to tell people about this!" I answered, "This is why we're writing the book!"

Saturday morning the Great Blue Heron was in the lake. <u>Power</u>!

Yesterday I flew to New York to help Linda when she has her finger surgery tomorrow. (She has a mucoid cyst on her right index finger which I think is due to her anger over her previous job plus her personal situation.) It was pretty exciting to walk into the terminal at La Guardia Airport yesterday and see the new counters we have been working on for Delta! After dinner Linda, her son Josh and I sat around reading daily items from the Dave Barry calendar and just roaring. It was so much fun! This morning Keith faxed us Dave's weekly column from the Atlanta paper and we howled at that, too.

This morning I was up early by myself and I went out to sit on the deck. It was cool and pleasant. After a bit I said, "Don't you have any wrens?" Sure enough, about two minutes later, a wren came hopping across the grass. Thank you!

This afternoon my son Mark drove out (he lives in Brooklyn) and we had a great time visiting. He entertained us by describing his trip to Borneo, as well as his adventure when his car broke down at the Holland Tunnel on the way to Newark airport. He enjoys living on the edge and has fun sharing his experiences! Mark brought me three trade magazines which feature him and his work in computer animation creating commercials for companies like Shell, Oldsmobile, Nestle, even

Barbie! He's an Artisan who is truly creating and it's pretty exciting. I feel very powerful for having parented such a together, self-aware and self-assured person. He is so competent as a department manager that in the past year not one of his 25 computer programmers has left, highly unusual for young people in such a fast-moving field. I am proud.

Incidentally, Tara said she saw me taking four trips this summer and this is number four, the unexpected one.

Aug. 28, 1995

Linda and I got up early to get her to the hospital by 7 AM. Josh and I brought her home around noon and she rested all afternoon. Then I served her dinner in bed and we had a wonderfully relaxed time talking, talking, talking. About everything. When I called our parents to let them know she was OK, they were just getting ready to call here and were so happy to hear from us. Mother actually said, "Tell her we love her. We love you both." Linda was just astounded. On Sunday she had played a CD with the song "Love Changes Everything." How true.

I had a very tender moment with Josh. After we brought Linda home and got her settled and she said, "Thank you," Josh said, "I'm happy to do it." I said to Josh, "It's a pleasure to help someone when you love them so much, isn't it." He grinned at me and we hugged.

Aug. 30, 1995

Linda's feeling much better now and we are just having loads of fun being together. She commented on how much energy I have and how happy I seem to be. I said, "Have I changed in any way?" Her answer thrilled me: "You're sprightly!" Nothing could be more wonderful than to be perceived the way my angel describes him/herself!

Sept. 5, 1995

Saw the eye doctor today and everything was fine. He said to come back in six months.

Paula and David are moving to Oregon on the 14th, the day after Keith and I leave for our vacation in Nova Scotia! So soon! I have really grieved over her moving away. We are taking them to brunch Sunday.

Sept. 26, 1995
It's been a pretty intense two weeks. We took Paula and David to brunch on a beautiful warm and sunny Sunday. As we were sitting in the restaurant, Keith, who was facing the window and the parking lot beyond, suddenly said, "The van is moving!" We looked out. I thought, "The van can't be moving," but it was. I was right next to a fire exit door. I opened it and stepped outside to see the van driving away with the alarm siren going full blast! David chased after it, but to no avail. We called the police, a frustrating exercise since they don't really seem to care. Keith was furious. Fortunately, we were not far from Paula and David's apartment. David walked home, got their car and drove us home.

The afternoon was intense and draining. Keith was so angry that he wanted nothing in the way of consolation or empathy. I tried to hug him and said I was sorry, but he remained aloof. I left him alone, but his negative vibration pretty much filled the whole house. About 7:30 the police called to say they had found the van in a parking lot at the airport and it did not appear to be badly damaged, just two broken windows and the starter. It had not been trashed. We were greatly relieved and were told how to claim it. Monday morning we went downtown to the police department, then to the impound area and then to the mechanic, who said they could make the repairs while we were on vacation. It was 1 PM when we finally arrived home, physically and emotionally exhausted.

Sept. 12, 1995 Of course, I had to ask the angels what was going on.
Ariel: Lois, while you and Keith are away, you will be given an opportunity to facilitate Keith's growth. Your ability to listen and love unconditionally can be a bridge for him to take some steps in his journey. You don't need to be a teacher, just an example. Curb your tendency to already "know" everything. Let yourself drop into a learning mode as you did with Linda and Josh.

Keith will see and do things in Nova Scotia that will trigger memories of his childhood. Avoid explaining events or memories to him. Allow your responses to come from your heart. Above all, relax in the knowledge of who you are and why you are here. As Keith sees you love unconditionally, his heart will be softened to look at himself. Do not judge his growth or overanalyze it. Keith is

on an upward spiral and is serving a multiple set of roles for you.
He helps you grow more than you realize.

The van was stolen to allow both of you to reflect on all the
events which can enter your lives, how suddenly life can change.
Thoughts, wishes or desires can sometimes be manifested in what
appear to be very odd ways.

We had a very enjoyable ten-day vacation in Nova Scotia. As we were
driving from the airport to Halifax, Keith said, "Boy, this sure looks like
the U.P." (the Upper Peninsula of Michigan). Keith's great-grandfather,
a miner from Cornwall, England, had come to Waverley, Nova Scotia, to
mine gold in the 1850's. Keith's grandfather was born in Waverley
before his parents moved to Michigan to mine iron ore. This turned out
to be the running thread throughout the entire trip, as Keith indeed saw
many, many artifacts in museums, landforms and buildings which
reminded him of his childhood, just as the angels predicted. I was
amazed. (When am I going to stop being amazed by these things?) We
stayed in Waverley and enjoyed visiting with the local historian whose
grandfather had founded the town. She found relevant birth and tax
records for Keith's family tree research and helped us explore the area.

My favorite day of the trip was when we woke up on Cape Breton to a
fierce Atlantic storm. Strong winds were driving pouring rain almost
horizontal, waves were crashing on the rocks below and it was so foggy
we could hardly see! After breakfast I wrote postcards for about an hour
and then Keith said, "Let's go into town." So we started driving. The
storm had let up some, but it was still foggy and windy. The picturesque
little towns are nestled around harbors with myriad colorful fishing boats
and stacks of lobster traps everywhere. Even the houses are painted
bright colors against the often cold and gray landscape. We drove down
the narrow side roads to wharves where we photographed and
videographed the wind, rain and huge waves. It was so dramatic and
somehow appropriate to experience this powerful, cleansing storm and
we wondered what it would be like to be out in a small fishing boat on a
day like that. Around lunch time we found a tiny, quaint restaurant
where we had steaming chowder and continued to watch the storm from
this cozy vantage point.

The weather abated by afternoon and we went back to the lodge. Keith wanted to rest, but I was so invigorated that I went out to walk one of the nearby trails. It was windy with alternating sun and clouds and everything was very shiny clean, refreshed after the rain. I wandered around for about an hour taking pictures and on my way back sat down behind the lodge facing the bay. A bald eagle flew across the entire wide vista of the sky from right to left, just out over the water. I felt like he was greeting me in that wondrous moment.

Sept. 26, 1995

We were surprised and disappointed to learn that the van had not been worked on while we were out of town.

Appointment with Dr. G. today. As the nurse was taking me back to be weighed, Dr. G. came out of her office. She looked at me with a rather surprised expression and said, "Hi!" When she came into the exam room she told me, "You caught my eye because you were standing up so straight and walking so fast!" In other words, I no longer move like a person who has rheumatoid arthritis! That was great news. Of course, she attributes my improvement to the Plaquenil and suggested that I increase the dosage to 1-1/2 tablets per day and stop the cortisone. My goal is to stop both the Plaquenil and cortisone! I told her I was getting massage and showed her how my fourth and fifth fingers on my right hand will now stay in the joints, instead of being ulnar deviated (slipping out of the joints and angled toward the right). She was somewhat surprised and credited the Plaquenil. "When it reduces the inflammation, these improvements can happen," she explained.

Last summer a likable young man came to the door selling magazines. I wanted to help him, but couldn't find a magazine that I needed or wanted to subscribe to. So I decided to send a subscription to *Parenting* magazine to Diane. It takes three months for the subscription to start and I thought, "Surely by that time she'll be pregnant." Well, Diane called last night because she got the notice about it. "It's hard," she said, "when I want to be pregnant and it isn't happening." I apologized. Darn. Sometimes following my first impulse doesn't seem to work out.

Oct. 12, 1995

More from the angels on the significance of animals:

Eagle: Power, Majesty. The eagle you saw was a confirmation of the rightness of where you are and that you should continue on your path.

Hawk: Predator. A sign of confirmation. You see a hawk as you break free from your self-imposed bonds. A hawk understands his place in the Universe and knows how to stay aloft and use the air currents to his advantage. Your vision is sharpened as you soar with the hawk.

Kingfisher: Another predator, but with a sneaky side. They represent a tendency to short-circuit the learning process. (Is this related to my impatience?)

Cardinal: War, anger, endurance. The cardinal is a sign for you that your anger is coming to the surface. Let it free itself in a constructive way or you will have to endure it, a much more painful option. (I love cardinals so much, that at first I resisted this one, preferring Ted Andrews' interpretation: "Renewed vitality through recognizing self-importance. Brightening the environment." However, I began to notice that often when my anger is triggered I will immediately hear or see a cardinal. I now know that the cardinal is reminding me to consciously release this anger instead of denying, nursing or repressing it.)

Crow: Blackness, the darker side. Crows are calling you to let go and see your spirit against the blackness of the Universe, an uncontaminated canvas on which your life can be projected. See yourself against this background of blackness which makes all colors more brilliant.

These signs are triggers for you to look into yourself, in your heart for the inner voice, the inner light of the moment. Remember to jot down your insights or use this little reminder:

Thank you, Spirit, for this understanding.
I receive it in my heart.
Bring it to my consciousness
When I choose to respond to its message.

Oct. 20, 1995

I was fascinated by these symbols and their meaning in my life. and couldn't resist asking for a few more because our home is so surrounded by nature.

Blue Jays: A reminder of the fleeting sense of time that you occasionally feel. They are brightly colored, as your flashes of insight tend to be. (This was interesting to me, since I have the chief feature impatience, based on a fear of there not being enough time. There are many blue jays in the woods around us and every spring we have a blue jay nest on the top of our patio column.)

Mockingbirds: These birds can take various voices, so it is necessary to develop your discernment. They are warning you to carefully evaluate the validity of some voices you hear and some thoughts which come to your mind.

Titmouse: Signs of joy. When you see them, let your Sprit soar. The heights to which you release yourself can be a wonderful confirmation of the good that lies ahead when you are in the midst/depths of a valley experience. Think of soaring up through the clouds.

All these birds have flight in common, which represents such freedom to mere mortals. This is just the birds' normal modus operandi. Each creature in the Universe has its own set of boundaries or constraints. Observation of the birds can offer glimpses of freedom. Rejoice in your powers of observation. Take these joys into your heart where they will grow and multiply.

Cockroaches: Fear of change. They sometimes scurry away, but often just sit there unmoved. When you kill them, they (others) always come back. You can soar with the eagles one minute and be consumed by a seemingly immovable fear the next. When you see a cockroach, acknowledge your fears and release the intellectual side of yourself. Look to the inner, emotional spirit side, which is an even greater and unshakable fact, and offer a "thank you" to Spirit for reminding you of your fears. Then move on, soaring or flying or resting serenely as a bird. Be confident in the knowledge of your heart.

My Planetary Guide predicted that the week of October 2-9 would be intense with the energy peaking on Wednesday when there would be twenty planetary aspects to put stress on everyone, plus some planets going direct. I could feel the energy pick up with the O. J. Simpson verdict on Tuesday. My Jewish neighbor said, "Isn't it interesting that this verdict is coming down on the eve of the Day of Atonement?" I got shivers. That afternoon it started raining. Hurricane Opal was surging around in the Gulf and Atlanta often gets a lot of rain from the periphery of these storms, so we were not surprised that it rained hard all night. The rain continued all day Wednesday as we worked hard to meet a couple of small deadlines. Opal made landfall in the Florida panhandle and was moving through Alabama, not losing strength as hurricanes usually do over land. I started feeling achy late in the day. When Keith asked me why, I said it was a combination of processing my last visit to Sue Ellen, the planetary aspects, the weather and the deadline stresses. Take your pick! I took 25 mg. of cortisone, some Darvocet, put the homeopathic gel on my hands and went to bed. The power went off at 10:15 PM. I woke up at 2 AM, relieved to be pain-free but a little surprised that it was still pouring rain. I didn't realize it at the time, but that was when Opal actually went through Atlanta knocking down 4,000 drought-weakened trees and wreaking havoc. A huge oak at the corner fell directly on the neighborhood transformer and we began five days of disabled existence. We have built our whole lives around electric power and when it is gone, it is like being sick. Everything just went on hold. I stayed with Diane and Hobie for four nights, feeling very blessed to have them so close at hand. (She was very disappointed to get her period while I was there. They are very ready to have a child, but it seems to be taking "a long time" to happen.). Finally, Monday afternoon the power came on, Tuesday afternoon our telephone service was restored and Wednesday cable TV was back. And best of all, Friday the van was ready. As I left Keith at the repair shop, tears came to my eyes. I said, "Please, God, let that be it for a while." We did agree that it could have been worse. None of us was hurt, the weather was warm enough that Keith and Lucky could stay in the house, it didn't happen while we were on vacation and I was physically OK.

Oct. 23, 1995

This day, this weekend, is one I will never forget. Several weeks ago Bonnie mentioned that she was wanting to have a "Mad Hatter Tea Party." I suggested that we could have the party at our house and jointly host it. The more we talked about it, the more excited we got. We would tell people to wear a hat. We decided to ask Tara Black to come and give mini-readings. Sue Ellen could do a healing demonstration on me. And then I got the idea to invite Howard and

Ruby from Columbia. Things started falling into place and Howard said he could come over on Friday evening and stay through the weekend. I found a picture of a Mad Hatter and taped it to the invitation, which I did up in several wild fonts on my computer and copied onto bright orange paper. I put out the word that Howard was coming and started making appointments for him. Bonnie said he could see people at her house, since she is all set up for bodywork. I was surprised when Diane said she wanted to see Howard, but she and Hobie had plans to go to her ten-year college reunion that weekend and wouldn't be back in town until Sunday evening. She has Mondays off, so I asked Howard if he could stay over until Monday morning to see her. He readily agreed.

Howard and Ruby arrived late Friday night. Saturday morning he started working on people, including me. Kenny and Elena both came and loved the experience. On Sunday he started again at 9 AM, worked on Keith and Bonnie and two others. I think he worked on Keith four times altogether. Howard is so dedicated to his work, he will just start in talking to you about your emotions or whatever you need to hear and then will start massaging your shoulders. He has a true drive to help people with his incredible gift. Kenny still intends to get his shamanic training from Howard, but hasn't yet made time or space for it.

We had a wild example of synchronicity on Sunday morning. When I came out into the living room, Howard was on the phone with a man who had advertised his car for sale in the newspaper. Howard wanted to see the car and asked the man if he would drive it over here. He asked me to give the man directions, which I did, and when I handed the phone back, I said, "This is a very nice person." Howard left for Bonnie's, the man with the car arrived and Ruby went for a test drive. When they returned, they were out in the driveway looking under the hood. I took a bag out to the trash and Ruby introduced us, saying, "He works for MARTA." I said, "Well, I have done specs for MARTA," and he said, "Why, yes, Lois, I know you. I've seen you in the hallways." Ruby decided to buy the car and they came into the kitchen. I told Keith that this man worked for MARTA (where Keith had worked when we first moved to Atlanta) and Keith went into the kitchen to find someone he used to go to lunch with! They had fun talking about everyone they knew in common When the car deal was complete, the man called his wife to come and pick him up. Guess what her name is: Angelyn!! She and Ruby started talking and found they had friends in common Well, isn't God paying attention!

People started arriving for the party right at 4 PM. Kenny and Elena were among the first to come and Keith noticed the delightful change in them. "They are like different people," he said the next day. She was happy and outgoing, the friendliest I'd ever seen her and Kenny's eyes are so much brighter than ever before. The hats everyone wore were a great ice-breaker. It was a wonderful group of friends and there were many connections. Tara was in demand for short readings.

After some high-intensity socializing, things calmed down and Sue Ellen and I announced that we would start the demonstration of Inner Nature's Integration downstairs. About ten people came to watch. The first thing that came up was that I was feeling unprotected. Then there was something about not having a role model for the feminine. There was a hole in my etheric web, fairly high above my body, about two inches in diameter which I needed to heal. And I then needed therapy for one of my organs—my bladder. The therapy was for everyone in the room to pray out loud, each in turn. I said I would start and I asked Howard to be the last. It was truly powerful and inspiring. And of course, I shed a few tears. After that, the session was over and she put me into timed processing. There were two other interesting sidelights to the praying time. I heard Lucky meowing outside, as if he were praying, too. And during that time, someone used the bathroom upstairs. We could hear very clearly the emptying of a bladder.

Sue Ellen told me later that she had seen two white doves while driving to church that morning and remarked to her son, "Something special is going to happen today." During the prayers for me she could feel the love in the room going from heart to heart and it was an extremely powerful experience for her. She also recounted that Howard had really helped her. I had seen the two of them talking very seriously in the kitchen early in the evening. After she worked on me, she said to him, "You want a session, don't you?" He was not going to ask for it, but she knew he wanted one, so she worked on him for about half an hour. Sue Ellen said that she was floating all through the next day.

My friend Vic was thrilled with the party and the people who came. He said, "I think you've started something here." He wants to get the group together every month! I was pretty wired after everyone left and it took me a long time to get to sleep.

Diane arrived on Monday morning, her beautiful, vibrant self. She and Howard sat in the living room and talked while Keith and I worked in the office downstairs. After about an hour and a half I heard them go out onto the deck and I went upstairs. Howard was inside and Diane was standing out on the deck in her bare feet, facing the lake. He motioned for me to go out and join her. She had the most wonderful expression on her face, a smile of blissful peace and love and joy. We hugged each other for a long time, whispering our love for each other and shedding tears of joy and gratitude as she stroked my hair and I patted her back.

It was a gorgeous fall morning with the autumn colors of the trees reflecting in the still surface of the lake and a brilliant blue sky above. Bonnie's fiancé had left one of those huge multiple bubble makers on the small table on the deck. Diane started making bubbles and they floated up to the sky. "Do you know what these look like, honey?" I asked. "Zygotes!" (Scholarly note: A zygote is a fertilized egg. The cell division which follows conception looks just like these bubbles!) We laughed and cried as she made more and more glistening, iridescent spherical rainbows. The breeze took them high, up to the Creator and up to the exquisite soul that is waiting to come in and be my grandchild. Howard came out with his video camera to capture this miraculous moment. When we came inside, I warmed up some of the leftover spiced cider from the party and we sat in the living room while Howard told some of his healing stories. It was a very comfortable and nurturing time. I was thrilled that Diane, a medical doctor, wanted to see Howard at all. I marveled at how receptive she was and that she seemed to be new and improved after such a short time with Howard! Her body must be in pretty good shape, because he only did a little release work on her shoulders.

After Diane left, I was overcome with more tears of love and joy. Ruby hugged me as I just dissolved, expressing all my feelings about the whole weekend: the sessions with Howard and Sue Ellen, giving the party, having company for four days, losing sleep, all culminating in my joyous experience with Diane. A moment later I saw two bluebirds in the tree right outside the kitchen window. Happiness is right!!

After lunch Howard and Ruby left in their two cars. I cleaned up the kitchen some more and then took a leisurely walk around the house and the lake. I looked at all the plants and trees, loving the earth, absorbing the light and the sunshine, feeling the feelings, overflowing with a few more happy tears, just being in the moment and in tune with life and my planet. After walking all the way around the lake I sat on the lower deck and stared into the water. The reflections of the clouds looked like so many angels. I dearly love my home and all that goes with it. My life is so blessed, so full of love. The miracles are happening one after the other and Dreams Really Do Come True.

EPILOGUE

On Tuesday after the big weekend, I had a headache and my neck was also somewhat stiff, probably due to my body's processing the sessions with both Sue Ellen and Howard. I took ten mg. of cortisone. The next day I felt much better and did not take any. Nor the day after that or the day after that. As the days stretched into weeks I realized my healing had reached a new level, and I rejoiced that I didn't need those steroids on a regular basis anymore.

About two weeks later I saw Sue Ellen and my body said to reduce the Plaquenil to 1/2 tablet per day! Then just before New Year's, my body said to stop taking nine of the supplements I had been taking. Progress, progress. More layers of that onion!

On December 5th I got a phone call from Diane. She said, "I just wanted to tell you that it's OK about the *Parenting* magazine." I was silent, afraid to ask, hoping against hope. "It's OK, Mom, I'm pregnant!" YES!! She is due in August, right after the Centennial Olympic Games in Atlanta. To say I was thrilled was a great understatement! Diane invited me to go with her for an ultrasound appointment in January and there we saw the first image of my first grandchild. The joy of having yet another of my dearest dreams come true is indescribable. It's just another confirmation of the way Spirit is continuing to work in my life and the lives of those around me.

We had a wonderful Christmas holiday in New York City. But when we came home, Lucky had disappeared. We searched and called and put up signs, but there was no trace of him until January 6th when neighbors found his body. Apparently he'd been killed in a fight with a bigger animal. We sadly buried him in the garden on that cold gray day. That night I went to bed and listened to a new tape called "Angel's Adoration." I just couldn't stop crying, wishing we had done this or not done that, feeling terrible about the violent way he had died. After about half an hour (which is a long time even for me to cry!) my tears suddenly stopped and I felt a huge sense of peace and love settle over me. It was as if Lucky was saying, "It's OK, don't worry. I'm fine. I love you, I love you, I love you." I was able to sleep and in the morning I had the sense that my grieving was complete. Of course, I still missed him and would choke up telling people what had happened, but the deep sense of loss was healed. It was an inspiring way to recover.

On February 13th I had another flare-up, but went to the emergency room at 1 AM instead of spending all night lying in bed hoping to get better. Part of it was what Dr. Christiane Northrup calls "the anniversary effect," as I recalled Valentine's Day the year before. Karmelah came by a couple of days later and she said, "You look great!" I said, "I do?" and told her about the flare. She closed her eyes a moment and then declared, "This was not a setback, it was a healing crisis. Your energy is very clear." Shortly after that I received the monthly Michael tape which said that a huge burst of emotional energy impacted the planet on Feb. 13 and 14! Well, I felt it. I am very sensitive to these energies!

I have learned that the course of my healing is not a straight line process. If it were graphed, it would look something like the stock market of late with intermediate ups and downs but an undeniable upward trend. I do not know how high it will eventually go, but I do know, looking back, that I have come a very long way. I am very grateful.

It is interesting to contemplate where my spiritual and emotional development might be without this gift of rheumatoid arthritis nipping so painfully at my heels. If I had left Jack in 1970 to pursue some challenge or other, would I not have needed such an encumbrance? Is there a parallel universe someplace where I stayed healthy and still grew spiritually? Or would I have manifested it regardless because of all those past lifetimes of not dealing with the issues and all those ancestral burdens? I don't know. I do know that I am thrilled beyond words to be who I am, where I am right this very moment. And all that matters is this moment.

Whatever lessons lie ahead, I welcome them, for I know that as long as we are on the physical plane, we are learning something and I plan to be around for quite a while yet to enjoy all the grandchildren that are on the way. The love of the Creator and the Angels and my family and my friends surrounds me and lifts me up. And as (the entity) Michael says, "Love is stronger than anything."

All the wild, wonderful, weird stuff I have tried is available in most towns and cities if you just look for it. The movement away from Western medicine is growing rapidly. Start with herb and health food stores, look for massage therapists in the phone book. They are usually networked into alternative healing. There are many magazines and newsletters and I have listed several in the Appendix. It is important to trust and like your healers. Above all, follow your feelings and don't give away your power. If something isn't working, try something or someone else. Be open to new ideas and new methods.

***

June 22, 1996

After one of my past life regressions in April of 1995, I looked down at the carpet in my room and saw a small, dark-amber colored bead which I had never seen before. I reached down to pick it up and asked Karmelah if it was hers. No, it wasn't. I put it on my "altar" with my candles and other gemstones.

About ten days ago I spent two evenings in my room sorting through stacks of papers that tend to collect in there, cleaning up the shelves and putting things in order. I made several piles of articles to file, paper to recycle, etc., and was very surprised to see an amber bead on the floor. I thought at first that it might be the same one I found a year ago but when I checked, the first one was still on the altar. I picked up this new one and placed it in the dish alongside the other. A little later I picked up a box of papers from one of the bookshelves and could hardly believe my eyes—two beads lying in it! So now I had four.

These beads are teardrop-shaped as if they were warm and molten when dropped from a height. They stick a little to the carpet and when I pull them off they have indentations of the carpet fibers in them, again, as if they were warm when they landed. They have not been drilled as for a necklace, but are whole. I have them all in a little agate dish and they tend to stick together like a resinous material, which, indeed, amber is.

The next night I resumed my cleaning task and within an hour received two more beads. And before the evening was over, three more came to me, the last appearing in the hallway just outside my room as I was going to bed.

Last Tuesday evening I drove over to Diane's to see the new nursery furniture. We had a lovely long and meaningful conversation sharing our feelings on many topics. I felt very warm and loving and so fortunate to have my daughter and her family so close at hand. The anticipation of my grandson's arrival is a delectable emotional treat that I am enjoying to the utmost. When I came home I went into my room and there was another amber bead on the floor!

I have now received 11 beads. In trying to figure out what this means, I can only conclude that they represent some sort of blessing. I asked Kenny and received this answer:

Angels: Lois, you have been manifesting the amber beads from the joy of your heart. You have uncovered the innermost part of Lois—the level at which you truly work. The therapy of producing the amber is a distillation of the lost years that are being restored to you for this lifetime. You have dealt with so much pain and hurt that you have often wished for this lifetime to be over. In your heart of hearts, you had subtracted eleven years from your lifetime. (Eleven is your number right now, but do not lock yourself to this time frame.) As the pain has begun to lessen, your essence has recognized the wonderful opportunities for growth and experience and now wants to continue this lifetime. The amber is a physical symbol of the power of your spirit at work. Go back and record your thoughts about each time you found beads. Look at your total experience each time. You are dealing from a much stronger hand than you often give yourself credit and this strength is the force that has manifested the beads. It was not someone else who made you feel good enough about yourself to let that energy come through. It was your strength that soared and recognized just who you are and what you want to manifest. It happened because of you. Diane did not do it. Recognize your own strength. Rejoice and be glad. Drop the need to figure out the physical.

All that exists is energy. Everything that we perceive as real is energy arranged in some form that we perceive as real or solid. The key to the Universe is the recognition of your perceptions. You are bound only by your self-imposed limits. The closer you get to understanding the forces of the I AM, the closer you come to slipping the bonds of time and space. Acknowledge where you have been. Prepare to soar with the eagles. You are ready.

Angels don't have wings for nothing. They use them!

PART THREE

Appendix

ACKNOWLEDGMENTS

As I sit here thinking of all the people who need to be acknowledged, I am overcome yet again by a wave of very deep emotion. I am reminded of a sympathy card which says, "Sorrow comes to carve out places in the heart for Joy," for I believe that my newfound capacity to know true Peace and Love and Joy is possible only because of all the pain and anger that are now past, transformed by the grace of Spirit and all those on and off the planet who have helped me along this pilgrimage.

Well, I have to start someplace—my family: My sister **Linda** has always been there for me. We would never have survived without each other's unwavering emotional underpinnings and the unconditional love and support we have for each other. Our parents unwittingly spurred us to these lessons which have led to incredible empowerment. My two offspring have brought me <u>so</u> much joy and pride. My son **Mark**, the creator of computer graphics for television commercials you have seen and great films you will see. One of my task companions, he has a brilliant mind and unique personality along with an unerring instinct for what I need to hear and how to make me laugh. My darling daughter and entity mate, **Diane**, the dermatologist, is a constant source of loving compassion. When she makes a suggestion or observation, I pay attention, for she is very wise and knows me so well. I thank them both for choosing me to be their mother in this lifetime. I also am grateful to Diane for finding **Hobie** and to the two of them for presenting me with my precious grandson, **Adam Grant Duvall**.

My husband **Keith** has taught me many lessons, both personal and professional, in our multi-layered, challenging relationship and he is a continuous source of growth, love and healing. A man of many talents, he took my photograph for the back cover.

Russ Rude first set me on the path of self-understanding. My very dear friend **Herman** stabilized me after my divorce and paved the way for Keith. Close friend **Merry McQuiddy** has always been there when I need someone to talk to or inspire me. **Beverly Tyler** introduced me to the channeled Michael Teaching, changing my life. **Joya Pope** has channeled Michael for me for years and has become an important member of my support group as well as a delightful friend. She is now my eagle-eyed, supportive editor and I am so grateful to have had her input on this project. **Michael** is my source of understanding how the Universe works in my life and I thank them for all their contributions and advice. Good buddy **Kenny** led me to my personal angel **Ariel**, the ultimate source of strength for this most recent leg of the journey. I am especially grateful to Kenny and his wife **Elena** for having the courage to let me tell their story. They are two of the strongest people I know.

Lynn Winch, my psychic, has taught me much and "seen" so many mysterious and wonderful symbols for me, frequently helping me over some very rough spots. **Howard Wills** and **Duane Hall** both helped me to release the stored-up, toxic emotions that I had put into my body. **Bonnie Mah Gibert** is gently but firmly coaxing my hands and feet back to normalcy and she has become an important member of my healing/friendship circle. **Karmelah Grevan Lancer** has refined my efforts to create a healing home and skillfully guided me to the past lives which needed healing. **Sue Ellen Renn** is a magician—I cannot imagine where I would be without her healing skills, love and friendship. Long-time special friend and fellow Scholar **Miriam Jones Murdoch** and my architectural colleague **Terry Dotson** read the manuscript and made invaluable suggestions. Close friends **Paula**, **Wendy** and **Kim** have enriched my life as we have shared our growth opportunities. Thanks to **Alan, Andy, Nicole** and the others whose life events are included here. I have changed the names of some of these friends to protect their privacy.

I gratefully acknowledge those who have so generously permitted me to quote their works. They are, in alphabetical order, *Ascending Times*, **Emily Baumbach, Ronna Herman, Sara Schurr, José Stevens** and **Andrew Weil, M.D**. **Debbie Rankin**'s inspiring cover artwork has been channeled from the angels and I am so pleased to find her again in this lifetime and have another instant best friend. Finally, I especially appreciate **Dave Barry's** granting me permission to share my discovery. Thanks, Wolfie!

What a group! How blessed I am! I love each of you in your own way. "Thank you" is so inadequate. I can only wish all of you the joys that Life and the Creator can bring as we continue The Adventure together.

Lois M. Grant
Atlanta, Georgia, 1996

LOIS GRANT'S TOP ELEVEN
RECOMMENDATIONS FOR HEALING

1. Meditate. Just do it!
2. Live in the moment.
3. The only person you can control is yourself.
4. If it don't feel right, it ain't right.
5. Follow your feelings.
6. Your opinion of me is none of my business.
7. One definition of insanity is: Doing the same thing and expecting different results.
8. The hardest thing there is to do on the planet is to have a long-term intimate relationship with another person. The second hardest thing is to get something built the way you want it.
9. "Age is a question of mind over matter. If you don't mind, it doesn't matter." Jack Benny
10. Don't sweat the small stuff.
11. It's all small stuff.

HEALING RESOURCES

HELLERWORK: Hellerwork is an integrating process which combines deep, soft tissue structural bodywork, movement education and dialogue in an exploration of how the body reflects the mind. The practitioner works to release chronic tension and rigidity in the body, while the client works to recognize ongoing attitudinal patterns and to become free of set patterns, both mental and physical.

Hellerwork International
406 Berry Street
Mount Shasta, CA 96067
(800) 392-3900
Hellerwork@aol.com

INNER NATURE'S INTEGRATION: An esoteric system of healing also called "Restoring Human Potential." Founded by a gifted and Divinely guided British physician Sulihin Thom, D.O., M.R.O., D.Ac., INI is able to detect a myriad of negative influences on the astral, etheric, emotional and mental bodies that are bogging down the physical body and preventing perfect health. Anything that is detected can be cleared and when the clearing is complete, the body heals itself.

Inner Nature's Integration
91 Berwick Road
Lake Oswego, OR 97034
(800) 304-4464
Fax (770) 751-0956

Some of the items mentioned in the text are explained here:
Integrity: Permits energy to move from the physical into the emotional part of the person. When the person is totally integrated in body, mind and spirit, he/she has true integrity and is open to guidance from Spirit.
Integrity of the Vessel: Enables a person to move away from outmoded ways of thinking and into a new way of looking at the Spiritual basis of life. The Vessel is the physical body which contains the Soul during the lifetime.

Miasm: From the Greek word for fog, in this case a fog that is penetrating the person's spiritual aspect.

The following is from a handout written by Sue Ellen Renn:

As most of us have observed throughout our lives, our minds frequently deceive us. Our bodies, however, never lie and will find ways to communicate with us when things are less that optimal within. Through the use of Clinical Kinesiology, the art of muscle testing, a therapist enables a client to communicate with his/her body and to identify those parts of the self that need attention. With the guidance of the therapist, the client's bodily responses reveal areas of previous experience, family patterns, beliefs and models of social or cultural coding from the current or previous lifetimes that have permeated the client's conscious or subconscious being and may be restricting his/her full development.

The process for communicating with the inner self involves the use of hand modes (positions) which communicate to the therapist the areas of life that need to be explored, such as inner pain, discomfort and emotional needs. Areas for exploration can include painful memories, fears, unwanted emotional baggage, limiting beliefs and decisions which may express themselves as difficulty in relationships, self-sabotage mechanisms, low self-esteem, health problems, prosperity blocks, co-dependency issues, addictions, over-sensitivity and blocks to creativity or intuition.

The process of communication with the inner self often goes beyond the dysfunction itself to help the client realize what is being said, what may be missing, what may be required to do or what may need to be released. The process educates both the client and the practitioner regarding factors that may be corrupting the client's core beliefs. The practitioner is able to provide therapies for the issues which come up for attention.

Inner Nature's Integration is a carefully researched modality which leads to a feeling of well-being and resolution because it brings about a new awareness of the Self and attention to the components of complete health: balanced spiritual, emotional and mental spheres.

THE MICHAEL TEACHING
A BRIEF OVERVIEW

"They" versus "He": Michael is a compound group with over a thousand fragments. Students differ on whether to use singular or plural pronouns when referring to Michael. This is just another choice. I prefer to say, "they," while others, including Joya, use "he." Take your pick. When Michael is being channeled, they say "we," but they don't really care which we use. They just want us to study and apply the parts of the teaching that feel attractive and useful to us!

SOUL AGES:

As an Essence moves through the cycle of the Physical Plane, the soul age advances with experience. Different lessons are emphasized at different soul levels,. The Soul Ages are Infant, Baby, Young, Mature and Old. Within each of these ages are seven levels. Essence enters the cycle on the Physical Plane as a first level Infant Soul and progresses through seven levels of Infant Souldom to first level Baby, second level Baby, etc., then to Young, Mature and, after many, many lifetimes, to seventh level Old. Since the journey from the Tao and back is circular, no soul level is "ahead of" or "better" than another and each soul age has certain advantages and disadvantages.

Infant Soul: The first of the five soul ages of the Physical Plane. Infant Souls learn how life works on the Physical Plane and usually confine themselves to simple or "primitive" cultures. A great deal of karma is usually created during these lifetimes.

Baby Soul: The second of the five soul ages of the Physical Plane. Baby Souls are concerned with structure, rules and civilization. They tend to be fearful and rigid.

Young Soul: The third of the five soul ages of the Physical Plane. Young Souls are concerned with power and monetary success and learning how to end up at the top of the Physical Plane heap. This soul age is the most enmeshed in the illusion of Personality and the Physical Plane and Young Souls tend to create many karmas.

Mature Soul: The fourth of the five soul ages of the Physical Plane. Mature Souls begin to see their connectedness to others and are concerned with opening to emotional issues and working with others on moral and ethical lessons. Mature Soul lifetimes tend to be passionate and dramatic as karmas are balanced or "paid back."

Old Soul: The last of the five soul ages of the Physical Plane. Old Souls begin to get philosophical and detach from Physical Plane excitement. They are concerned with spiritual growth and learning the ultimate lesson of agape or unconditional love.

Transcendental Soul: The level at which all Essences from an entity recombine on the Causal Plane where they continue learning and teaching. A Transcendental Soul can incarnate in a single body to create one person with the wisdom and experience of the entire entity. Examples are Mahatma Gandhi, Pope John XXIII, Yogananda and Meher Baba.

Infinite Soul: A manifestation of the Tao which takes on a physical body while retaining total consciousness. The Infinite Soul incarnates to teach and assist planetary growth. Jesus Christ, Buddha, Krishna and Lao Tsu were Infinite Souls. There will be several new manifestations of the Infinite Soul over the next twenty years, both male and female.

OVERLEAVES

The elements of personality which Essence chooses each lifetime in order to facilitate the lessons, karmas, agreements and creative purpose it has set up for the particular lifetime. These elements are: Goal, Mode, Attitude, Centering and Chief Feature. Note that there are seven of each element and one of each of these is chosen for each lifetime. Complete descriptions may be found in *The World According to Michael* and other Michael books.

Personality: The chosen overleaves.

Attitude: The chosen perspective on life. The stance from which a person views life. The seven Attitudes are: Skeptic, Idealist, Stoic, Spiritualist, Cynic, Realist and Pragmatist.

Chief Feature: Personality's primary stumbling block which is chosen by Essence when the person is about 21 years old after experimenting with all or several during adolescence. The seven Chief Negative Features are: Greed, Self-Destruction, Arrogance, Self-Deprecation, Impatience, Martyrdom and Stubbornness. Essence considers it to be "good work" to erase the Chief Feature by the end of the lifetime.

Goal: The chosen underlying accomplishment Essence aims for in a given lifetime. The seven Goals are: Acceptance, Discrimination, Growth, Re-evaluation, Dominance, Submission and Stagnation.

Mode: The chosen means of attaining the goal. The seven Modes are: Caution, Power, Reserved, Passion, Perseverance, Aggression and Observation.

Positive/Negative Poles: Each overleaf, role and soul level has a positive and negative aspect, like two sides of a coin. The positive pole carries personality in a more spiritual direction, while the negative pole takes the personality farther away from Essence and more into the illusion of the Physical Plane. The negative poles make up False Personality, which Michael also refers to by the Hindu term "Maya."

Role: The chosen role through which Essence experiences all the planes of existence during a cycle. This role remains the same during the entire cycle. The seven Roles are: King, Warrior, Priest, Server, Sage, Artisan, and Scholar.

CENTERS:

An individual chooses to primarily use one of the three ordinal energy centers: Emotional, Intellectual and Moving.

Instinctive Center: The energy center at the base of the spine, the first or root chakra, which rules unconscious, automatic body functions and contains the record of all you were born with. It includes survival instincts, instinctual fears, reflexes and past life memories.

Emotional Center: The energy center at the fourth chakra, the heart, which controls intuition and the full range of emotions. A person who is emotionally centered responds to an event by having feelings about it.

Intellectual Center: The energy center at the sixth chakra, also called the third-eye, is chiefly concerned with intelligence, reasoning, words, concepts and ideas. Intellectually centered people respond to an event by thinking and analyzing.

Moving Center: The energy center at the third chakra or solar plexus causes the body to move. This can be expressed as random, restless, nervous energy or in a disciplined form such as dance or sports. Those who are moving centered tend to respond to an incident physically, to do something like taking a walk.

Higher Emotional, Higher Intellectual and Higher Moving Centers: The enlightened versions of centering which put the person in touch with the exalted levels of Love, Truth, and Beauty, respectively.

Part: The secondary centering, Emotional, Intellectual and Moving. See Centering above. A person first responds to an event with their primary centering, then secondly according to the part. For example, a person who is Intellectually centered in the Emotional part will first think about something that happened and then will feel the feelings. It is difficult for them to have the feelings until they have thought it through.

PLANES OF EXISTENCE:

Physical Plane: The plane where energy moves slowly enough to be solid. An Essence in a human body on the Earth is on the Physical Plane.

Astral Plane: Essence moves to the Astral Plane after completing the lessons of the Physical Plane. Here Essence eventually reunites with its entire entity. Essence also visits the Astral Plane when the body is sleeping and dreaming or unconscious and also between the death (completion) of one lifetime and birth (incarnation) of the next.

Causal Plane: The plane where Essences as part of their reunited Entity go after completing the lessons of the Astral Plane where intellectual lessons concerning the structure of the Universe are learned. The entity Michael teaches from the Causal Plane.

OTHER DEFINITIONS:

Agape (ah-gah**-pay or ah-gah-pay)**: The Greek word for unconditional love and acceptance. The goal of Essences as they progress through the cycle. The goal of the Michael teaching.

Chakra: An energy center in the body.

Channel: A person on the Physical Plane who receives information through non-physical means from another Essence or entity which is usually on another plane, such as the Astral or Causal. The information is translated by the channel, often verbally, but sometimes through physical contact, such as massage, or automatic writing by hand, typewriter or computer.

Cycle: A series of approximately 50 to 400 lifetimes on a particular planet during which the Essence learns the lessons of life on that planet by progressing through all the levels of all the soul ages on all the planes. Cycles may be experienced sequentially on many planets in many galaxies, one cycle at a time.

Entity: A group of about a thousand Essences or fragments who agree to learn lessons together through the seven planes of existence. Fragments are separate, though often familiar with each other on the Physical Plane, and recombine into a single unit on the Astral Plane after all physical lives are completed by all members of the entity.

Essence: That part of us which continues from lifetime to lifetime, also commonly called "soul." Essence is in the game of life to learn lessons about the nature of life. The role, focused vs. creative energy balance, and energy frequency are aspects of the Essence which do not change and are carried from lifetime to lifetime. The Soul Age of the Essence evolves with earth experience. Essence decides which lessons will be learned and pushes in the direction of karma and intensity. And Essence decides when the lifetime is complete and it is time to leave the body.

Essence Twin: Two Essences, usually of different roles, who agree to come from the Tao to the Physical Plane at the same moment. Essence twins do lessons together throughout most of their lifetimes and have a profound effect on one another. When they meet on the Physical Plane, essence twins usually enjoy an intense relationship. After many lifetimes together, the qualities of each role begin to "rub off" onto the other.

Imprinting: The training received from parents and culture from birth to age 14 about how to be in society and how to think, act and react. Essence chooses the parents for each lifetime with an eye to the type of imprinting they will provide to enhance or challenge the experience and lessons of the lifetime.

Karma: One of the most basic laws of the Universe, that "what goes around comes around." If one person murders another in a lifetime, in some future lifetime the victim may murder the other or the murderer may save the victim's life with her own. Karmic acts are intense and create the drama of life by taking away the victim's choices. All karma will be "burned" or balanced before an Essence chooses to cycle off.

Monad: An agreement between two essences to participate in a relationship on the physical plane. The agreement is made before coming into the lifetime. Some common monads are: parent-child, husband-wife, student-teacher, hopelessly loving-hopelessly loved, leader-follower. An essence must complete at least one of each type of monad before cycling off. For more on monads see *Tao to Earth* by José Stevens.

Reincarnation: The process of coming into a new body for a new lifetime after so-called "death." During the time between lifetimes the Essence goes to the Astral Plane, ponders the lessons just learned and then decides what to tackle in the next lifetime and which overleaves will best enable the new lessons to be learned.

Tao (dow): The total consciousness of the universe. The whole of which we are all a part or fragment. The Infinite Soul. God/Goddess/AllThatIs. Father/Mother/God.

Task Companion: A spiritual agreement between two essences that they will work together on the physical plane to accomplish a given assignment. This can be a brief one-time project or a lifelong relationship, such as a business partnership. These relationships are usually mutually enjoyable and without the emotional intensity of karma.

FURTHER MICHAEL READING:

Pope, Joya, *The World According to Michael, An Old Soul's Guide to the Universe*, 1992, Emerald Wave, Fayetteville, AR

Stevens, José, Ph.D., *Earth to Tao, Michael's Guide to Healing and Spiritual Growth*, 1989, Bear & Co., Santa Fe, NM

Stevens, José, Ph.D., *Tao to Earth, Michael's Guide to Relationships and Growth*, 1988, Bear & Co., Santa Fe, NM

Stevens, José, Ph.D., and Simon Warwick-Smith, *The Michael Handbook*, 1990, Warwick Press, Sonoma, CA

Stevens, José, Ph.D., *Transforming Your Dragons*, 1994, Bear & Co., Santa Fe, NM

Yarbro, Chelsea Quinn, *Messages from Michael*, 1979, Berkley Books, New York, NY

INFORMATION ON PRIVATE CHANNELING:

Joya Pope c/o P.O. Box 969, Fayetteville, AR 72702, Telephone: (501) 575-0019, e-mail JoyaPope@aol.com

Michael Educational Foundation at P.O. Box 675, Orinda, CA 94563 Telephone: 510 254-4730 e-mail: michael@ccnet.com or http://www.spiritguide .com

OVERLEAVES:

Here is a list of the overleaves/soul profiles of most of the people in this book and in my life. It may be more than anyone except another Michael Scholar wants to know! The overleaves are listed in the following order: Name, Soul Age and Level, Role/Essence Twin Role, Goal, Mode, Attitude, Chief Negative Feature, Centering and Part. An arrow > means that the person tends to slide from one to another. Each of these overleaves is defined and discussed in more detail in the Michael books listed above.

Lois: Old 2, Scholar/Server, Dominance>Submission, Observation, Pragmatist> Cynic, Idealist, Impatience>Martyrdom, Intel/Emot

My Mother: Mature 1 (heavy Baby Imprinting), Server/Sage, Discrimination, Repression>Passion, Spiritualist>Stoic, Impatience>Marytrdom, Emot/Moving

My Father: Mature 4, King/Scholar; Growth; Power; Idealist; Stubborn>Greed, Arrogance, Impatience; Intel/Moving

Andy (Chapter Four):   Mature 4; Artisan/Scholar; Dominance; Observation> Perseverance; Aggression; Skeptic;

Stubborn>Greed, Arrogance, Martyrdom, Impatience; Emot/Intel

Beverly (Introduced me to Michael): Old 2, Scholar/Priest, Acceptance, Power , Idealist, Stubborn>Greed, Arrogance, Impatience, Intel/ Moving

Bonnie (My massage therapist): Old 1, Warrior/Artisan, Growth, Passion>Reserved, Stoic>Spiritualist, Stubbornness>Arrogance, Emot/Moving

Curt (Keith's son): Mature 5, Sage/Artisan, Acceptance, Observation>Passion, Idealist, Arrogance>Self Deprecation, Emot/Intel

Diane (My daughter): Old 5, Priest/Scholar, Acceptance, Passion, Idealist, Impatience, Intel/Emot

Elena (Kenny's wife, Chapter Eleven): Young 2 (Baby Imprinting), Priest/Scholar, Submission, Perseverance>Aggression, Idealist>Skeptic, Stubborn, Intel/Emot

George (Kenny's son): Young 1, Priest/Scholar, Dominance, Perseverance, Pragmatist, Stubborn>Impatience, Intel/Moving

Henry (Co-worker, Chapter Seven): Mature 6, Artisan/Server, Growth, Power>Caution, Skeptic, Arrogance, Emot/Intel

Herman (My very dear friend): Mature 7, Artisan/Scholar, Acceptance, Observation>Passion, Reserved, Spiritualist, Arrogance/Self Deprecation, Intel/Emot

Hobie (Diane's husband): Old 1, Sage/Priest, Growth, Reserved>Passion, Idealist, Greed, Emot/Moving

Howard (Kahuna Healer): Old 4, Sage/Artisan, Acceptance, Passion, Spiritualist, Stubborn, Emot/Moving

Jack (My ex-husband): Mature 5, King/Artisan, Discrimination, Power, Pragmatist, Greed, Intel/Emot

Jan (Jody's wife): Mature 6-7, Sage/Server, Growth, Aggression, Stoic>Spiritualist, Stubborn, Intel/Emot

Jody (Keith's nephew): Young 6, Warrior/Sage, Growth, Power>Caution, Pragmatist, Impatience, Emot/Intel

Johnny (Chapter Four): Mature 5, Artisan/Sage, Growth, Passion, Idealist>Skeptic, Greed>Self-Destruction, Emotional/Moving

Josh (Linda's son): Mature 2, Warrior/Server, Dominance, Pragmatist, Power>Caution, Moving/Intel

Joya (Michael channel and author): Old 6>7, Sage/Warrior, Acceptance, Power, Realist, Impatience, Intel/Emot

Keith (My husband): Mature 6, Warrior/Sage, Growth, Perseverance, Realist, Arrogance, Intel/Moving

Kenny (My engineer friend and Angel channel): Mature 6>Old 2, Artisan/Priest, Growth, Passion>Reserved, Spiritualist>Stoic, Self Deprecation/Arrogance, Emot/Moving

Kim (Friend): Mature 6, Warrior/Priest, Dominance, Perseverance, Idealist, Impatience, Intel/Moving

Laurie (Kurt's wife): Mature 3, Priest/Scholar, Growth, Reserved, Stoic, Stubborn, Intel/Moving

Linda (My sister): Mature 7, Warrior/Artisan, Acceptance, Passion, Spiritualist>Stoic, Greed (light), Emot/Intel

Lynn (My psychic): Old 2, Warrior/Sage, Growth, Perseverance, Idealist, Greed, Emot/Intel

Mark (My son): Mature 5, Artisan/Warrior, Growth, Skeptic>Idealist, Arrogance, Emot/Intel

Merry (Long-term friend): Old 2, Priest/King, Dominance, Passion, Spiritualist, Arrogance, Intel/Moving

Nicole (Chapter Four): Old 1, Priest/Scholar, Submission, Aggression, Realist, Impatience, Intel/Moving

Paula (Friend): Old 4, Priest/Scholar, Dominance, Passion, Spiritualist, Impatience, Intel/Emot

Rick (My former boss): Mature 5, Priest/Scholar, Discrimination, Power>Caution, Cynic, Arrogance, Intel/Moving

Scott (Keith's son): Mature 7, Artisan/Server, Growth, Caution>Power, Idealist>Skeptic, Greed, Intel/Emot

Sue (Scott's wife): Old 3; Scholar/Artisan; Submission; Observation; Stoic>Spiritualist; Stubborn>Self-Dep, Martyrdom; Emot/Intel

Sue Ellen (My Inner Nature's Integration healer): Old 5>6, Priest/King, Acceptance, Power, Pragmatist>Idealist, Stubborn>Impatience, Intel/Emot

Wendy (Friend): Old 6, Scholar/Priest, Acceptance, Caution, Spiritualist, Stubborn, Emot/Intel

HELPFUL ARTICLES and MEDITATIONS

MEDITATION FOR PROSPERITY

From *Tao to Earth* by José Stevens, published by Bear & Co., Santa Fe, NM Reprinted with permission

Sit quietly, close your eyes and be aware of your body, your thoughts and your feelings. Put all those things to one side.

Think of a quantity of energy. This may be easiest in monetary terms such as an annual salary. Or you can think of it as a quantity of love, or a measure of getting the most out of life. Draw that amount of energy out of the earth and up into your feet. Be aware of reprogramming the very cells of your body to a higher level of havingness.

Move the energy up your legs to your torso. Pay special attention to the joints, such as ankles and knees. Energy tends to stick in the joints.

Eventually move the energy up through your head and imagine it as a fountain pouring out of the top of your head. Let the energy cascade down the outside all around you at about a one to two foot radius. Pay special attention to your back.

As this energy flow hits the ground draw it around and in again to your feet. Now increase the amount to a higher level—for example think of raising your worth as a salary. Check to see if you feel comfortable with this higher level. If it is uncomfortable, lower it to where it is comfortable. The aim however is to gradually get it higher and higher.

So draw in that increased amount of energy into your feet and up through your body. Be aware now of the overall circulation of energy and let it circulate for a few minutes.

Finally seal off your feet and your head and when you feel complete, draw the meditation to a close.

This meditation can in fact be done several times during the day fairly quickly. You can do it while jogging or sitting in a car in traffic, or sitting at a desk, or while walking.

It is a powerful meditation and strongly recommended. Within weeks or at most months you will notice results.

YOUR BODY THE LAST RESORT

From *Spirit Speaks* Magazine, Issue Number 42, Channeled from
Aranya by Sara Schurr. Reprinted with permission

Health is the natural state of your body. Illness is merely a
statement by your physicality that something is out of whack—period.
From my point of view, it is useful to look at illness and to realize, "Oh,
this is a message from my physical body about what is going on with me
on other levels that I don't want to deal with."

I always say that your body is a means of last resort. If you
won't listen to your self on a mental level, if you won't listen to your
self on an emotional level, then you'll put it where you *will* listen—your
body. It's real hard to ignore a broken leg, a stuffed-up head, laryngitis,
a sprained ankle, whooping cough, or cancer. People manage, I know,
but it's hard.

It is relatively easy for many of you to ignore those little
messages that say, "I need a break. Gee, it would be nice to go away. I
am really angry about that. I don't want that, I hate that. Gee, nobody
appreciates me." Emotionally it's really easy to just sort of say, "Don't
want to deal with it this week. I shouldn't feel that. Nice people don't
think that. I couldn't possibly be feeling that." Eventually you push it
down and deny it enough that it comes out as a physical message, an
illness.

You all know about those wonderful *dis*eases that are considered
psychosomatic. Hysteria, that wonderful thing which Dr. Freud
generated, comes from the Greek root word *hystera*, meaning *womb*.
Women are better at being hysterical when it comes to *dis*eases. They
are more talented at taking their emotions and putting them into their
bodies than are men, and they are a little more creative with things that
don't make sense physically, so doctors can go "Tsk, tsk, tsk."

In truth, all *dis*eases are hysterical. They start in your head and
then they get put into your body. All *dis*eases start somewhere in your
spiritual/emotional being and move up into your head, where a little
alarm system goes off in terms of ideas or noted emotional states of
whatever, and you say, "No," and then they go into your body.

The doctor who says to you, "This is really due to your nerves,"
is telling you the truth. Everything that you create that is "wrong" with

your body is an emotional/spiritual alarm system. It's an opportunity for you to stop and address something that you have been unwilling to address. You move in sequence, starting with aches and pains and minor problems—you know: the common cold, the sprained ankle, the bump on the head, the runny nose, the headache. All those things are small alarms. We are not talking about a five-alarm fire here, but a minor little alarm that goes off and says, "There is something here to be addressed.

If it's not addressed at that point, it moves into the big time, into *dis*eases that are not transient—degenerative *dis*eases, chronic *dis*eases. Instead of getting a cold, you get asthma. Instead of just having a stuffed-up nose, you get allergies. Instead of getting a stiff elbow, you get arthritis. Instead of having aches and pains in your chest, you get heart disease. Instead of having occasional indigestion, you move to ulcers and fancy gastroenteritis and gastritis and all of that good stuff.

Notice in that list that none of those are terminal. They are uncomfortable and chronic, but not terminal. It's very hard to die of asthma or hay fever. Arthritis is very uncomfortable, but it doesn't kill you. They are the next level of alarm: "There is something that is to be addressed here. It is important. Something is not being looked at." Now, if you continue to ignore that, you go to the doctor, who gives you a pill, and the pain goes away—you know, the stuffy nose goes away. You get a little inhaler for your asthma. You take pills to make the pain of arthritis go away. You take a little this or that for your heart disease, and everything is fine. The discomfort goes away—except the issue doesn't.

So then you up the ante. You turn up the heat. Then you have not just mild heart disease, you have coronary heart disease, and soon you need a heart transplant. You get degenerative osteoarthritis and you are going to fall apart. You have a stroke. You get cancer. You get AIDS.

The final sequence of events in the process of denial of issues is death. You say, "I would rather die of cancer than deal with this issue," and you take the coronary heart disease or the AIDS or the osteoporosis or the diabetes to its logical end. It is not that those *dis*eases are by necessity terminal. It's the issues associated with them. By the time you get those diseases, usually you have already said, "No way in hell am I going to address that issue. I would rather die than deal with that. I would rather die than admit that I hate the world, that I love humanity but can't stand people. I would rather die than admit that I hate myself. I would rather die than admit that I have issues about supporting myself, that everybody else is more important than I am. I would rather die than say *I won't* about whatever it is."

THE RULES FOR BEING HUMAN
Anonymous

1. YOU WILL RECEIVE A BODY. You may like it or hate it, but it will be yours for the entire period this time around.

2. YOU WILL LEARN LESSONS. You are enrolled in a full-time informal school called LIFE. Each day in this school you will have the opportunity to learn lessons. You may like the lessons or think them irrelevant or stupid.

3. THERE ARE NO MISTAKES, THERE ARE ONLY LESSONS. Growth is a process of trial and error, experimentation. The "failed" experiments are as much a part of the process as the experiment that ultimately "works."

4. A LESSON IS REPEATED UNTIL IT IS LEARNED. A lesson will be presented to you in various forms until you have learned it. Then you can go on to the next lesson.

5. LEARNING LESSONS DOES NOT END. There is no part of life that does not contain its lessons. If you are alive, there are lessons to be learned.

6. "THERE" IS NO BETTER THAN "HERE". When your "there" has become a "here," you will simply obtain another "there" that again, looks better than "here."

7. OTHERS ARE MERELY MIRRORS OF YOU. You cannot love or hate something about another person unless it reflects to you something that you love or hate about yourself.

8. WHAT YOU MAKE OF YOUR LIFE IS UP TO YOU. You have the tools and resources you need: What you do with them is up to you. The choice is yours.

9. THE ANSWERS LIE INSIDE YOU. The answers to life's questions lie inside you. All you need to do is look, listen and trust.

WORLD HEALING MEDITATION

by the Atlanta Commission for World Peace
To be used at sunrise on New Year's Day.

In the beginning, In the beginning God. In the beginning God created the Heaven and the Earth. And God said, "Let there be Light." And there was Light.

Now is the time of the new beginning. I Am a co-creator with God and it is a new Heaven that comes as the Good Will of God is expressed on Earth through me. It is the Kingdom of Light, Love, Peace and Understanding and I Am doing my part to reveal Its Reality.

I begin with me. I Am a living Soul and the Spirit of God dwells in me, as me. I and the Father are One and all that the Father has is mine. I Am Truth, I Am the Christ of God.

What is true of me is true of everyone, for God is All and All is God. I see only the Spirit of God in every Soul, and to every man, woman and child on Earth I say, "I love you, for you are me. You are my holy self."

I now open my heart and let the pure essence of unconditional love pour out. I see it as a Golden Light radiating from the center of my Being and I feel its Divine Vibration in and through me, above and below me.

I Am One with the Light. I Am filled with the Light. I Am illumined by the Light. I Am the Light of the World.

With purpose of mind, I send forth the Light. I let the radiance go before me to join the other Lights. I know this is happening all over the world at this moment. I see the merging Lights. There is now ONE LIGHT. We are the Light of the World.

The One Light of Love, Peace and Understanding is moving. It flows across the face of the Earth, touching and illuminating every Soul in the shadow of the illusion and where there was darkness, there is now the Light of Reality.

And the Radiance grows, permeating, saturating every form of Life. There is only the vibration of the One Perfect Life now. All the kingdoms of the Earth respond, and the Planet is alive with Light and Love.

There is total Oneness, and in this Oneness we speak for the World. Let the sense of separation be dissolved. Let humankind be returned to Godkind.

Let Peace come forth in every Mind. Let Love flow forth from every Heart. Let Forgiveness reign in every Soul. Let Understanding be the common bond.

And now from the Light of the world, the One Presence and Power of the Universe responds. The activity of God is healing and harmonizing Planet Earth. Omnipotence is made manifest.

I Am seeing the salvation of the Planet before my very eyes as all false beliefs and error patterns are dissolved. The sense of separation is no more; the healing has taken place and the World is restored to sanity.

This is the beginning of Peace on Earth and Good Will toward All. As Love flows forth from every heart, Forgiveness reigns in every Soul, and all hearts and minds are one in Perfect Understanding.

It is done. And it is so. I Am.

SEVEN STRATEGIES of SUCCESSFUL PATIENTS
From Chapter 17 of *Spontaneous Healing* by Andrew Weil, M.D., 1995,
Alfred A. Knopf, New York
Reprinted with permission

Successful Patients:
1. Do not take "no" for an answer, but find their own answers.
2. Actively search for help.
3. Seek out others who have been healed.
4. Form constructive partnerships with health professionals.
5. Do not hesitate to make radical life changes.
6. Regard illness as a gift.
7. Cultivate self-acceptance.

RECOMMENDED READING

Andrews, Ted, *Animal-Speak, The Spiritual & Magic Powers of Creatures Great & Small*, 1995, Llewellyn Publications, St. Paul, MN

Bach, Richard, *Illusions, The Adventures of a Reluctant Messiah*, 1977, Delacorte Press, New York, NY

Barry, Dave, *Dave Barry Is Not Making This Up!*, 1995, Random House, New York, NY

Batmanghelidj, F., M.D., *Your Body's Many Cries for Water, You Are Not Sick, You Are Thirsty!*, 1995, Global Health Solutions, Inc., Falls Church, VA

Baumbach, Emily, *Michael Medicine, Your Holographic Body*, 1997, Causalworks, San Rafael, CA

Benson, Herbert, M.D., *The Relaxation Response*, 1975, William Morrow and Company, Inc., New York, NY

Borysenko, Joan, M.D., *Minding the Body, Mending the Mind*, 1987, Addison-Wesley Publishing Company, Inc., Reading, MA

Brans, Jo, *Take Two, True Stories of Real People who Dared to Change Their Lives*, (Lois Grant is the subject of Chapter 3), 1989, Doubleday, New York, NY

Burnham, Sophy, *A Book of Angels*, 1989, Ballantine Books, New York, NY

Chopra, Deepak, M.D., *Ageless Body, Timeless Mind*, 1993, Harmony Books, New York, NY

Chopra, Deepak, M.D., *Perfect Health*, 1991, Harmony Books, New York, NY

Chopra, Deepak, M.D., *Quantum Healing, Exploring the Frontiers of Mind/Body Medicine*, 1990, Bantam Books, New York, NY

Chopra, Deepak, M.D., *The Seven Spiritual Laws of Success, A Practical Guide to the Fulfillment of Your Dreams*, 1994, Amber-Allen Publishing, San Rafael, CA

Condron, Daniel R., D.M., D.D., M.S., *Permanent Healing*, 1993, SOM Publishing, Windyville, MO

Daniel, Alma; Wyllie, Timothy; Ramer, Andrew; *Ask Your Angels*, 1992, Ballantine Books, New York, NY

Denning, Melita and Phillips, Osborne, *Psychic Defense & Well-Being*, 1980, Llewellyn Publications, St. Paul, MN

Dyer, Dr. Wayne W., *Real Magic*, 1995, HarperCollins*Publishers*, New York, NY

Dyer, Dr. Wayne W., *The Sacred Self, Making the Decision To Be Free*, 1995, HarperCollins*Publishers*, New York, NY

Gerber, Richard, M.D., *Vibrational Medicine, New Choices for Healing Ourselves*, 1988, Bear & Company Publishing, Inc., Santa Fe, NM

Hay, Louise L., *Heal Your Body*, 1984, Hay House, Inc., Carson, CA

Hay, Louise L., *You Can Heal Your Life*, 1982, 1987, Hay House, Inc., Carson, CA

Herman, Ronna, *On Wings of Light, Messages from Archangel Michael*, 1996, *Star*Quest*, Alpine, CA

Huffines, LaUna, *Bridge of Light, Tools of Light for Spiritual Transformation*, 1989, Simon and Schuster, Inc., New York, NY

Huffines, LaUna, *Healing Yourself with Light, How to Connect with the Angelic Healers*, 1989, Simon and Schuster, Inc., New York, NY

Kabat-Zinn, Jon, Ph.D., *Full Catastrophe Living, Using the Wisdom of Your Body and Mind to Face Stress, Pain and Illness*, 1990, Dell Publishing, Inc., New York, NY

Ketch, Tina, *Candle Lighting Encyclopedia, Volume I,* 1991; *Volume II* 1993, Stone Mountain, GA

Levine, Barbara Hoberman, *Your Body Believes Every Word You Say, The Language of the Body/Mind Connection,* 1991, Aslan Publishing, Lower Lake, CA

MacLaine, Shirley, *Going Within, A Guide for Inner Transformation,* 1989, Bantam Doubleday Dell Publishing Group, Inc., New York, NY

Marciniak, Barbara, *Bringers of the Dawn, Teachings from the Pleiadians,* 1992, Bear & Company Publishing, Inc., Santa Fe, NM

Murray, Michael T., N.D.; *Arthritis, How You Can Benefit from Diet, Vitamins, Minerals, Herbs, Exercise, and Other Natural Methods;* 1994, Prima Publishing, Rocklin, CA

Northrup, Christiane, M.D., *Women's Bodies, Women's Wisdom, Creating Physical and Emotional Health and Healing,* 1994, Bantam Books, New York, NY

Patent, Arnold, *You Can Have It All,* 1995, Beyond Words Publishing, Inc., Hillsboro, OR

Pope, Joya, *The World According to Michael, An Old Soul's Guide to the Universe,* 1987, 1992, Emerald Wave, Fayetteville, AR

Pope, Joya, *Upcoming Changes, Prophecy and Pragmatism for the Late Nineties,* 1995, Emerald Wave, Fayetteville, AR

Roman, Sanaya and Packer, Duane, *Creating Money,* 1988, H. J. Kramer, Inc., Tiburon, CA

Rossbach, Sarah, *Interior Design with Feng Shui,* 1987, The Penguin Group, New York, NY

Smith, Penelope, *Animal Talk, Interspecies Telepathic Communication,* 1989, Pegasus Publications, Point Reyes Station, CA

Stauffer, Edith R., Ph.D., *Unconditional Love and Forgiveness,* 1987, Psychosynthesis International, Diamond Springs, CA

Stevens, José, Ph.D., *Earth to Tao, Michael's Guide to Healing and Spiritual Growth*, 1989, Bear & Co., Santa Fe, NM

Stevens, José, Ph.D., *Tao to Earth, Michael's Guide to Relationships and Growth*, 1988, Bear & Co., Santa Fe, NM

Stevens, José, Ph.D., *Transforming Your Dragons*, 1994, Bear & Co., Santa Fe, NM

Two Disciples, *The Rainbow Bridge*, 1981, The Triune Foundation, Rainbow Bridge Productions, Danville, CA

Weil, Andrew, M.D., *Spontaneous Healing, How to Discover and Enhance Your Body's Natural Ability to Maintain and Heal Itself*, 1995, Alfred A. Knopf, New York, NY

Weiss, Brian L., M.D., *Many Lives, Many Masters*, 1988, Simon and Schuster, Inc., New York, NY

Weiss, Brian L., M.D., *Through Time into Healing*, 1992, Simon and Schuster, Inc., New York, NY 10020

Whitney, Catherine, *Uncommon Lives: Gay Men and Straight Women*, 1990, New American Library, NY

Wright, Machaelle Small, *Behaving as if the God in All Life Mattered, A New Age Ecology*, 1987, Perelandra, Ltd., Warrenton, VA

Wright, Machaelle Small, *MAP The Co-Creative White Brotherhood Medical Assistance Program*, 1990, Perelandra, Ltd., Warrenton, VA

Yarbro, Chelsea Quinn, *Messages from Michael*, 1979, Berkley Books, New York, NY

TAPES

Bass, Robert, On Wings of Song, *Om Namaha Shivaya,* Spring Hill Music, Boulder, CO

Hamm. Marcy, *Inward Harmony,* Music by Marcy, Richardson, TX

Hay, Louise, *Love Your Body,* Hay House, Inc., Carson, CA

Howell, Kelly, *Sound Sleep, Sound Waves that Move Your Mind,* Brain Sync Corporation, San Rafael, CA

Kabat-Zinn, M.D., Jon, *Mindfulness Meditation, Guided Sitting Meditation,* Stress Reduction Tapes, Lexington , MA

Young, Cynthia Rose, *Angel's Adoration*, Spiritus Sanctus Records, Atlanta, GA

Zygon, *SuperImmunity Brain Supercharger,* Zygon Mind Research Laboratory, Thousand Oaks, CA

PERIODICALS, WEB PAGES

Aquarius, A Sign of the Times, Atlanta's monthly metaphysical magazine; 984 Canton St., Roswell, GA 30075 (770) 641-9055, (770) 641-8502 fax; e-mail: aquarius@atlanta.com.; web site: or http://www.earthchannel.com/aquarius

Angel Times, Bi-Monthly Magazine, 4360 Chamblee-Dunwoody Road, Suite 400, Atlanta, GA 30341-9826

Ascending Times, bi-monthly magazine, P.O. Box 100, Simpson, Saskatchewan, Canada S0G 4M0 (504) 634-7848

Michael Educational Foundation, P.O. Box 675, Orinda, CA 94563 Telephone: 510 254-4730 e-mail: michael@ccnet. com; Web Site: http://www.spiritguide.com

Natural Health Magazine, P. O. Box 7440, Red Oak, IA 51591

Dr. Christiane Northrup's "Health Wisdom for Women", Monthly newsletter; Phillips Publishing, 7811 Montrose Road, Potomac, Maryland 20854, (301) 424-3700

PhenomeNEWS, Michigan's monthly metaphysical magazine; 18444 West 10 Mile Road, Suite 105, Southfield, MI 48075

Dr. Andrew Weil's "Self Healing Newsletter, Creating Natural Health for Your Body and Mind," P.O. Box 787, Mt. Morris, IL 61054-0787

BOOKS BOOKS BOOKS

☼ *Spirit at Work: A Journey of Healing* Lois Grant.......$15.00

☾☆ *Eight Cards – Best Affirmations and Prayers*............$7.00
The most beautiful and inspiring affirmations and prayers from *Spirit At Work*, beautifully designed & colored, fold-over wallet-sized cards.

The World According to Michael
An excellent introduction to the Michael material about soul ages and personality overleaves. Includes info on essence twins, task companions, imprinting, and male & female energy. Joya Pope........$10.95

⊘ Upcoming Changes:
Prophecy and Pragmatism for the Late Nineties
Illuminates patterns behind world political, social, weather and earth changes occurring now and in the near future. A powerful guide to understanding your present and the shifts of the near future. Overviews and specifics.   Joya Pope...................$13.95

The Journey of Your Soul:
A Channel Explores Channeling & the Michael Teachings
Intelligent. Highly readable. Addresses the structure of the soul, parallel lives, body types, life plan, relationships, karma, reincarnation, entities, etc. 448pp   Shepherd Hoodwin..........$19.95

Earth to Tao
Michael on spiritual growth, the chakras, healing, acceleration, our human relationship to nature, plus more. Jose Stevens............ $12.95

Tao to Earth
This Michael book covers the variety of human relationships, the laws of karma, the laws of prosperity, support groups, and how a life gets planned....from the astral.   Jose Stevens........ $12.95

Loving from Your Soul: Creating Powerful Relationships ♡
Topics include the nature of love, sexuality, anger, loneliness, boundaries, listening, finding a mate, alternative lifestyles and body image.   Shepherd Hoodwin.............................$11.95

The Michael Handbook ↔
Thorough, lots of tables, graphs and comparisons. All the basics, in detail.   Scholarly types love it. Jose Stevens, Simon Smith $14.95

BOOKS BOOKS BOOKS

☆ Ask Your Angels
Learn practical ways to connect with angels (and higher energies, higher self, your guides and bosom buddies on the astral). Excellent. Chronicles how angels are currently reaching out in new ways to humanity.   Daniel, Wylie, and Ramer.........................$12.00

Animal Talk: Interspecies Telepathic Communication
How to connect. Helpful coaching from a woman who has communicated with animals for 25 years. Increase your fun with animals & psychic sensitivity too.   Penelope Smith....................$8.95

Interior Design with Feng Shui
The wise old Chinese way of fixing energy flow or *chi* in your living space to make it healthier and more life-supporting.   Eye-opening, easy to comprehend and do; sometimes necessary for physical, emotional or financial health.   by Sarah Rossbach............$15.00

Further Spiritual Dimensions of Healing Addictions
Goes magically further than 12-Step programs & more old soul too. Covers food, sugar, caffeine, tobacco, alcohol, grass, heroin & cocaine addictions, finding unique & different issues behind each and different "fixes" too.   Donna Cunningham......................$9.95

Transforming Your Dragons: Turning Personality Fear Patterns into Personal Power
Transforming your personal dragon, i.e. your chief negative feature of impatience, greed, martyrdom, self-deprecation, etc. into a pussy-cat which has no power to trip you up.   Jose Stevens......................$12.95

Michael's Gemstone Dictionary
Stones to calm your first chakra or rev up your second. And much more. This is a more essential old-soul reference book than you might imagine! It describes what happens to your energy field if you were to drop one of over 600 gems or minerals into your pocket. Well done. Highly recommended.   Judithann David & JP Van Hulle............$18.95

☆ 10% discount on 5 titles or more ☆

see next page

BOOKS BOOKS BOOKS

ORDERING BOOKS

U.S. Postage & Handling:
$2.00 first book,
$1.00 each thereafter

Canada: $3.00 first book, $1.00 thereafter
European Postage: air, $6 to $11 each.......please
estimate using book price, or use Mastercard or Visa

Arkansas residents, add 7% sales tax

Send Check or Mastercard or Visa number
plus Expiration date and Exact Name.

**NEW SAGE, BOX 969
FAYETTEVILLE, AR 72704**
email sagebooks @aol.com

☆ 10% discount on 5 titles or more ☆

Bookstores:
Order directly from Bookpeople, New Leaf,
Moving Books or Baker and Taylor

BOOKS BOOKS BOOKS

New Sage Books, Box 969, Fayetteville AR 72702

Send to:

Name_____

Street_____

State & Zip_____

Title	#Copies	Price	Total
Spirit At Work	_____	$15.00	_____
8 Cards, Prayers & Affirmations	_____	$ 7.00	_____
The World According to Michael	_____	$10.95	_____
Upcoming Changes	_____	$13.95	_____
The Journey of Your Soul	_____	$19.95	_____
Earth to Tao	_____	$12.95	_____
Tao to Earth	_____	$12.95	_____
Loving From Your Soul	_____	$11.95	_____
The Michael Handbook	_____	$14.95	_____
Ask Your Angels	_____	$12.00	_____
Animal Talk	_____	$ 8.95	_____
Interior Design with Feng Shui	_____	$15.00	_____
Further Healing Addictions	_____	$ 9.95	_____
Transforming Your Dragons	_____	$12.95	_____
Michael's Gemstone Dictionary	_____	$18.85	_____
		Subtotal:	_____

10% off for 5 books or more Discount Amount: _____

New   Subtotal: _____

$2.00 first title, $1 each additional Postage: _____

AR residents add 7% sales tax   **Tax:** _____

Visa, Mastercard, Check or Money Order: **Total:** _____

For Visa and Mastercard:

Full exact name oncard_____

Billing Address_____

Expiration Date _____   Telephone_____

Signature_____

BOOKS BOOKS BOOKS

ORDERING BOOKS

U.S. Postage & Handling:
$2.00 first book,
$1.00 each thereafter

Canada: $3.00 first book, $1.00 thereafter
European Postage: air, $6 to $11 each.......please
estimate using book price, or use Mastercard or Visa

Arkansas residents, add 7% sales tax

Send Check or Mastercard or Visa number
plus Expiration date and Exact Name.

NEW SAGE, BOX 969
FAYETTEVILLE, AR 72704
email sagebooks @aol.com

☆ 10% discount on 5 titles or more ☆

Bookstores:
Order directly from Bookpeople, New Leaf,
Moving Books or Baker and Taylor

BOOKS BOOKS BOOKS

New Sage Books, Box 969, Fayetteville AR 72702

Send to:

Name_____

Street_____

State & Zip_____

Title	#Copies	Price	Total
Spirit At Work	_____	$15.00	_____
8 Cards, Prayers & Affirmations	_____	$ 7.00	_____
The World According to Michael	_____	$10.95	_____
Upcoming Changes	_____	$13.95	_____
The Journey of Your Soul	_____	$19.95	_____
Earth to Tao	_____	$12.95	_____
Tao to Earth	_____	$12.95	_____
Loving From Your Soul	_____	$11.95	_____
The Michael Handbook	_____	$14.95	_____
Ask Your Angels	_____	$12.00	_____
Animal Talk	_____	$ 8.95	_____
Interior Design with Feng Shui	_____	$15.00	_____
Further Healing Addictions	_____	$ 9.95	_____
Transforming Your Dragons	_____	$12.95	_____
Michael's Gemstone Dictionary	_____	$18.85	_____
		Subtotal:	_____

10% off for 5 books or more Discount Amount: _____

New Subtotal: _____

$2.00 first title, $1 each additional **Postage:** _____

AR residents add 7% sales tax **Tax:** _____

Visa, Mastercard, Check or Money Order: **Total:** _____

For Visa and Mastercard:

Full exact name oncard_____

Billing Address_____

Expiration Date _____   Telephone_____

Signature_____